The Globalization of Wine

Also available from Bloomsbury:

Food and Globalization, Alexander Nuetzenadel and Frank Trentmann
The Globalization of Food, David Inglis and Debra Gimlin
Wine and Culture, Rachel E. Black and Robert C. Ulin
Veiling in Fashion, Anna-Mari Almila

The Globalization of Wine

Edited by
David Inglis and Anna-Mari Almila

BLOOMSBURY ACADEMIC
LONDON • NEW YORK • OXFORD • NEW DELHI • SYDNEY

BLOOMSBURY ACADEMIC
Bloomsbury Publishing Plc
50 Bedford Square, London, WC1B 3DP, UK

BLOOMSBURY, BLOOMSBURY ACADEMIC and the Diana logo are trademarks of
Bloomsbury Publishing Plc

First published in Great Britain 2020

Copyright © David Inglis, Anna-Mari Almila, and Contributors 2020

David Inglis and Anna-Mari Almila have asserted their right under the Copyright, Designs and Patents Act, 1988, to be identified as Editors of this work.

All rights reserved. No part of this publication may be reproduced or transmitted in any form or by any means, electronic or mechanical, including photocopying, recording, or any information storage or retrieval system, without prior permission in writing from the publishers.

Bloomsbury Publishing Plc does not have any control over, or responsibility for, any third-party websites referred to or in this book. All internet addresses given in this book were correct at the time of going to press. The author and publisher regret any inconvenience caused if addresses have changed or sites have ceased to exist, but can accept no responsibility for any such changes.

A catalogue record for this book is available from the British Library.

A catalog record for this book is available from the Library of Congress.

ISBN:	HB:	978-1-4742-6499-0
	PB:	978-1-4742-6498-3
	ePDF:	978-1-4742-6501-0
	ePub:	978-1-4742-6500-3

Cover design by Dani Leigh
Cover image © Howard Sokol/Getty Images

Typeset by Integra Software Services Pvt. Ltd.
Printed and bound in Great Britain

To find out more about our authors and books visit www.bloomsbury.com and sign up for our newsletters.

This book is a tribute to:

Davide of Salerno and Glasgow
and
Renato of Gidleigh Park

Two great men who really knew their wines

Contents

List of Contributors — viii

1. Introduction: The Travels and Tendencies of Wine
   David Inglis and Anna-Mari Almila — 1

2. Wine Globalization: Longer-term Dynamics and Contemporary Patterns *David Inglis* — 21

3. Reflexive *Imbrications*: Burgundy and the Globalization of *Terroir* *Marion Demossier* — 47

4. Building and Sustaining Legitimacy in an Emerging Wine Region: The Case of North Carolina, USA *Ian Malcolm Taplin* — 65

5. From Post-Socialist to Pre-EU: The Globalized Transformation of the Republic of Macedonia's Wine Industry *Justin Otten* — 83

6. Globalization and Reputation Dynamics: The Case of Bordeaux Wines *Pierre-Marie Chauvin* — 103

7. Fluid Modernity: Wine in China *Björn Kjellgren* — 115

8. The Globalization of the Wine Industry in Hong Kong: A Local and Global Perspective *Hang Kei Ho* — 133

9. Enduring Wine and the Global Middle Class *Peter J. Howland* — 151

10. Natural Wine and the Globalization of a Taste for Provenance *Jennifer Smith Maguire* — 171

11. Wine, Women and Globalization: The Case of Female Sommeliers *Anna-Mari Almila* — 191

Index — 213

List of Contributors

Editors

Anna-Mari Almila is Research Fellow in Sociology of Fashion at London College of Fashion, UAL. She writes in the fields of cultural, global and historical sociology, and her topics include the historical/political construction of urban spaces, the materiality of dressed bodies and their environments, fashion globalization, history of fashion studies, and gendered wine mediation and consumption. She is the author of *Veiling in Fashion: Space and the Hijab in Minority Communities* (I.B. Tauris, 2018) and the editor (with David Inglis) of *The Routledge International Handbook to Veils and Veiling Practices* (2017) and *The Sage Handbook of Cultural Sociology* (2016).

David Inglis is Professor of Sociology at the University of Helsinki. Before that, he was Professor of Sociology at the University of Exeter and the University of Aberdeen. He holds degrees in sociology from the Universities of Cambridge and York. He writes in the areas of cultural sociology, the sociology of globalization, historical sociology, the sociology of food and drink and social theory, both modern and classical. He has written and edited various books in these areas, most recently *The Sage Handbook of Cultural Sociology* and *The Routledge International Handbook to Veils and Veiling Practices* (with Anna-Mari Almila). He is founding editor of the Sage/BSA journal *Cultural Sociology*. His current research concerns the sociological analysis of the global wine industry.

Other contributors

Pierre-Marie Chauvin is Associate Professor of Sociology at Sorbonne University. He has been Vice Dean for Human and Financial Resources (Sorbonne University, Arts & Humanities Faculty) since 2018. His research interests include economic sociology, sociology of reputations and visual sociology. His PhD focused on the construction of reputations in the Bordeaux wine community (*Le Marché des Réputations. Une sociologie du monde des Grands Crus bordelais*, Bordeaux, Féret, 2010) and has been awarded by the Académie Nationale des Sciences, Belles-Lettres et Arts de Bordeaux and by the Gourmand Awards (Best Book for Professionals). Since then, he has especially been working on a more general theory of reputations, not only in the wine industry but also in other economic, artistic and social worlds.

Marion Demossier holds a Chair in Anthropology in the Department of Modern Languages and Linguistics at the University of Southampton. She has previously taught French and European politics and society at the University of Bath. She holds a PhD in Social Anthropology from the EHESS (École des Hautes Études en Sciences Sociales) in Paris. She has published more than twenty scholarly articles in leading academic journals in Britain, France and the United States, including the *Journal of the Royal Anthropological Institute, Cultural Analysis*, the *Anthropological Journal of European Cultures* and *Modern and Contemporary France*. She has recently completed her third monograph on the anthropology of wine and *terroir: Burgundy: a Global Anthropology of Place and Taste* (Berghahn, 2018). She has also written widely for a student audience, contributing chapters to prestigious series such as *A Companion to the Anthropology of Europe* and *Culinary Taste*.

Hang Kei Ho is Lecturer in Globalization and Development in the Department of Technology and Society Studies within the Faculty of Arts and Social Sciences at Maastricht University. He previously worked as a Postdoctoral Fellow in the Department of Social and Economic Geography at Uppsala University, Sweden. He also worked in the UK as Postdoctoral Researcher in the Department of Sociology at the University of York and Visiting Research Fellow at Goldsmiths, University of London. His current research themes include the geographies of consumption in relation to cultural identity, the global alcohol industry with a specific focus on wine consumption in Hong Kong, the changing identity of Hong Kong with respect to mainland China and the West, and the super-rich and the flow of capital from South East Asia to the UK property market. He obtained his PhD in Geography from University College London with a thesis entitled *Drinking Bordeaux in the 'New' Hong Kong: Exploring Changing Identities through Alcohol Consumption*. Before academia, he worked in education, real estate consultancy, IT and engineering. He also holds an MSc in Geography from University College London, an MA in Digital Culture and Technology from King's College London, and an MEng (Hons) in e-Commerce Engineering from Queen Mary, University of London.

Peter J. Howland is a lecturer in sociology at Massey University in New Zealand. Formerly a journalist (by mistake) and an anthropologist by training, Peter has an enduring interest in wine production, consumption and tourism, and particularly its implications for the various expressions and enactments of middle-class identities (including reflexive individuality), distinctions and values, and associated constructions of place, leisure and sociality. He is the editor of *Social, Cultural and Economic Impacts of Wine in New Zealand* (Routledge, 2014) and co-editor (with Assoc. Prof. Jacqueline Dutton, University of Melbourne) of *Wine, Terroir and Utopia: Making New Worlds* (Routledge, 2019). Peter also researches lotto gambling, gifting and dying/death.

Björn Kjellgren is Associate Professor at KTH Royal Institute of Technology, Stockholm, Sweden. He has a PhD in Sinology and has previously worked as a researcher in social anthropology at the Chinese University of Hong Kong and Stockholm University, where his main research interests have been related to identity, communication and other forms of social interaction.

Justin Otten is an adjunct professor at Indiana University's Russian & East European Institute, where he teaches area studies coursework focusing on the post-communist and ongoing changes occurring in Central & Eastern Europe. Otten previously resided and worked in the Republic of Macedonia and the wider Balkan region through work with the US Peace Corps and American Councils, where he then conducted research for his doctorate in social anthropology from the University of Kent, Canterbury.

Jennifer Smith Maguire is Professor of Cultural Production and Consumption in Sheffield Business School, Sheffield Hallam University. Her research focuses on processes of cultural production and consumption in the construction of markets, tastes and value, often set within the empirical context of super-premium wine markets and market intermediaries. She has published her research in such journals as *Journal of Consumer Culture* and *Consumption, Markets & Culture,* and is the author of *Fit for Consumption: Sociology and the Business of Fitness* (Routledge, 2008), editor of *Food Practices and Social Inequality* (Routledge, 2018) and co-editor of *The Cultural Intermediaries Reader* (Sage, 2014).

Ian Malcolm Taplin is Professor of Sociology, Management and International Studies at Wake Forest University, North Carolina. He has published extensively on the wine industry, in North Carolina, Napa and Bordeaux. The latter two areas are part of a collaborative project examining trends in ultra-premium or iconic wines and how they are changing in the face of increased global markets for wines. His earlier work was on work relations in the clothing industry. He teaches courses on business and society and international business.

1 Introduction: The Travels and Tendencies of Wine

DAVID INGLIS AND ANNA-MARI ALMILA

We walk into a shop that sells wine, located in a city somewhere in north-western Europe. We scan the shelves, which contain wines that have travelled to this country from all over the world. They range from well-known regions like Burgundy to emerging (or re-emerging) areas like Georgia. We seek out what we hope will be an interesting white wine to go with dinner that evening. A bottle from the north-east of Italy catches the eye, not just because it is proclaimed to be organic but also because of a striking label design: a plain white background with a large image of a hashtag. Next to the image is a line where you can write in your own name or anything you feel like putting. On the reverse label, at the bottom, there is a small message in English. It says that the wine is the alter ego of the winemaker, who gives his name, a typically 'Italian'-sounding one. Purchasers of the bottle are politely requested to send photos of them enjoying the wine to a telephone number registered with the Whatsapp social media app. We go back home and while cooking dinner we send via the app a picture of us drinking the wine in the kitchen, adding in a message that we like the wine a lot. A little later we get a cheerful response from the winemaker, thanking us for sending the photo and saying that he hopes that we enjoy the wine. We finish it off and then open another bottle, this time a Pinot Noir from Chile. It is much more basic in character but goes well with the food. There is no winemaker to contact this time, which is the usual case with almost any wine we have ever bought. It gets us thinking about why there is not usually some mechanism mentioned on bottle labels for consumers directly to get in touch with winemakers if they want to ...

Wine is today 'one of the most widespread and complex commodities produced globally' (Huber 2011: 89). An 'ordinary' bottle of wine that middle-class drinkers across the Developed World may open on any given day is in some ways just like other comestibles consumers regularly buy from supermarkets: the green beans in their evening meal may have come from Kenya, the strawberries might have come from Mexico. This is part of much broader trends in agricultural globalization, involving significant levels of dietary 'de-localization', whereby what we eat may have travelled tens of thousands of miles, having negative impacts on the environment while on the way (Murray 2007). What could be more apparently delocalized than enjoying a glass of Chilean wine in, for example, northern Finland? But the label on the bottle wants to assure the consumer that it came from somewhere very 'local' indeed. This is a *re-localizing* move upon a delocalized commodity, seeking to assure the buyer that this product has true character and 'provenance' (see Smith Maguire in this volume) and is not just any old faceless and characterless globalized entity.

The real-life vignette above captures some of the dynamics and phenomena of the globalization of wine (or *wine globalization*, if you prefer), which this book is concerned with. Some of the factors involved in wine globalization, which are pursued throughout this book, can be summarized under these headings: *wine production* (involving a globalization of 'wine world(s)'), *wine consumption* (involving globalization of 'wine culture(s)') and *wine discourse* (involving globalization of 'wine field(s)').

Wine production

- The long-distance and transnational movement of both wines and the containers they come in, moving through complex financial systems and distribution channels.
- The spread in multiple ways, and at various scales and levels, of wines and wine-related entities, practices and ideas, across multiple sorts of borders, including geographical, political and cultural boundaries, and the reworking of those borders themselves.
- The increasing intricacy of trans-oceanic and cross-continental networks, linkages and partnerships.
- Interactions between the so-called 'Old' and 'New' Worlds, and their increasing complexification and mutual influencing of each other.
- The presence of both massive companies and tiny boutique producers, as well as a range of more medium-sized businesses.
- Wine as both bulk, undifferentiated, mass market commodity, and as hyper-differentiated, singularized, elite object of desire.
- Partnerships between firms located in disparate regions of the planet, and 'clusters' of businesses located in certain regions and endowed with diverse forms of knowledge and expertise.
- The appearance of new economic actors, some of which are interested in diverse forms of investment, ploughing money into both established and start-up wineries.
- The integration of winemaking facilities into the global(ized) tourist economy and leisure industries.
- The various roles that scientific knowledges and technological forms of know-how play in how wine is made.
- Globally recognizable classifications of quality standards and price levels, such as the widely-used nomenclature that divides wines into *Basic*, *Premium*, *Super Premium*, *Ultra Premium* and *Icon* categories.

- Various counterblasts to what some regard as the overly technologized orientations of much contemporary winemaking, and the creation of alternative, apparently more 'natural' ways of making wine.
- Controversies about how winemaking impacts both on natural environments and on the workers whose labour, usually in the vineyards, wine depends on; the effects of climate change on winemaking activities.

Wine consumption

- The efforts of wine producers, located across ever more diverse parts of the planet, to enchant consumers sufficiently that their wares will be purchased, this being done through multiple mechanisms of promotion and marketing, including how bottles are labelled and how wines are packaged.
- The tastes, purchasing power, impacts on wine production, and sociopolitical sensibilities of (primarily) middle-class consumers (Koo 2016) – who may be culturally 'omnivorous' or younger, more 'hipster'-style drinkers – located across the Developed World (and increasingly elsewhere too).
- The creation of transnational, 'cosmopolitan' drinking cultures, which spread similar forms of wine-related thought and practice across the richer parts of the world.
- The apparent democratization of wine drinking, making it less of an elitist pursuit than before in some ways, but at the same time affording opportunities for new forms of social division, elite arrogance and snobbery.
- Buying wines at auctions and other locations for reasons of financial speculation.
- The mutation and transnationalization of cultural intermediary roles, such as wine critics and sommeliers, who sell and represent wines to consumers.
- A ubiquitous 'shopping list' of stock words and phrases to describe scents, colours and flavours, which is a kind of global – and globalized – wine talk.
- Retail display mechanisms that can be found practically anywhere where wine is sold to private customers (the cheapest bottles at the bottom of the racks, the most expensive at the top, the bottles the seller wants consumers to trade up to located at eye level).
- Widely available styles of glassware, including those designed by leading companies like Riedel, to enhance flavours and scents, aimed both at wine professionals and at more discerning amateurs across all countries.
- The apparently inevitable presence of certain brands, such as Champagne marques like *Veuve Clicquot*, in putatively 'upscale' retail outlets the world over, alongside other generic, branded commodities like 'designer' perfumes and sunglasses (Ritzer and Ryan 2002).

Wine discourse

- The transnational diffusion of globalized models of how to make and appreciate wine, and multiple indigenizing adaptations of these by people in many different places.
- The operation of a globalized wine cultural industry, involving mass-market books, magazines, courses for non-professionals, tours and vacations, all of which do not just sell wine but also help to frame and stabilize judgements among consumers as to what wine 'is', how it should be part of one's lifestyle, which wines and regions are the best or the most trendy, what environmentally conscious drinkers should be interested in, etc.
- The construction and contestation of regimes of valuing and legitimation, as well as 'good' and 'bad' taste.
- The construction and reconfiguration of what counts in wine terms as 'old' and 'new', 'virtuous' and 'pernicious', etc.
- Defences and inventions of 'tradition' and 'locality'. The interplay between constructions and defences of what counts as the 'local' and 'locality' in winemaking, and reconfigurations of what is 'local' and of what counts as indigeneity, authenticity and provenance. The perception of threats to locality deriving from senses that wine globalization is a massive force tending towards a global homogenization of wines and winemaking styles.
- Disputes over the highly contentious term *terroir* (Ulin and Black 2013).
- The influence of often controversial cultural politics of wine on legislation, both national and transnational, and vice versa, the negotiation and contestation of different legal apparatuses by diverse sorts of actors.
- The roles played in constructing the value of wines, and choosing which wines to buy, by such 'judgement devices' (Karpik 2010) as the reviews and scores offered by influential critics – such as Robert Parker and his globally transportable, comprehensible and influential 100-point scale (McCoy 2005).
- The influence of publications such as *Decanter* magazine, and the transnational influence of the quality and other sorts of judgements made in them.

Mapping wine globalization

The categories above are in some ways artificial classifications. All the factors listed above impact upon all the others in myriad ways. One task of the social scientist is therefore to map this multi-level and poly-causal complexity. Different schools of thought narrate the history of wine globalization in differing but overlapping ways, especially as regards the New World coming to challenge the Old World. Institutionalist economists, for example, focus on how New World companies reduced transaction costs by closely aligning grape-growing, processing, marketing and distribution in strategies of vertical integration, giving them significant advantages over Old World competitors. Regulationist economists, meanwhile, emphasize how changes in the wine world are often responses to broader structural and demographic changes nationally and transnationally, such as changes in consumption habits due to lifestyle shifts among the middle classes across the Developed World. Actor Network Theory-inspired scholars tend to focus on how new marketing strategies connected New World producers to Old World consumers, taking market share away from European companies (for the different paradigms, see Itçaina et al 2016). In what follows here and in Chapter 2, we will draw selectively on these models.

Wine consumers like to imagine – and are very much encouraged by people in the wine business to believe – that a particular person called a 'winemaker' made what they drank, and that they made it in a particular place, and that the wine somehow reflects and expresses the nature of that location. But when one investigates who is 'responsible' for the wine, it is almost always never just a single person, even if a singular (meaning rhetorically 'singularized') person is the public face of the wine and its winery. Those 'responsible' for the wine, in one way or another, include not only those who actually turn the grapes into what is conventionally called 'wine', but also the people who grew the grapes, who pick them, who own the fields and the wineries, who invent and disseminate the scientific knowledges and the technologies that inform the winemaking process, and many others too, especially those involved in shipping and marketing. Wine is a *collective* and *distributed* product, made by different sorts of people, all acting in tandem, and sometimes interacting in conflictual ways too.

Put very schematically, the kinds of actors involved in the physical making, distributing and consuming of wine across borders look like this (following Simpson 2011):

Growers (of grapes) – Makers/producers (of wine) – Technical specialists (e.g. scientists, advisors, marketers) – Merchants – Importers – Retailers – Consumers.

As changes occur in the various relations connecting the various types of people in the chain, so too may the nature of the participants *themselves* change. For example, when new means of transportation of wine arrive on the scene, they may help to change what existing producers and consumers do, while possibly helping to create new types of producer and consumer.

Different relations between the various groups indicated above have pertained at different times and places. Sometimes a single company can play more than one role in the chain. For example, in the nineteenth century, in much of the so-called New World (primarily North and South America, South Africa, Australasia), growers often owned winemaking facilities, and so the grower and maker roles were combined, whereas in much of Europe (the so-called Old World), growing was often separate from production, which in turn was often separate from marketing. Merchants would blend the grapes of small family producers and sell it to consumers under their names rather than those of the producers. In this way, the consumer learnt to trust and like brands that did not reveal who grew the grapes or made the wine. However, a counter-trend also developed, whereby producers, who were sometimes also growers, sought to market their wine to consumers under their own name, reducing the power of the merchants and importers.

One of the major features of wine globalization today is a tendency towards very large companies being involved in, and thus being able to control, multiple parts of the chain. These outfits may control everything, from what is grown in vineyards and how it is grown, to the placing of the bottles on the shelves of shops. Major actors here include massive drinks conglomerates and certain large supermarkets, especially British ones like Tesco and Asda. Both these sorts of companies have the financial clout to control what wine gets made, how it is distributed, and how it is sold. They have great influence upon which wines get to consumers and which wines consumers find palatable and worth paying for (Veseth 2012).

Globalization processes have complicated the collective and distributed nature of wine production, drawing into the web that makes wine and wine drinking possible in the first place, ever more variant types of people, who are located, in complex but patterned ways, across large swathes of the planet. Examining the sorts of social relationships that exist between all these different kinds of people involves attending to things that are cultural, economic, political and spatial in nature, or blends and hybrids of these. One might therefore more precisely define the globalization of wine as *the increasing social, cultural, economic, political and spatial complexification across the planet of how wine is made, how it is distributed, how it is drunk, and what people think it means to them.*

The globalization of wine never involves just one single big process. Instead, wine globalization is made up of multiple processes, all overlapping and affecting each other but not necessarily cohering or heading in any one unified direction. The globalization of wine is made up of clashing and contradictory processes, and it is precisely that which means things usually becoming more complicated over time. The globalization of wine is also always tied up in all sorts of ways with wider processes of globalization, themselves being social, cultural, economic, political and spatial in nature. Wine globalization is strongly shaped by these factors and the ways in which they intertwine, as well as to some degree acting upon them in turn too.

There is of course no one accepted definition among scholars as to what 'globalization' is and involves, and which theoretical and empirical accounts of it should be deployed. Yet wine globalization is of far too great a complexity for the diverse processes involved in it to be adequately captured by any one theory or paradigm. Nonetheless, students of wine globalization have drawn, and in future can draw, on certain theoretical vocabularies so as to highlight and understand better the particular phenomena, forces and trends that they are particularly concerned with. Theoretical positions that have already been useful in this regard, or could be further utilized, include (in a non-exhaustive list):

- Marxist political-economic and neo-Marxist accounts of the globalization of neo-liberal economic ideas and practices (Harvey 2014), as well as world-systems analysis of cores, semi-peripheries and peripheries of wine worlds (Wallerstein 2004).
- Understandings of, and attempts to model, the nature of global forms of complexity (Urry 2003).
- Geographic analysis of the construction and operation of diverse scales and levels of globalization, and the resulting forms of spatiality and positionality (Sheppard 2002).
- A focus on the interrelated processes of *de-territorialization* – involving a set of processes 'in which the constraints of geography on social and cultural arrangements recede and in which people become increasingly aware that they are receding' (Waters 1995: 3) – and *re-territorialization* – where locality and place once again become objects of political concern and motivating forces for action.
- A focus on the 'stretching' of social relations across vast distances, connecting different sorts of people in novel ways (Giddens 1990).
- Morally engaged critique of transnational practices which exploit humans and non-humans alike (Bauman 1998), and the creation of spiralling forms of anxiety and risk (Beck 2000).
- Analyses of trends towards global cultural homogenization (Seabrook 2004) and similarities of thought and practice in diverse locations, as well as counter-trends towards forms of resistance to perceived homogenization (Castells 1997), and dynamics involving increased cultural heterogenization and hybridization (Robertson 1992).
- Understanding the diffusion of globalized models, templates and ideas around the planet (Meyer 2010), as well as forms of adaptation and indigenization of them (Appadurai 1996).
- Culturalist accounts of the complex interplays between more 'global' and more 'local' phenomena, and how each of these constitutes the other, including through processes of 'glocalization' (Robertson 1992), and 'the loss of the "natural" relation of culture to geographical and social territories' (Garcia-Canclini 1995: 107).
- Anthropological analyses of complicated forms of cultural 'friction' (Tsing 2005) and 'imbrication' (Demossier in this volume).

Returning to the schematic chain of actors indicated above, it is limited in at least two ways. It omits consideration of other sorts of human actors who are involved, as well as ignoring non-human 'actants'. Wine is, after all, located in complicated ways between 'nature', agriculture and human culture(s). How it is made and sent around the world is always part of broader dynamics in the world agriculture industries

(Alston and Pardey 2014). At the same time, wine is a *cultural* industry. Just like fashion, pop music and films, the wine world is centrally concerned with selling and marketing products, and with generating enough interest in those products among potential customers to shift them off the shelves. Whether a wine travels or not very strongly depends on whether conditions are right for its portability to generate profits for different sorts of people. The factors involved here encompass phenomena as diverse as the costs of the wages of the labourers who pick the grapes (part of the global agricultural industry), through to the fees incurred in hiring designers to produce appealing labels on bottles (part of the global cultural industries). All these impact on how far, by what means, and eventually to whom, a wine will travel.

We suggest looking at these sorts of issues through some useful distinctions made by the American sociologist Priscilla Parkhurst Ferguson (2004) (while acknowledging that not all scholars would agree with this conceptualization). When we talk of the *wine world*, we primarily mean the sphere of wine *production*, which is made up of networks of all the different sorts of people involved in growing grapes and making and selling wines. When we refer to *wine culture*, we mean the sphere of wine *consumption*, encompassing what people do when they buy wine (to drink it, to store it, to have it as an investment in storage that they will never drink, etc.) and the various sorts of ideas and values which drive their buying of it. Finally, when we refer to the *wine field*, we refer to how people talk about, construe, debate, polemicize about and imagine wine, both in general and in terms of specified bottles, grapes, wineries, regions, nations and suchlike. This is a field of competing and conflicting values and opinions. It mediates between the wine world and wine culture, as it shapes both what consumers consume and what producers produce. It is not only a field populated by people like professional critics and wine instructors; it is also made up of anyone who has an opinion about wine that is expressed publicly in one way or another, such as amateurs who go to wine-tastings or people who blog about wine for fun.

Globalization processes have had and are having multiple effects on the wine world, the wine culture and the wine field. One could argue that today a wine world, a wine culture and a wine field exist which intersect with each other and which are truly 'global' in scope, insofar as people in practically every part of the world are participants in them and therefore are connected to each other by virtue of being participants. Each of these domains crosses the globe, traversing and often troubling national and other borders. But they are complicated domains, in large part because nested within them are both *national* and *regional* (and sometimes *subregional* and perhaps even very *local*) wine worlds, cultures and fields. For example, the Médoc subregional world, culture and field are nested within their Bordeaux regional, French national and global equivalents. The more particular Médoc domains have their own specified logics, dynamics and concerns, which feed into their more regional, national and global counterparts in complex ways. At the same time, the forces and phenomena produced through, and operative within, the latter come to impact upon the more specific Médoc domains in multiple ways.

We could therefore further define wine globalization in this way: the *dialectics of 'local', 'sub-regional', 'regional', 'national' and 'global' wine worlds, cultures and fields*. The geographical terms are in inverted commas because they are not essences, even if much wine parlance presents them that way. Instead we should recognize at least two aspects of the (so-called) *'local', 'sub-regional', 'regional', 'national'* and *'global'*: actors rhetorically construct and dispute these terms constantly, and each of these domains should be seen to co-constitute all the others in multiple ways. One task of the wine-focused social scientist is to map out these multiple and complicated processes of co-constitution.

This is still a human-centred picture of wine-related matters. It omits the fact that in the production of wine there are more than just human actors; there are also – to use the terminology of Actor Network Theory – non-human 'actants' involved (Latour 2003). These also 'make a difference' to the totality of the processes that wine involves. The non-humans which need to be considered in order to give a more adequate picture of both wine and wine globalization include the vines (and the human and non-human scientific and technological labour that went into making them what they are); the grapes in their multiple forms and types; the pests that afflict grape crops; the insects and other animals that live in the vineyards; the weather and climate (including climate change); the soil and other features of the wine-growing terrain; the scientific knowledges and technological apparatuses, such as filtering mechanisms, used to transform grapes into viable juice, and juice into viable wine; the yeasts, 'natural' or 'artificial', which are necessary for fermentation; the winery buildings, including the scientific laboratories often found inside them today; the fermenting vats; the storage barrels; the additives, preservatives and stabilizers added to the wine, such as sulphites; the containers used for shipping, as well as the vehicles deployed for that purpose; the bottles and bags wine is sold in; the decanters, filters and glasses used to drink it, and various other non-human entities. All of these are just as much players in the 'co-creation' of winemaking and drinking, and therefore of wine globalization, as are the human actors involved.

A note on *terroir*

So important is the notion of *terroir* in wine-related thought, practice and politics today that a few remarks about the term are in order at this point. The notion that a wine must be the product of a given *terroir* strongly influences how people across the world today think about wine's provenance (Parker 2015). Notions of *terroir* have spread across the world, especially over the last forty years. The ubiquity and taken-for-granted nature today of *terroir* ideas across the world is itself a sign and product of globalization. The term was not used much in English language discussions of wine until the 1980s, at which point its usage rose hugely (Matthews 2015: 148). There is now an 'international cult of terroir' (Hannickel 2013: 12).

The idea of *terroir* has a very long history in France, stretching back to the Renaissance period. But the cultural consecration and marketing of it is a twentieth-century phenomenon. Burgundy in the 1920s and 1930s can be argued to be a pioneering region, where intellectuals and journalists popularized *terroir* notions. They staged a new, media-savvy range of wine festivals, gastronomic fairs and newly invented brotherhoods of the vine carrying out supposedly arcane wine rituals at public events, which weaved together 'natural resources, historical memory, marketing strategies and cultural performance'. These new activities and institutions emphasized *terroir*'s 'eternal, transcendent and metaphysical properties' (Whalen 2009: 68, 76). The need to present this message on foreign markets was well understood (Whalen 2009: 95). So successful was this strategy, encompassing globally-aimed publicity and encouraging international tourism, that it was widely copied by other French regions, and then in winemaking regions around the world, where interested parties want to present to the world that their wines are expressions of *terroir* and a very particular sense of place (Crenn 2015).

This sort of marketing of wine can help to create a sense of a coherent 'regional' food culture, even if that is a fabrication which hides local political tensions as well as the possible presence of exploited (often minority ethnic) labour and of globalized capitalist agribusiness (Peace 2006). Both visitors and the personnel on-site who handle them will in most cases be overwhelmingly of white ethnicity, testament to the highly ethnically skewed nature of wine worlds, cultures and fields across the world (Howland in this volume). Ideas of *terroir* are widely deployed in touristic wine promotion, and internationally recognizable words like 'chateau' and 'domaine' operate as reproducible signifiers, connoting that either the humblest or the most mass-market wineries are somehow part of a wider noble tradition (Gade 2004).

For social scientists sceptical of *terroir* claims, 'reputation and tradition are constructed while helping to disguise the reality of social change' (Demossier 1997: 56). Critics also allege that *terroir* ideas imply a kind of environmental determinism – somehow the earth 'speaks' through the wines. It then becomes potentially awkward for the winemaker to describe their own role in the process. Are they just 'midwives', allowing the *terroir* to speak for itself? If so, how does one account for the fact that the winemaker is actively involved in all sorts of ways in making the wine (Matthews 2015)? Wine marketing often relies on globally spread *terroir* imagery, disguising the scientific and technical basis of most modern winemaking (Beverland and Luxton 2005). According to some, *terroir* thinking is in fact mostly or wholly a marketing strategy (Laudan 2004). *Terroir* is a way of constructing the 'local' in order to circulate it globally and to accrue profit from it (Heath and Meneley 2007). *Terroir*-based marketing claims that the wine comes from an authentic rural idyll, rather than from the generic, highly industrialized and scientized environments it actually was made in (Beverland and Luxton 2005). As Demossier (2010: 210) trenchantly argues, winemakers in all parts of the world can play 'the local, traditional and natural cards even when they are almost entirely detached from their social environment, do not cultivate their land or do not even make the wine themselves'.

One outspoken critic of *terroir* ideas, Mark Matthews (2015), suggests that science and technology can trump *terroir* such that almost identical wines can be made in radically different environments – which is precisely what advocates of *terroir* would vehemently deny. Conversely, Genevieve Teil (2012) argues that *terroir* is neither simply 'real' nor 'fake'. It is a changing entity widely distributed among many winemakers, an ongoing collective production provisionally dependent every year on collective actions by multiple people. The qualities of the wines are 'the plural, diverse and relatively unpredictable result of a production process' involving multiple actors across time (Teil 2012: 490). Teil's approach may be a way for social scientists to look at *terroir* which avoids buying into one side or the other in the deeply polarized debates about *terroir* – whether it is real or imaginary, whether it is under threat or thriving – that go on across the world.

We can also say that 'globalization' and 'terroir' are not necessarily diametric opposites, even if highly politicized rhetoric in wine fields often constructs things that way. When people in a particular place worry that the wines made there may lose their special *terroir*-based characteristics, as wine production becomes seemingly ever more 'globalized', what they will most likely not be fully aware of is that it was already as a result of globalizing forces that the very notion that wines in that place express a *terroir* will have arrived in that location in the first place. Paradoxically, at a time when the French branch of the wine world seems to be under threat and in a state of crisis apparently like never before, because of the forces of 'globalization', at the same time the globalized wine world is thoroughly underpinned and animated by originally French – but now trans-nationally present – ideas about what wine is, and how it should be made, sold, and enjoyed (Demossier 2010).

Some trends and dynamics

As will be noted in Chapter 2, wine globalization in our view should be understood in the light of consideration of long-term processes. There are good reasons for claiming that, up until the eighteenth century CE, wine involved certain *proto*-globalization processes, but it was not until the eighteenth or nineteenth centuries that one can really speak of 'wine globalization' as such beginning. Regardless of such periodizations, one can certainly say wine and its globalization have clearly become much more complex over the last forty years or so, mirroring much wider trends towards global complexity (Urry 2003). Since the 1970s and (especially) 1980s, a series of new developments have occurred, consideration of which captures much (but not all) of what might reasonably be characterized as 'wine globalization' in a strong sense of that phrase.

If we first of all consider changing patterns of wine production, trade and export, we can see that the wine world was still very centred on Europe as recently as the 1960s, with France and Italy predominating, both in terms of production levels and of prestige. As wine production everywhere has since then shifted from a focus on pure volume to higher quality levels, the total amount of production across the world has dropped considerably (Anderson and Pinilla 2018). In the middle half of the nineteenth century, France, Italy and Spain produced more than three quarters of global production. It was not until 2006 that their share fell below 50 per cent, being affected by massively increased production in the New World (Anderson and Pinilla 2018).

Most wine made until the 1960s was consumed relatively close to its geographical source. More than half of the total global wine export trade in the period immediately after the Second World War was comprised of cheap Algerian imports into France (Veseth 2012). The trend share of global wine production that was exported from the country of origin remained flat at about one-eighth across the first six or seven decades of the twentieth century (Anderson and Pinilla 2018). Only circa 10 per cent of total wine production by volume was traded internationally in the 1960s. The corresponding figure was still less than 15 per cent by 1990 (Anderson and Pinilla 2018). That figure had risen to 25 per cent by 2001. From the late 1980s through to the early 2000s, the international wine trade nearly doubled in size. The share of wine production that was exported grew more rapidly in the New World than the Old. For the big producing countries of Europe (France, Italy, Spain), the ratio of the volume of exports as a percentage of total production rose from 20 per cent in the late 1980s to 33 per cent in the early 2000s, while the corresponding figure for New World countries went up in the same period from 3 per cent to 20 per cent (Anderson 2003; Anderson et al 2004).

The take-off of New World exports started in the late 1980s and then accelerated in the 1990s. Having accounted for less than 9 per cent of the value of global wine exports before 1990, the New World's share rose to 37 per cent in the first decade after 2000, before reaching a plateau in the second decade (Anderson and Pinilla 2018). By 2006, Australia exported half of its total wine production, while France exported one quarter (Duncan and Greenaway 2008). By 2012, the annual volume of wine traded internationally was about 24 per cent of total world production. Much of that trade was over relatively short distances (e.g. from Italy to France). The New World countries accounted for 30 per cent of wine exports by volume, while Italy, Spain, France, Germany and Portugal made up most of the remaining 70 per cent (Smith et al 2013). Spain and Chile have the highest level of exports per capita today, while Argentina and South Africa have dramatically increased export levels over the last few decades (Anderson and Pinilla 2018). There has been a major trend over time towards convergence between Old and New Worlds in terms of both production levels and consumption per capita (Anderson and Pinilla 2018).

Export trends have been very much bound up with changing patterns of drinking among consumers. The top seven wine-consuming countries accounted for 77 per cent of total wine consumption in the period 1959–63, but this dropped to 61 per cent in the period 2009–13, indicating a wider spread of countries consuming ever larger proportions of the global total (Anderson and Pinilla 2018).

Another very general trend since the 1970s, with particularly marked ramifications in the Old World, has been a decline in wine drinking in producer countries. In Western Europe, the volume of alcohol, including wine, consumed fell steadily after 1990. This has forced Old World producers to seek more value from export markets. Across all countries there was a marked trend away from old-fashioned local and regional *vin ordinaire* table wines and towards consumption of 'premium' wines, with more of the latter than the former being consumed across the board by the mid-2000s (Smith et al 2013). With higher average income levels, the level of expenditure per bottle increased, as consumers in Europe especially raised the quality level of their purchases (Anderson and Pinilla 2018).

There have been rises in consumption in non-wine-producing countries (or those with very small local wine industries, such as Denmark) but mostly from very low starting points (Anderson and Pinilla 2018). The biggest percentage-rate rises of levels of national wine consumption in Europe between 1970 and 2010 were as follows: Ireland (+960 per cent), Finland (+573 per cent), UK (+566 per cent) and Denmark (+323 per cent). The biggest falls in consumption in the same period were in wine-producing countries: Italy (−61 per cent), France (−53 per cent), Spain (−54 per cent) and Portugal (−30 per cent) (Smith et al 2013). At the same time, the fastest growing market for wine was China, undergoing an unprecedented economic boom and a concomitant forging of a new conspicuous consumption-driven elite and a broader upper- and middle-middle class (Smart 2004; Smith et al 2013; Capitello et al 2016; for detailed discussion of China, see Ho and Kjellgren, both in this volume).

In all Developed World countries where the mass drinking of wine was a new phenomenon, there was a high correlation between wine consumption and the social level of consumers, as measured by level of education. In European wine-producing countries, declining consumption was strongly connected to the shrinking of the 'old' working class, through deindustrialization processes destroying employment in heavy industries and the decreasing role of agricultural work in the economy. It became less common and less socially approved to drink wine during the working day, while national governments enacted ever stricter rules on drunk driving, while highlighting health concerns to do with alcohol consumption (Lukacs 2012). Even in France, which both French people and foreigners have imagined as a bastion of everyday wine consumption, consumption levels of all types of alcohol fell from the 1970s onwards, with a marked shift away from wine to mass-market beer and branded spirits, and away from the old-style anonymous table wines towards branded products (Sulkunen 1989).

By contrast, in the UK, Ireland and other parts of north-west Europe including the Nordic countries, the drinking of branded, often New World wines developed greatly in the 1980s and onwards due to a range of factors. This included the rise of aspirational lifestyle-conscious middle classes and their newly developed orientation to buy wine in supermarkets and drink it in the booming restaurant market (Anderson et al 2004).

While the UK has for centuries been an important consumer of premium wines, especially from Bordeaux, it accounted for under 1 per cent of global wine sales before the early 1970s (Anderson and Pinilla 2018). There had been a rise in wine consumption in the UK in the later nineteenth century, but that had fallen before the

Second World War to the same level it was at the time of the Napoleonic wars. This was less to do with tariffs on imports blocking consumption, and more to do with the fact that the amount and quality of wine being imported could not keep pace with the consistency of the supply chains for other mass-market branded comestibles, such as chocolate and tea (Simpson 2011). But in the 1980s there became available a steady supply of palatable and cheap mass-market wines from the New World. By the early 2000s, one could say that 'more of the world's wines [were] … available in the UK than any other country' (Stening et al 2004: 136). By the 2010s, the British consumed 5 per cent of total world wine production by volume, but 17 per cent of all world wine imports, the highest proportion in the world, followed by consumers in Germany and the United States. The UK was also responsible for a massive 20 per cent of the total money spent per year in international wine exchanges (Veseth 2012: 53).

In North America, wine became a fashionable interest in the 1980s and 1990s for higher fractions within the broad 'middle class' (Pinney 2005). Across the Developed World, there was the rise of what Demossier (2010) calls the 'wandering drinkers', who increasingly supplanted in importance the old-style upper bourgeois drinker with unchanging tastes (as in the British case, for example, for styles and regions like claret and Port). These new entrants were middle-class people, especially younger ones, with disposable income, often working in service jobs in the neo-liberal economy, with interests in trying out new alcoholic drinks, and having no strong affiliations to any particular wine style or region. Capturing their attention, as well as supplying a mass market of less adventurous consumers who would buy basic table wines from supermarkets, became an important part of wine marketing in the 1990s and after. That in turn had important effects on which wines were made, which styles were elaborated, and where they were made. Many of these newer consumers were female, in white-collar work, and equipped with disposable income, and wine marketing increasingly targeted the growing female market (Stening et al 2004; for wine and gender, see Almila in this volume).

In a strongly neo-liberal economic situation, massive disparities in wealth are created with a small group of super-rich at the top, who vastly surpass in buying power more ordinary middle-class drinkers. Particularly since the 1980s, the use of wines from prestigious regions – pre-eminently Bordeaux, but also areas such as Burgundy, Tuscany and parts of Northern California – as investments by the very wealthy has grown apace, a trend magnified by the entrance of Chinese buyers into the game from the early 2000s. As prices in both classic regions of the Old World and prestigious parts of the New World have gone up, in some cases astronomically, more demand has arisen for the development of 'new' regions that will produce wine that large numbers of more modestly endowed middle-class drinkers can access. For example, the rapid renaissance of regions in northern Spain and southern Italy, now producing mid-market wines aimed at international audiences rather than the *vin ordinaire* of the past, which only would have been consumed locally, is a consequence of, and further contributing factor to, these global market dynamics (Lukacs 2012). An indicator of the degree to which people all across the world now drink the same sorts of wines is that 12 to 14 per cent alcohol volume is today standard pretty much everywhere across the wine-producing regions of the world – although some areas, such as Germany and Alsace, specialize in lower alcohol white wines, reaching certain niche markets of consumers, including the apparently 'health-conscious' (Nossiter 2009).

The rest of the book ...

The various chapters in this book unpick and go into more detail on the various issues mentioned above. The complexity of wine globalization issues means that it is not enough to approach them from the viewpoint of any one theoretical perspective or academic discipline – which is why the definitions of wine globalization offered above are deliberately general and open to varying forms of operationalization. Throughout this book, chapter authors draw on a range of disciplinary sources, such as sociology, anthropology, geography, and history, among others, seeking to develop more comprehensive accounts of how wine globalization works in practice. Each chapter seeks to do more than just report on particular conditions in some part of the world where wine is made, sold or drunk, although that is obviously fascinating and worthwhile in itself. They also seek to show how broader globalization processes are at work in such locations, as well as suggesting how consideration of particularities may refine or change our understandings of those wider dynamics. Moreover, chapters have been designed to represent a variety of interconnected locations – physical and symbolic – across wine worlds, cultures and fields. These include both Old and New Worlds, both 'classic' (e.g. Bordeaux, Burgundy) and 'emerging' (e.g. Peru, Republic of Macedonia, North Carolina) regions, both well established (e.g. European capital cities) and novel (e.g. Hong Kong, China) places and spaces of intermediation and consumption. Authors draw out wider implications, and draw upon and sometimes modify existing models, while their empirical data provide the reader with the opportunity to compare the reported contexts with other locations they may know about.

Chapter 2, by David Inglis, provides background and contextualization for the later chapters by concentrating on some of the major and general dynamics of wine globalization, as these have occurred both historically and more recently. In Chapter 3, Marion Demossier discusses the interrelatedness of more local and more global narratives in Burgundy, arguing that there is a global hierarchy of values that each winemaking location must define itself through. She analyzes the struggles in and through which different groups of wine professionals redefine themselves and their region in the world wine market.

The next two chapters raise broader issues to do with emerging (or re-emerging) wine-producing regions. In Chapter 4, Ian Taplin discusses the case of winemaking in North Carolina. During recent decades actors in the region have managed to (re)establish it using thoroughly transnational means, such as deploying knowledges taken from more established regions, planting globally known grape varietals and hybrids, starting wine education programmes, establishing a local *appellation*, and promoting wine tourism, in so doing creating a new and viable form of local 'authenticity'.

In Chapter 5, Justin Otten discusses the Republic of Macedonia, a location with a long history of winemaking through the times of the Roman and Ottoman Empires, the Communist era, the period of the post-Communist privatization of markets, and now candidacy for EU membership. The Macedonian case illustrates certain trends typical of the former Communist Bloc as a whole, while it also displays some dynamics particular to that country itself. Partly despite politics and partly because of them, the country has begun to be established as a producer of more than just cheap bulk wines. A range of globalized strategies have also been involved here, as in North Carolina, such as planting internationally known varietals and realizing the potential value of indigenous grapes for discerning foreign consumers. Yet the country's wine world still struggles, for various more localized and more globalized reasons.

Other chapters consider the forms of global connectivity that stretch across and into geographically disparate parts of the globe. In Chapter 6, Pierre-Marie Chauvin sets out how a reputation system for wines operates in one of the most prestigious regions in the world, namely Bordeaux, arguing that globalization processes have been involved in the creation of that system for a considerable time. Already the famous 1855 classification of elite producers was a production of both French and international actors, created in large part for international marketing purposes. All elements of the reputation system, such as classifications, grades, prices and winemaker signatures, are globalized, and transnational factors are crucial in the system's operations. With current changes in the region, such as new owners with no previous winemaking skills, new actors have emerged, notably transnationally operative wine consultants, whose signature has emerged as an alternative currency instead of the reputation of traditional winemaking families.

Chinese money has radically changed aspects of Bordeaux recently, and in Chapter 7 Björn Kjellgren describes how China has become a major global wine actor, not only in terms of consumption but also in terms of actual grape-growing and winemaking. He recognizes the long history of these in China (Li et al 2018), as well as more recent developments in importing wine and the great influence that French winemaking has had on China's wine culture today. Local winemakers often struggle to find a coherent identity for selling their products but nonetheless can tap into various globalized imageries, involving symbolism of urban cosmopolitanism, Chinese heritage and Bordeaux-derived stylistics. This is a combination of perceived tradition and aspirational modernity that can be found in different ways across the globe today.

One of major ways that finer wines, including those from Bordeaux, reach Chinese buyers and consumers is through wine auctions in the intermediary location of Hong Kong. This is Hang Kei Ho's focus in Chapter 8. He reflects upon Asia becoming a central location for the globalized fine wine trade over the last two decades. There have been elaborate governmental efforts to support the development of wine retailing in Hong Kong, focused on investment, trade and tourism.

Hong Kong wine events today are globalized in multiple ways. While running a wine business in Hong Kong can be challenging, involving all sorts of intermediaries and complicating factors, the distinctive wine culture there is attracting many new kinds of entrant, at the same time as cultural transformations are at work that legitimize wine drinking and wine knowledge as valued forms of cultural capital. One can also note here the apparently very high levels of wine fraud in Hong Kong, with rich buyers being sold fake versions of grand wines from Bordeaux and other classic regions (Chan 2017).

Issues of cultural capital, cultural legitimization, cultural intermediaries, and old and new middle-class consumers are all crucial aspects of wine worlds, cultures and fields today, and they are elaborated upon by Peter J. Howland, Jennifer Smith Maguire and Anna-Mari Almila in Chapters 9, 10 and 11 respectively. Howland discusses globalized middle-class tastes in wine and how they operate in and through the burgeoning area of wine tourism. He argues that such tastes are not in any simple sense universal, but rather are simultaneously hybridized and globalized. While for consumers and tourists there is a certain sense of adventure involved when exploring new winemaking regions, there is also a sense of transnational recognizability: vineyards opened for visitors seem to be similar everywhere, and are run along similar lines, which creates a sense of familiarity and safety for the affluent wine tourist. Howland argues that a globalized system of influences – encompassing multiple media, commentators, websites, and events – has created a complexly globalized wine culture that traverses the whole of the Developed World.

Smith Maguire raises similar sorts of issues but this time with reference to how the sociocultural legitimacy and prestige of 'natural' wines has been created by the evoking of symbols of purity, heritage, genuineness and *terroir*. She argues that the rise of more 'omnivorous' cultural dispositions among middle-class consumers in multiple locations has helped the spread and legitimation of 'natural' wines. She recognizes the important role of influencers in the globalized wine field, such as wine critics and journalists writing for wine magazines, in promoting this new category of wines. She discerns a certain level of democratization of both wine production (enabling production in new or hitherto less prestigious areas, often by novel sorts of winemakers) and wine consumption (opening up access to complex wines to consumers who were previously scared off by more traditional ways of appreciating wine). 'Natural' wines are particularly appealing for those who have more cultural than economic resources, especially younger, hipper drinkers in big city locations around the Developed World. These new consumers are helping to develop broader definitions of wines' provenance, possibly in the direction of 'post-terroir' sensibilities.

The influence of cultural intermediaries on patterns of wine consumption is also taken up by Anna-Mari Almila. The globalized idea of the sommelier today is still primarily of a job carried out by persons who are 'male and pale'. But by focusing on the entry of more women into the traditionally male-dominated profession of sommelier, Almila considers the mutating nature of this influential wine profession, and also points to more general issues to do with the highly gendered nature of wine in national and transnational contexts. Wine globalization processes have created opportunities for women to participate, often for the first time, in all sorts of wine-related work, and have also allowed for different types of mobilities, both social, economic and geographical. While research has been carried out on female winemakers (Matasar 2006), women who operate in other wine-related professions remain under-explored, a gap which Almila's chapter starts to fill.

Each of the chapters that follow has, as it were, its own distinctive nose, bouquet and body, while resonating with and illuminating each other. None are, we believe, 'dry' in the academic sense of the word. All reveal themselves beautifully, in so doing illustrating and interrogating many crucial aspects of the globalization of wine. We trust that the reader will enjoy what each has to offer, perhaps accompanied by a good glass of something or other, drawn from the multiple and manifold wine options that the world presents us with at the present time…

References

Alston, J.M., and Pardey, P.G. (2014), 'Agriculture in the Global Economy', *The Journal of Economic Perspectives*, 28(1):121–46.

Anderson, K. (2003), 'Wine's New World', *Foreign Policy*, 136:46–54.

Anderson, K., Norman, D., and Wittwer, G. (2004), 'The Global Picture', in Anderson, K. (ed.), *The World's Wine Markets: Globalization at Work*, Cheltenham: Edward Elgar, 14–58.

Anderson, K., and Pinilla, V. (2018), 'Global Overview', in Anderson, K., and Pinilla, V. (eds), *Wine Globalization: A New Comparative History*, Cambridge: Cambridge University Press, 24–54.

Appadurai, A. (1996), *Modernity at Large: Cultural Dimensions of Globalization*, Minneapolis: University of Minnesota Press.

Bauman, Z. (1998), *Globalization: The Human Consequences*, Cambridge: Polity.

Beck, U. (2000), *What Is Globalization?*, Cambridge: Polity.

Beverland, M., and Luxton, S. (2005), 'Managing Integrated Marketing Communication (IMC) through Strategic Decoupling: How Luxury Wine Firms Retain Brand Leadership While Appearing to Be Wedded to the Past', *Journal of Advertising*, 34(4):103–16.

Black, R.E., and Ulin, R.C. (eds) (2013) *Wine and Culture: Vineyard to Glass*, London: Bloomsbury.

Capitello, R., Charters, S., and Menival, D. (eds) (2016), *The Wine Value Chain in China: Consumers, Marketing and the Wider World*, Amsterdam: Chandos.

Castells, M. (1997), *The Power of Identity, The Information Age: Economy, Society and Culture*, Vol. II, Oxford: Blackwell.

Chan, B. (2017), 'Is Hong Kong Awash with Fake Wines?', *South China Morning Post*, 2nd March.

Crenn, C. (2015), 'Ethnic Identity, Power, Compromise, and Territory: 'Locals' and 'Moroccans' in the Sainte-Foy-Bordeaux Vineyards', in MacClancy, J. (ed.), *Alternative Countrysides: Anthropological Approaches to Rural Western Europe Today*, Manchester: Manchester University Press, 61–81.

Demossier, M. (1997), 'Producing Tradition and Managing Social Changes in the French Vineyards: The Circle of Time in Burgundy', *Ethnologia Europaea* 27:47–58.
Demossier, M. (2010), *Wine Drinking Culture in France: A National Myth or a Modern Passion?*, Cardiff: University of Wales Press.
Duncan, A., and Greenaway, D. (2008), 'The Economics of Wine – Introduction', *The Economics Journal*, 118(529):F137–41.
Ferguson, P.P. (2004), *Accounting for Taste: The Triumph of French Cuisine*, Chicago: University of Chicago Press.
Gade, D.W. (2004), 'Tradition, Territory, and Terroir in French Viniculture: Cassis, France, and Appellation Contrôlée', *Annals of the Association of American Geographers*, 94(4):848–67.
Garcia-Canclini, N. (1995), *Hybrid Cultures: Strategies for Entering and Leaving Modernity*, Minneapolis: University of Minnesota Press.
Giddens, A. (1990), *The Consequences of Modernity*, Cambridge: Polity.
Hannickel, E. (2013), *Empire of Vines: Wine Culture in America*, Philadelphia: University of Pennsylvania Press.
Harvey, D. (2014), *Seventeen Contradictions and the End of Capitalism*, Oxford: Oxford University Press.
Heath, D., and Meneley, A. (2007), 'Techne, Technoscience, and the Circulation of Comestible Commodities: An Introduction', *American Anthropologist*, 109(4):593–602.
Huber, T.P. (2011), *Wine: An American Provence*, Boulder: University Press of Colorado.
Itcaina, X., Roger, A., and Smith, A. (2016), *Varietals of Capitalism: A Political Economy of the Changing Wine Industry*, Cornell: Cornell University Press.
Karpik, L. (2010), *Valuing the Unique: The Economics of Singularities*, Princeton: Princeton University Press.
Koo, H. (2016), 'The Global Middle-Class: How Is It Made, What Does It Represent?', *Globalizations*, 1(1):1–14.
Latour, B. (2003), *Reassembling the Social*, Oxford: Oxford University Press.
Laudan, R. (2004), 'Slow Food: The French Terroir Strategy, and Culinary Modernism', *Food, Culture and Society*, 7(2):133–144.
Li, H., et al (2018), 'The Worlds of Wine: Old, New and Ancient', *Wine Economics and Policy*, 7:178–82.
Lukacs, P. (2012), *Inventing Wine*, New York: W. W. Norton.
Matasar, A.B. (2006), *Women of Wine: The Rise of Women in the Global Wine Industry*, Berkeley: University of California Press.
Matthews, M.A. (2015), *Terroir and Other Myths of Winegrowing*, Berkeley: University of California Press.
Meyer, J.W. (2010), 'World Society, Institutional Theories, and the Actor', *Annual Review of Sociology*, 36:1–20.
McCoy, E. (2005), *The Emperor of Wine*, New York: HarperCollins.
Murray, S. (2007), *Moveable Feasts: The Incredible Journeys of the Things We Eat*, London: Aurum.
Nossiter, J. (2009), *Liquid Memory: Why Wine Matters*, London: Atlantic.
Parker, T. (2015), *Tasting French Terroir: The History of an Idea*, Berkeley: University of California Press.

Peace, A. (2006), 'Barossa Slow: The Representation and Rhetoric of Slow Food's Regional Cooking', *Gastronomica*, 6(1):51–59.
Pinney, T. (2005), *A History of Wine in America: From the Beginnings to Prohibition*, Los Angeles: University of California Press.
Ritzer, G., and Ryan, M. (2002), 'The Globalization of Nothing', *Social Thought & Research*, 25(1-2):51–81.
Robertson, R. (1992), *Globalization: Social Theory and Global Culture*, London: Sage.
Seabrook, J. (2004), *Consuming Cultures: Globalization and Local Lives*, London: New Internationalist.
Sheppard, E. (2002), 'The Spaces and Times of Globalization: Place, Scale, Networks, and Positionality', *Economic Geography*, 78(3):307–30.
Simpson, J. (2011), *Creating Wine: The Emergence of a World Industry, 1840–1914*, Princeton: Princeton University Press.
Smart, J. (2004), 'Globalization and Modernity—A Case Study of Cognac Consumption in Hong Kong', *Anthropologica*, 46(2):219–29.
Smith, D.E., et al (2013), *International Business of Wine*, Chengdu: Nordic International Management Institute Press.
Stening, S., et al (2004), 'The United Kingdom', in Anderson, K. (ed.), *The World's Wine Markets: Globalization at Work*, Cheltenham: Edward Elgar, 124–40.
Sulkunen, P. (1989), 'Drinking in France 1965–1979. An Analysis of Household Consumption Data', *British Journal of Addiction*, 84(1):61–72.
Teil, G. (2012), 'No Such Thing as Terroir?: Objectivities and the Regimes of Existence of Objects', *Science, Technology, & Human Values*, 37(5):478–505.
Tsing, A. (2005), *Friction: An Ethnography of Global Connection*, Princeton: Princeton University Press.
Urry, J. (2003), *Global Complexity*, Cambridge: Polity.
Veseth, M. (2012), *Wine Wars*, Lanham: Rowman and Littlefield.
Wallerstein, I. (2004), *World-systems Analysis: An Introduction*, Durham: Duke University Press.
Waters, M. (1995), *Globalization*, London: Routledge.
Whalen, P. (2009), '"Insofar as the Ruby Wine Seduces Them": Cultural Strategies for Selling Wine in Inter-War Burgundy', *Contemporary European History*, 18(1):67–98.

2 Wine Globalization: Longer-term Dynamics and Contemporary Patterns

DAVID INGLIS

Introduction

In this chapter we will consider the long-term development of both wine globalization and what we call 'proto-globalization' (that is, trends before the eighteenth and nineteenth centuries CE), looking at these especially in terms of wine production (that is, the 'wine world'). By taking a long-term perspective, we aim to get a clear idea of trends and continuities across time, as well as periods of novelty and innovation – of which the most obvious are the movement towards transoceanic wine production and distribution in the eighteenth and nineteenth centuries, and the complexification of these processes again from the 1980s onwards.

Wine is usually sold to us today as deeply redolent of the place where the grapes that went into it were grown. But almost certainly some part of the total set of factors involved in making a wine will have travelled from somewhere else to the place where the wine was made. What is often occluded in the marketing of wine is the *trans-local, trans-regional*, *trans-national* and *cross-border* nature of wines, vines and winemaking techniques. The borders that they cross include those that are cultural, symbolic, political and physical (Huber 2011). Wine has historically been much more likely to travel over long distances as a circulating commodity than other fermented drinks. It has had strong capacities for forging economic, social and cultural (and sometimes political) linkages between geographically disparate places (Dietler 2006).

Multiple grape species have grown wild across the world. But it is just one single Eurasian grape species, *Vitis vinifera* L. subsp. *Sylvestris*, which is the source of 99 per cent of the world's wine today. In its wild, uncultivated form, *Vitis vinifera* grows from Central Asia to Iberia, spanning a distance of about 6300 kilometres within a north-to-south band of about 1300 kilometres. In globally warmer times in the past, it probably grew outside of its current area (McGovern 2003). All domesticated grape varietals derive from it in an astonishing variety of shapes, sizes, combinations of sugars and acids, and flavours. There are today as many as 10,000 cultivars or clonal types. The plant's 'pliable, almost chimeric nature' is perhaps its most notable feature (McGovern 2003: 13).

It is this capacity that has made possible the tremendous variety of styles of winemaking, both historically and in our own globalizing epoch, as viticulturalists have exploited *Vitis vinifera*'s tremendous potential for being altered, manipulated and transplanted to new places. Roughly speaking, cultivated grapes historically have grown between 30 and 50 degrees latitude in both the Northern and Southern hemispheres (Taber 2005). But in recent years, as both expression and driver of wine globalization, viticulture has been developed nearer to Equatorial regions in places with relatively hot climates like India, Thailand, Peru and Brazil, as entrepreneurs seek to exploit new regions for production and to supply both old and new consumer markets. As this has happened, so too have new hybrids been developed to grow effectively in novel grape-growing environments (Huber 2011).

Wine vessels – be they ancient amphorae, wooden barrels, metallic tanks filled with bladders, or glass and plastic bottles – are intended to preserve the wine adequately so that it is *potable and portable*, over shorter or longer distances. Finished wine has been travelling for millennia. In general, the nearer we come to our own time, the greater the distances that can be travelled, both in terms of viable transportation mechanisms and the economies, financial and cultural, that make it worth sending over long distances. But even in the quite distant past, wine could travel considerable distances if there was sufficient demand for it (McGovern 2003).

The 'proto-globalization' of wine

The slow but steady spread of grape-growing and winemaking across parts of Eurasia in ancient times can be construed as a kind of proto-globalization of wine – that is, as a set of processes that involve wine's geographical and cultural spread across places and borders. The earliest evidence of making grape wine dates from about 6000 BCE in the Caucasus, where modern Georgia is located (Kassam and Davis 2017). There was a wine industry in Egypt and Lower Mesopotamia circa 3000 BCE. The writing on wine jars, and the stamps on clay seals put onto them, sometimes indicated quite detailed information: vintage year, vineyards, vintner name, and classified quality level. All these were important indicators for traders and buyers of where the wine had travelled from (Meneley 2007). In the third millennium BCE, 'wine was an object of trade … [but] generally a costly good consumed only by elite strata', while lower strata often drank beer (Dietler 2006: 233). In the second millennium BCE, winemaking spread westwards to Crete by 2200 BCE (McGovern 2003). Phoenician traders from Tyre and Lebanon took grape vines to North Africa, Italy and Iberia, importing a wine culture there (McGovern 2003: 202–3). Greek settlers colonized southern Italy in the eighth and seventh centuries BCE, planting so many vines there that the Greeks called southern Italy 'Enotria', the Land of Vines (Millon 2013).

The development and travels of wine have historically been profoundly bound up with social relations of trade and commerce on the one side, and empires and imperial conquest on the other. This occurred across the centre of Eurasia, in the Assyrian, Persian and Chinese empires. The Roman Empire, which made the whole Mediterranean Sea its central highway, can be viewed as a major mechanism of ancient proto-globalization of wine. Within its massive territory, stretching from

Iberia and Britannia in the West through to the Near East, there was a massive movement and churning up of people, ideas, goods and commodities (Inglis and Robertson 2008), including vines, winemaking techniques and finished wines. The poet Virgil said Italy had an uncountable number of different grapes and wines. The author Pliny said that the wines of Campania were famous across the whole world, indicating that the concept of global reputation for especially fine wines is not new (Geraghty 2007). The Greco-Roman world understood the agricultural trinity of wheat, olives and wine as profound symbols of civilization (Serventi and Sabban 2002: 163). Elite drinkers at formal dinners liked to alternate between Italian and foreign wines, the latter being called *transmarina* (from across the sea), hailing from Greece and Asia Minor (Dalby 2000). Wines expressed 'Western-ness' and 'Eastern-ness', an ancestral form of modern *terroir* thinking, and not unlike the way that wine cultures and fields today distinguish between so-called Old and New World styles. Winemaking and drinking by the indigenous inhabitants of colonized lands, in imitation of Roman practice, were important parts of the Romanification process (Sweetman 2007). Such developments were partly made possible by large-scale transportation of wine-bearing *amphorae* all around the empire (Hingley 2005). For example, an estimated 55–65 million amphorae of wine were imported into Roman Gaul over the course of the hundred years spanning the second to first centuries BCE (Dietler 2006).

Keeping wine from spoiling while it travels over long distances has prompted different sorts of technological fixes at different times. Wines from the Eastern Mediterranean intended for long-distance travel to Western parts of the Roman Empire usually had brine and/or spices added for preservative purposes. Over time, drinkers got a taste for these flavours, so they were added for aesthetic reasons – an anticipation of different sorts of modern technological interventions to make wine appeal to the palates of drinkers located at significant geographical and cultural distances from the point of production (Lukacs 2012).

After the so-called fall of Rome, much winemaking knowledge was kept alive by the inhabitants of Christian monasteries. Some of these operations continue still today, mostly in Germany, exhibiting nearly a thousand years of ongoing winemaking practices (Millon 2013). In medieval Europe, the wine trade was relatively simple, with merchants seeking to make profits by selling wines mostly to social elites located in places where wine was not made. There was little market differentiation, the main distinction being between more sweet styles from the Mediterranean and more dry wines from further north (Unwin 1991). The major wine-trading routes involved water-borne transportation: from the Mediterranean by sea and land to Poland and the Baltics, the southern German trade via the River Rhine to Northern Germany and Scandinavia, and the sea trade from Western France to England and Flanders (Phillips 2000). Wine in medieval Europe was often bitterly complained about because of spoilage problems. Barrels replaced ancient *amphorae* as the solution to making wine portable (Murray 2007). But barrels were often sealed poorly, and the wine inside could rapidly oxidize. Even when barrels worked properly, once they were opened the wine was good for only a few days before turning sour. The advent of the new transport technology of the glass bottle and cork from the sixteenth century CE eventually dispensed with the need for adding spice to wine (Millon 2013). The spread of bottle and cork technology was a significant part of early modern wine proto-globalization. Much later, in the twentieth century, the standardization of bottle sizes into metric measures – including the now ubiquitous 75cl size – significantly rationalized the exporting of wines across the globe (Pinney 2005).

To understand the nature of long-standing wine regions today – vis-à-vis both their more localized features and their relative positions in the global wine field – we need to consider their long-term history. Roger Dion (1959) showed that the nature and relative status of winemaking regions have shifted often dramatically over time. Shifts up and down the prestige scale have often strongly been linked to forms of political and economic power. One important reason why Burgundy enjoys such a high global reputation today is that in the medieval period the Dukes of Burgundy had sufficient political clout to put their terrain on the winemaking map, and to influence elite opinion around Europe that the region's wine was outstanding (Moran 1993). The vineyards were close to major travel routes, so the wines could easily be transported to other locations, and there was a constant stream of elite visitors from all over the continent to the monasteries where the monks had mastered advanced viticultural techniques (Pitte 2002: 16).

Ulin (2002, 2004) has shown how the rise to eminence, first in Europe and then across the world, of Bordeaux, was strongly bound up with political and economic factors. The English kings controlled large parts of Western France in the twelfth and thirteenth centuries CE, and they awarded privileges to the Bordelais producers of wine over their rivals located further inland. This stimulated Bordeaux's exporting of wine to England and other countries, sowing the seeds of the strong orientation to world, rather than simply national, markets in the region evident today (Colman 2008). Bordeaux's reputation for wines of serious quality was also intertwined with world-level market forces. Competition that arose in the seventeenth century from Spain, Portugal and Italy led to Bordelais growers replacing high-yielding crops which produced more basic wines with lower-yielding vines and higher-quality production. These wines found ready markets in places as far away as North America and Russia. Since the twelfth century CE, Bordeaux has been profoundly shaped by the dominant political power in the region, and then the world, at any given time: first the English, up until the immediate post–Second World War period, then the Americans in the later twentieth century, and then the newly economically empowered Chinese (Nossiter 2009: 92).

By the fifteenth century CE, social elites in north-western Europe regularly drank wines from areas such as western France, Germany, Spain, and the eastern Mediterranean. About eighty different kinds of wine were reported in London in the early sixteenth century (Colquhoun 2007). In the early eighteenth century, Daniel Defoe remarked on the fast-changing fashions in drinking in London, with cheaper, more basic Portuguese and Spanish wines increasingly being relinquished by those with sufficient spending power in favour of more expensive Bordeaux, Burgundy and Champagne (Dillon 2004).

The availability of this variety of wines was made possible by a range of changes within contexts of production throughout the early modern period. New wine styles were developed in established European locations, entrepreneurs doing so with the expectation of increased profits. Traditional forms of feudal land tenure gave way to more capitalist economic relations, involving the expansion of wine production and the increasing use of wage labourers to pick the grapes and make wine (Unwin 1991). Rapidly burgeoning urban populations in Northern Europe created more demand for mass-market wines made cheaply in large quantities. In response, social elites began to desire higher-quality wines, partly to distinguish their drinking habits from those of the lower classes. In this way, the characteristically modern bifurcation of wine markets and trade into premium wines and table wines was begun (Guy 2003). Producers have often survived by moving into quality wine production for those more far-flung consumers who could still afford to pay premium prices in times when local demand was weak (Unwin 1991).

Towards globalization

One could argue that wine only truly becomes 'globalized' at the point when production and distribution of it becomes trans-oceanic in scale and when oceans, rather than rivers alone, become regular highways for wine's movement from producers to ever more distant consumers. Such a turning point is reached in early modernity.

Between the sixteenth and eighteenth centuries CE, more money was invested in wine production itself and not just in the processes whereby it was traded across distances (Unwin 1991). Investment for the purposes of speculative profit went into more far-flung and non-European winemaking regions. These were now in play because of two interrelated developments: colonial expansion and new transportation technologies. The world's oceans became navigable and viable trading routes. Spanish Jesuits began wineries in Peru in the seventeenth century, and Franciscan monks did the same in Mexico, and then in California, in the late eighteenth century (Colman 2008). In both cases, the motivations were religious – the production of communion wine – rather than commercial. But novel winemaking locations set up to make profits out of distant consumers right from the start included the Portuguese-controlled island of Madeira and the Dutch colony of the Cape in Southern Africa. The Madeira vineyards were begun after the colonial sugar cane trade had been shifted to the Caribbean and Brazil (Murray 2007). The new regions did not only produce bulk wine. Constantia wine from the Cape in South Africa already had a high pan-European reputation as early as the seventeenth century.

Production for far-off customers increased in the eighteenth century. The Atlantic now operated more as a highway between continents than as a moat between them (Hancock 1998, 2005). Trading networks stretching from Europe to the Americas operated as information channels between diverse wine-related actors. This was a world of small- to medium-sized wine-trading companies. Firms located in Madeira had commercial contacts that stretched from Edinburgh and London to Jamaica, New York and Bengal. Actors in the networks these firms created and made a living out of included North American farmers (whose grain might be traded for wines), Swedish barrel-makers (who made the containers that rendered trans-Atlantic trade possible), and French brandy exporters (whose product was added to the wine to stabilize it on its travels), as well as buyers and consumers in European and colonial markets (Hancock 1998, 2005).

Madeira's global success led to the manufacture of cheap imitations from Tenerife, sold in at least one store in upstate New York as 'Made, here, a' (Hancock 1998). As wine came to consumers more regularly from far-away places, so too did levels of uncertainty rise as to its provenance. Such anxieties led to more demands for market regulation. There is some evidence to suggest that a legally recognized region of wine production was running in Paris as early as the twelfth century CE, although the border apparently was not fully legally codified until the early fifteenth century. Claims have also been made for eighteenth-century Tuscany, Portugal and Hungary as the sites of the first substantial legal recognition of distinctive winemaking areas (Matthews 2015). In 1756 the Marquis de Pombal set up geographical boundaries to guarantee the authenticity and quality of Port wines for their major market, British merchants and consumers (Stening et al 2004). The French AOC (*Appellation d'Origine Contrôlée*) legal apparatus started to take shape in the early twentieth century. A 1935 law created the regulatory agency the *Institut National des Appellations d'Origine* (INAO) to formulate and enforce AOC regulations (Trubek and Bowen 2008). An AOC appellation and the *terroir* it regulates is a complicated – and possibly ambiguous – 'assemblage' of nature, culture, land, plants, technologies and practices (Meneley 2007). Appellation rules were (and today still are) about *restrictions:* as to which grape varietals may be planted in the area, how large yields per hectare may be, allowed and disallowed winemaking methods ('traditional' ones are allowed, those defined as non-traditional likely not), permitted minimal alcohol levels, etc. (Moran 1993). The INAO and AOC are often presented as developments purely internal to the French nation state's territory. But it was from the start about winning international prestige and making money in foreign markets (Whalen 2009).

Returning to the spread of winemaking across the world in the nineteenth century, this was in large part due to the broader trajectories of European colonialism and consequent mass migration across oceans and continents. As many as 100 million people migrated in the nineteenth century, half of them Europeans, and wine was bound up with such massive movements of people (Held et al 1999). In terms of imperialist politics, the administrators of European empires had certain symbolic concerns about the need to introduce winemaking to the colonies. They believed that viticulture allowed the landscapes of conquered territories to be located within a Western imperialist narrative of world history, which 'claimed that all powerful nations, since antiquity, had transcendent grape cultures'. Making and drinking wines was part of 'an international set of colonial tactics for transforming landscapes and for propagating a particular worldview of cultivation and control' (Hannickel 2013: 15). Colonial authorities were also driven by more pragmatic concerns of gaining new sources of supply. The British governmental elite of the 1820s regarded Australia as a potential source of wine supply that would allow the mother country to circumvent reliance on imports from an unfriendly France. German colonists were introduced to Australia by the authorities in the 1830s to begin winemaking activities, followed by others such as Swiss and Dalmatians.

Throughout the rest of the century, migrants from winemaking regions of Europe colonized parts of the New World and brought vines and winemaking techniques with them (Unwin 1991). The winemaking Spanish, Italians and other Europeans who migrated to places like California, Argentina, Chile and Brazil certainly can be viewed as pioneers of wine globalization (Cinotto 2012; Peck 2009). Their efforts lead 'to a significant diversification in the world production of wine', as well as more production (Pinilla and Ayala 2002: 55). In the 1870s, California wines, often made by Italian immigrants, were being exported to places as diverse as Australia, Peru, China and Denmark, while being shipped to the US East Coast in 100,000-gallon containers (Unwin 1991).

Much discussion of the history of wine in the United States focuses on Italian migrants in California, but this occludes two issues. First, Hungarians, Germans and French were among other nationalities also involved. Already in the mid-nineteenth century, such people discussed whether new winemaking technologies could substitute for the traditional soils and winemaking practices of the long-established European regions, a theme that arose recurrently throughout New World winemaking circles in the twentieth century (Geraci 2004; Simpson 2011). Second, winemaking appeared in locales beyond California. The Finger Lakes district in New York State produced high-quality German-style wines in the late nineteenth century until Prohibition in the 1920s wiped the industry out there, as was also the case in North Carolina. These are areas that have only recently made comebacks in terms of national and global wine maps (see Taplin in this volume). In Latin America, Italian migrants settled in places like Southern Brazil, producing basic table wines for primarily Italian immigrants in the Brazilian cities. Like hitherto obscure areas in the United States, such regions are nowadays coming back onto the global wine radar (Nossiter 2009).

One reason Europeans took their winemaking skills to other continents was the devastating spread of the phylloxera disease across European wine-growing regions from the 1860s to the early 1900s. Phylloxera spreads when tiny insects feed on the roots and leaves of vines, eventually killing off the plants. The disease wreaked havoc across Europe. By the start of the twentieth century, nearly all vineyards in the affected regions had had to be uprooted and replanted with resistant rootstocks (Campbell 2004). Phylloxera was thoroughly transnational in both nature and consequences. It spread rapidly across European borders. While railways could take finished wines to ever more distant consumers, they also helped move around Europe the blight that seriously threatened the very existence of the industry (Macedo 2011). The pest originated in North America, brought over the ocean by steamship. The eventual solution to it was trans-oceanic too. European vines were grafted onto more phylloxera-resistant American rootstocks. North America was therefore source of both catastrophe and salvation for European wine (Campbell 2004). The disease was recognized as a profoundly transnational problem. International congresses devoted to dealing with the threat were held in the 1870s, creating what today might be called an international 'risk community' (Beck 2011).

There were numerous important consequences of phylloxera and the attempts to stem it. A new topography of vineyards came into existence, intended to make the disease monitorable. This involved much more surveying of wine-growing areas than hitherto, involving the new technology of photography, which rendered in visual terms for the first time a sense of the *terroir* of specific locations (Macedo 2011). Scientific forms of monitoring and control of vineyards became more systematic and more commonplace, paving the way to the situation dominant by the late twentieth century where vineyards and wineries were as much spaces of applied science and technology as of 'nature'. Wines made in the immediate post-phylloxera period, from grafted vines, probably in many cases tasted more generic than those made before the disease, paving the way for new, more homogeneous and trans-local wine flavours (Lukacs 2012).

Just as the ancient Romans had set up North Africa as a massive source of wine production, so too did the late nineteenth-century French set up Algeria as a vast source of supply (Pinilla and Ayala 2002). As the local peasantry were thrown off the land in favour of a small number of large industrial wineries owned by big companies, French colonial wine production rose greatly, from 1 million hectares under vine in 1885 to 8.4 million hectares in 1910 (Simpson 2011). French winemaking influence extended along the coast to Tunisia and Morocco, as well as to Lebanon, where fine French-style wines are still made today and have global recognition (Hyams 1965). The Algerian case points to a historically recurring feature of colonial and postcolonial contexts of winemaking concerning the scale of production. When new territories for winemaking were opened up by colonial expansion, the scale of production was generally much larger than in Western Europe, where a free peasantry owned smallholdings over multiple generations. At the time of the emperor Nero, only six proprietors controlled *all* wine production in Roman North Africa, a situation of massive concentration mimicked by the French experience there two millennia later (Johnson 1989).

In areas such as California, Mendoza in Argentina and Rio Grande do Sul in Brazil, by the late nineteenth century wine-growing was densely concentrated, and levels of production grew rapidly, creating homogeneous bulk wines in large quantities. This was made possible by a combination of the natural endowments of land and climate, where huge amounts of grapes could be cultivated, plus the use of modern farming technologies (Unwin 1991). These were fertile terrains for the growth of large industrial wineries Already in the late nineteenth century, much New World winemaking was highly concentrated, with about 70 per cent of wine in Australia and the United

States produced by the top five companies in each, while the corresponding figure for Argentina and Chile was about 50 per cent. European winemaking was still firmly based on small family and cooperative enterprises (Simpson 2011). Large winemaking enterprises, producing basic wines on an industrial scale, have been a hallmark of much New World production ever since.

The large companies in the New World engaged in 'forward integration', moving into the distribution and marketing of wine as well as its production. They also drew on the latest scientific and technological developments coming from Europe. New technologies allowed producers to make consistent wines in hot climates year upon year. These wines could be kept longer than before, and so were particularly susceptible to being sold under brand-names. Such technical winemaking innovations of the late nineteenth century facilitated both the beginnings of a slow shift in the balance of power from Old to New Worlds, and also major shifts in production trends in Europe, most markedly in France, with ever more wine being made in the hotter south of the country and in Algeria (Simpson 2011). In the early twentieth century, France occupied a paradoxical position of being by far the main producer *and* the largest importer of wines in the world – most of the imports coming from Algeria – and accounting for more than three quarters of total world wine imports (Pinilla and Ayala 2002).

But while production increased in the New World, producers struggled to find viable markets. There had been a rise in cross-border trade from the 1860s in a wave of liberalization made possible through international trade agreements. Yet by the end of the century, high tariffs on wine were erected by some European governments to protect their domestic industries (Pinilla and Ayala 2002). In a period of a major fall in international trade more generally, the United States and Argentine governments brought in protectionist measures to defend their own agricultural economies and build up national wine industries. New World producers in some instances also confronted local populations that were not accustomed to drinking wine, as in the cases of Australia and California. They also faced the challenges of shipping wine over very long distances to European consumers, which, coupled together with the power of a relatively small number of wine importers in Europe, all held New World sales back in the late nineteenth century (Simpson 2011). Facing periodic crises of overproduction, producers often turned to more easily marketable and transportable brandy, as well as crude table wines for primarily local consumption. It would only really be in the 1980s that it became generally profitable to export basic table wines over oceanic distances, when transportation costs fell and technology had been developed to prevent spoilage. While production was increasingly potentially globalized just before the First World War, at the same time distribution and consumption were not nearly so globalized (Simpson 2011).

This gap between potential supply and actual demand was exacerbated by the fact that production and distribution were generally handled by different companies, undercutting the ease of getting wine made in one place to consumers in far-off places (Unwin 1991). Moreover, northern European countries, excluding France, constituted very limited markets for wine consumption at this period. Levels of wine imports remained stagnant in northern Europe in the first three decades of the twentieth century, falling even further during the Great Depression (Pinilla and Ayala 2002). It would only really be in the 1970s and after when vertical integration of the different branches of the winemaking process, from growing grapes to selling wines off the shelf, would occur in major ways. What was lacking in the late nineteenth century came to fruition about a hundred years later: the dynamic presence of very large companies systematically connecting production in the New World with consumption in Europe, North America and elsewhere, through the systematic control of distribution and retail channels (Unwin 1991).

Neo-liberalization and related matters

The production and selling of wine have been thoroughly bound up with broader processes of neo-liberalization. The latter involves pronounced trends in the global economy since the late 1970s, and especially after the fall of Eastern European Communism in the late 1980s, towards the dominance of financial capital and markets over other economic activities, and the transformation of national governments from being concerned to tame transnational markets to being facilitators of them (Harvey 2014). In wine world terms, what neo-liberalization has in part meant is increasingly lowered national governmental tariff protections of domestic wine production, with wine producers becoming ever more directly exposed to global market forces. Some actors have been able to take advantage of these, while others have suffered seriously or gone out of business. To survive in new, harsh liberalized market conditions, wine companies have had to adjust by relinquishing old-style table wines and making new, more smoothly 'international', 'easy drinking' styles of wine that can sell abroad (Pont and Thomas 2012). In Chile, for example, out of the 300 million litres of wine made each year in the early 1990s, 20 per cent of that was exported and 80 per cent remained within the country. Yet by 2006, of the greatly increased annual production of 800 million litres, 75 per cent went to export. Some companies became very large indeed through these processes. The Concha y Toro group was by the early 2000s selling wines to 110 countries across the world, accounting for more than 25 per cent of all Chilean wine exports (Gwynne 2008).

There has also been a complexification of patterns of investment and ownership, with greatly increased numbers of investors and owners coming from outside the locales where wine is made (Curran and Thorpe 2014). Foreign investment has often come from very large companies, which are themselves products of changes in the beverage industry since the 1970s. There have been marked trends towards smaller enterprises being bought up by larger ones, with the resulting conglomerates having interests not only in wine but in multiple alcoholic beverages. These were taken over in turn by huge multi-sector corporations. Massive entities like Constellation Brands engaged in corporate takeovers of well-known winemaking operations like Mondavi in California and Mouton Cadet in Bordeaux. The French luxury brands conglomerate LVMH, which sells luggage and handbags as well as wine, owns wine properties on five continents. Their luxury-branded Champagnes and cognacs are sold across the planet in upscale retail outlets and airport duty-free lounges (Colman 2008). Apparently independent smaller-scale wineries are also often owned by corporations, although the branding usually implies otherwise. This has led to vast contrasts of scale in some regions, where owners of tiny plots sit next to vineyards owned by massive globe-spanning corporations (Pinney 2005).

It was the fall of Communist political systems in Eastern Europe which promoted further neo-liberalization across the world economy. Eastern European wine producers found themselves in the 1990s and after in a paradoxical situation, for the region constituted a kind of New World in, or at the eastern border of, the so-called Old World of Western Europe (for treatment of Macedonia in this light, see Otten in this volume). The transition to capitalist economies and putatively democratic political systems meant large-scale privatization of previously cooperative vineyards and wineries, as well as the inflow of some foreign investment (Noev 2007). Some former COMECON countries, notably Bulgaria, had been singled out by the USSR as the locales where the bloc's wine consumption needs would be catered for – a kind of Soviet globalization of wine production in the decades after the Second World War. Basic Eastern European table wines were exported to Western Europe as bargain-basement offerings in the 1990s, but were largely superseded by hugely increased New World exports in the 2000s. Winemakers in the former Communist bloc have struggled with a wide range of challenges. These include Byzantine levels of governmental bureaucracy and corruption among state apparatchiks, preventing easy access to European Union funding that would allow for the marketing of wines abroad, as well as a slow uptake of ideas as to making and marketing wines understood as coming from distinct *terroirs*. A winemaker needs to show to international audiences that their products are sufficiently standardized to gain a foothold in foreign markets – for example, their Cabernet Sauvignon must taste something like its rivals from other parts of the world. Yet this demonstration involves reducing, both materially and symbolically, the distinctiveness of the wines and the terrains they come from, and presenting such distinctiveness is also a crucial part of gaining the wines international recognition (Jung 2011).

Winemaking and wine marketing personnel circulate transnationally and learn from each other. Many of them hold university qualifications in wine production and/or management, from institutions in France, Australia, South Africa, the United States and elsewhere. These offer increasingly identical curricula, usually in English, which express convergent assumptions about how wine should be made and marketed (Roger 2010). This convergence is partly due to academics and practitioners who teach such programmes sharing knowledge and engaging in cross-border pedagogic collaborations (Geraci 2004). Teachers and pupils operate with increasingly similar scripts, whether they are trained in California, Bordeaux or Stellenbosch.

Massive corporate 'vintibusinesses' drive the vertical integration of grape-farming, winemaking, distribution and marketing today (Geraci 2004). The American giant Gallo makes eight times as much wine every year as do all the regions of

New Zealand put together (Veseth 2012). More specifically wine-focused enterprises, like the Italian Antinori company, own properties in regions in diverse countries like the United States, Chile, Hungary and Romania. Bordeaux- and Champagne-based operations have invested in locales in California and Latin America. Powerful regional players, with world-spanning market presence, have also emerged, such as Guigal in the Rhone and Torres in Catalunya (Lukacs 2012).

Over the last thirty years, power in wine worlds has shifted downstream, from primary producers to processors and marketers. Branded wines sold in massive quantities in Europe and North America, such as South Africa's major brands Arniston Bay and Two Oceans, which are not tied to particular vineyards or even specific regions, began to be the primary sorts of wines that average Developed World consumers would experience (Ewert and du Toit 2005). Yet despite these trends towards bigger companies with large market shares, across the EU in the early 2010s there were still 1.2 million wine-production entities that had less than 1 hectare of vines each (Smith et al 2013).

Neo-liberal doctrine is apparently hostile to state intervention in markets. Yet the rise to prominence of Australian wines was partly due to state planning. In the 1990s, the Australian government promoted the *Strategy 2025* policy, whereby the national wine industry would aim first for more volume of exports to target markets like the UK, then secure rising value per bottle, and then achieve overall pre-eminence over Old World producers. This strategy was copied by other governments and national industries, such as in South Africa (Ewert and du Toit 2005), illustrating broader issues to do with policy convergence across nation-states (Alasuutaari 2009).

Contemporary wine globalization involves the rise of new kinds of experts with novel skill sets. A transnationally operative 'wine consultant' may know about such diverse but interconnected fields as technical and scientific vineyard and winery knowledges, economics and global markets, and marketing know-how (Gwynne 2008, Chauvin in this volume). The highest-flying ones are also rich in social capital, enjoying connections to multiple sorts of power-brokers, ranging from the owners of prestigious properties to influential critics and the organizers of international wine fairs (Pont and Thomas 2012). The more winemaking is oriented to exports travelling very long distances, the less direct connections there are between producers and consumers. The high geographical mobility of the transnational adviser seems able to bridge such gaps, allowing the wine to travel to accurately defined consumer groups. This new breed of experts no longer comes only from Europe, but also from areas that up until the 1970s had been regarded as peripheries but which subsequently became prestigious, like California, Australasia and South Africa. Some who have risen to the greatest global prominence – such as the Bordelais Michel Rolland, who was heavily criticized as the unpalatable face of wine globalization in the documentary film *Mondovino* (2004) – have themselves become symbols of universally recognized styles and brands (Chauvin in this volume). Such consultants help create what Lagendijk (2004) calls the 'inter-connected locales' of the globalized, neo-liberalized wine world. Winemaking information of various types flows from multiple locations, in both Old and New Worlds, to receiving areas in both regions. Personnel move across the world, taking knowledge back and forth, disseminating it through multiple pathways, sometimes fitting in two harvest seasons per year by flitting between hemispheres. This is one crucial element of the sometimes radical *delocalization* of winemaking practices (Anderson et al 2004).

Itinerant consultants and technical personnel spread knowledges and practices across the continents, with vineyards and wineries the world over becoming subject to identical forms of control. The new 'techno-science' of wine has been, particularly from the 1970s onwards, the product of transnational cooperation between research facilities in major locations like California, South Africa, Australia and France. The technical know-how was then disseminated transnationally (Pinney 2005). Innovations spread rapidly around globe-spanning professional circuits. New knowledges can be taken up quickly because most sizable wineries have laboratories and personnel, often trained in university winemaking faculties, who are competent in applying such innovations. Large companies have taken up new knowledges with alacrity, as they offer the possibility of creating ever more reliably similar-tasting wines year after year, seasonal variations being brought under control by varied techno-scientific interventions (Lukacs 2012). Innovations include trellising and irrigation systems; the planting of vines at prescribed distances from each other; more intensive pruning earlier on in the growing season; delaying of the harvest to maximize ripeness of berries; the use of stainless steel tanks for fermentation (allowing dry wines to be made in warm, or even hot, climates); precisely managed induced malolactic fermentation and the use of artificial yeasts; and imported, often French, oak barrels for maturation and storage. A side effect of the latter is massive worldwide demand in the barrel-making industry (Colman 2008).

Travelling professionals have promoted the planting of the now-ubiquitous 'international' varietals, such as cabernet sauvignon, merlot, pinot noir and riesling (Lagendijk 2004; Pinney 2005). Grape varieties have always travelled both within and between countries, but the further back in the past this happened, the slower the travelling was, and probably the more unremarked upon. New grapes and wine styles slowly became indigenized and were understood to be quintessentially 'local'. In the pursuit of wines that Developed World consumers would find appealing, especially from the 1990s onwards winemakers planted grape varieties in large numbers in areas not previously associated with those types (Huber 2011). Nowadays the spread of a grape can seem dizzyingly fast. This is especially so if the new arrivals are planted at the expense of uprooting varietals that have been grown in a region for decades or even centuries, but which have come to be perceived as having no market value outside the region or even within it (Gade 2004). Such developments have stimulated fears by small producers and some observers that there is occurring a massive homogenization of tastes and flavours in favour of bland, characterless mass-market wines where 'case one taste[s] the same as case one million' (Colman 2008: 104). This is wine that critics feel could be made *anywhere*, regardless of the terrain, having low acids and tannins, soft textures, fruit-driven flavours, and relatively high residual sugars.

Critics regard these as 'technically well-made, globally palatable, interchangeable "wine products" of no perceptible origin or identity' (Nossiter 2009: 69).

Today mass-market wine may travel long distances in shipping containers with 24,000 litre bags inside them (Murray 2007). These shipping methods have allowed for the bulk transportation of even the cheapest wines in the world, whose predecessors would never have left their region. At the lowest-quality end, cheap Chilean wine sent in bulk to China may end up labelled as 'Chinese wine' when it reaches its destination. Pinot noir sold under a California-based brand may come from less prestigious parts of France and Italy (Veseth 2012). But at the same time, New World producers have also moved into the promotion of certain regions and varietals as being at least as good as classic European regions, seeking to entice higher-end consumers (Corby 2010; Sternsdorff 2013).

Mass-market wines are sold through a globalized system of semiotics on labels, involving bold colours, easy-to-read text with standardized stories about flavours and the supposed natural endowments of the places of production (even if the wines were made more in the techno-scientifically-driven winery than in the vineyard). There is often a foregrounding of one of the internationally recognizable grape varietals on the label too (Veseth 2012). Such labelling stands in contrast to the arcane and cryptic labels of many Old World producers. Such labels require higher levels of cultural capital on behalf of consumers to decipher which grapes may have been used and what the wine tastes like. Such producers have come under ever more pressure to revise their labels and market their wines in a more apparently user-friendly, 'New World'-style direction (Peck 2009).

Developed World consumers tend to buy their wine for everyday drinking from supermarkets rather than specialist wine merchants. As the wine economy became ever more neo-liberalized, a new kind of player emerged: the supermarket wine-buyer. This was particularly so in the UK, an increasingly important market for wine imports from the late 1980s onwards. Supermarket chains like Asda, Tesco and Sainsbury's came to have huge purchasing power. With that came the capacity to dictate which sorts of wines were to be made, first by New World – and then later by Old World – producers. Supermarket buyers bargain very hard, are keen to drive prices down, and impose stringent sanitary and technical requirements on producers (Ewert and du Toit 2005). From the 1990s UK supermarkets moved away from just reselling products bought from and branded by others, towards directly finding their own suppliers of wine and then putting their own brands on the bottles. This has had huge effects on how producers manage quality control, supply chains and the wines themselves. These were increasingly made from the internationally recognizable varietals, and according to ever more convergent, worldwide standards and taste conventions (Gwynne 2008). This mirrors broader 'McDonaldization' trends, whereby every part of a production process is engineered to fit tightly defined templates (Ritzer 2007). A winemaker becomes a manager making standard products for the perceived consumer tastes that are thought to drive global markets (Pont and Thomas 2012). This process in turn sets up the possibility of rebellion from such prescribed roles, by defiantly presenting oneself as someone who makes wines according to personal taste, a position markedly present in the 'natural' wine movement (see below).

Old World/New World

One of the most discussed aspects of wine globalization over the last fifty years has been the so-called rise of the New World at the expense of the Old World, creating crisis conditions in the latter, notably in France. One important aspect here is the New World's symbolic challenging of Old World (especially French) hegemony.

One aspect of this is the mythology surrounding the so-called 'Judgment of Paris'. The term refers to a blind tasting of high-end French and Californian wines in Paris in 1976, organized by the English wine merchant Steven Spurrier. The elite French critics rated some of the mostly unknown Californian wines higher than the very established French ones. Effects on the wine field outside of the United States were much less rapid and dramatic than subsequent myth-making would have it, which claims that it was immediately clear to all that California 'had arrived' on the world wine scene (Asher 2002: 172). The *Judgment* was not really 'a vinous shot heard round the world', as a reporter on the *Wall Street Journal* at the time called it, not least because wine fields were more nationally than transnationally organized at that time (Matthews 2015: 189). Nonetheless, many Americans thought that the French had for the first time recognized that world-class wines could be made in California. Moreover, reflections and debates about the *Judgment* were productive of at least two ways of thinking: either California (and by extension, the New World) is a place that can have *terroir* quite as much as grand regions in Europe can, or that great wine can be made in places without the sorts of *terroir* that French thinking regards as essential to it. Maybe great wine comes from the process in the winery, not the land itself (Matthews 2015: 203)? The image of California as literally *world* class asserted that Old World terrain and methods were not the only route to the highest quality in wines, and implied that perhaps those methods were now looking out of date.

The myth of the *Judgment* was used by the Californian wine business, and especially by powerful players within it such as Robert Mondavi of the pioneering Mondavi company, to forge a collective memory, mobilize other actors, build coalitions and create new networks. All this was done with the aim of imposing a perception of California's importance in world winemaking, to raise its status to the level of the classic European regions, and to upset the latter's strong symbolic mastery over 'great wine' (Itçaina et al 2016). This sort of coalition-building, through the creation and circulation of collective images and myths, was copied in other regions, such as Mendoza and North Carolina (see Taplin in this volume).

The New World also came to challenge the Old World in general, and France in particular, in the 1980s and 1990s because of successful coalition-building which upset the long-established dominance of French thought and practice (Roger 2010). New World actors in the US, Australia and South Africa were able to challenge the older French model. They enjoyed close ties both to big, powerful wine companies like Gallo in the United States, and to national governments which were ambitious to extend the export potential of national industries. The figure of the 'new consumer' was formulated and disseminated both by commercial operations and by academics in universities like Stellenbosch and the University of California, Davis. It was promoted through such mechanisms as international conferences and journals, which brought scholars and business professionals together in a common cause (Roger 2010). That was crystallized in the notion that the main focus of attention of the industry should be the 'new consumer'. This was conceived of as a middle-class person, interested in easy-to-drink wines, presented in bottles with labels that spelled out in simple terms the grape varietal and the flavours of the wine. This figure was implicitly juxtaposed against an outdated 'old consumer', someone who drank 'difficult' wines that needed aging and who could decipher cryptic labels. Being formulated by New World wine actors, the 'new consumer' was defined as someone who in effect wanted to drink New World wine, shunning the complex and arcane symbolism that had built up around French and some other Old World wines over the previous centuries (Roger 2010).

Business and academic actors from the New World developed this imagery and sought to impose it throughout the transnational(ized) wine world. To do so, they built up a coalition with other types of people who also had interests in ensuring the types of wines that the new consumer supposedly wanted became dominant. These included plant scientists and biochemists, who were focused on interventionist winemaking techniques involving microbiology such as artificial yeasts and filtration (Roger 2010). Industry and academic actors also enlisted econometrists, who claimed to be able to predict the 'right' price for wines on global markets, and marketing specialists, who claimed that 'new consumers' were much less interested in provenance and *terroir*, and much more oriented towards reliable, never-changing brands (Roger 2010). International organizations were set up by this coalition to promote these New World principles and ideas. A powerful binary discourse was deployed – stagnation versus dynamism, parochial versus global – which defined the Old World's *terroir*-oriented dispositions as badly out of date. The figure of the 'new consumer' became in some quarters ever more unquestioned, and started to be perceived as a self-evident fact, not a rhetorical construction (Roger 2010). The 'new consumer' eventually came to inform fundamentally the EU's new wine policy in 2006, which demanded a shift from an 'artisanal' to an 'industrial and more competitive' model of winemaking across the bloc. Old World producers would have to imitate New World producers and make easy-to-drink wines, made using the latest techno-scientific manipulations, sell them under branded labels, drop *terroir*-based marketing on mass market wines, and put the grape varietal(s) on the label (Roger 2010). While some bigger European companies' interests were well served by this shift, many smaller, supposedly 'old-fashioned', producers were greatly disadvantaged, fuelling the senses of grievance about perceived 'globalization' that had been around for some time.

Nowhere has this been seen more dramatically than in France. 'Globalization' ('mondialisation') is seen by both the political left and right as perniciously striking at the very heart of France, namely its (apparently) traditional *terroir*-based agriculture, and the foodstuffs and cuisine which derive from it. The term *terroir* is the antonym of unceasing and rootless globalization, and a rallying cry against it (Waters 2010). The winemaker, like the peasant more broadly, stands as either a tragic or heroic figure, depending on how successful they are in combatting the destructive forces of globalized markets and predatory foreign capital, of which American money is the most distrusted (Demossier 2010). This was well dramatized in the so-called *l'Affaire Mondavi*, when in the early 2000s the Californian Mondavi company pulled out of a venture in the Languedoc in response to bitter criticism from local activists (Jones 2003).

Fears of the end of *terroir* involve worries about the destruction of the French countryside, rendering it into a series of empty, placeless zones, populated by massive industrial food monocultures and ersatz entertainment sites for tourists (Heller 2007). In the leftist version of this discourse, popularized by the farmer-activist José Bové, who has become a global media star of the anti-globalization movement, the defence of *terroir* is not politically reactionary. Instead, small-scale and artisanal production rooted in place, standing in opposition to mass-market factory production that could be made anywhere, is defined as cosmopolitan rather than parochial (Bodnar 2003). Sometimes the defence of tradition has taken direct and violent forms. For example, in the Languedoc, protests at perceived government inaction in protecting the region's winemaking from global markets have led to various violent and illegal protests (Colman 2008).

While 'globalization' and *terroir* are often presented in political discourse as opposites, they need not be construed that way in social scientific terms. Globalizing forces do not just assail or transform existing wine regions and *terroirs*; they can also help produce new ones too. For example, what is presented as the distinctive *terroir* of the New Zealand region of Marlborough was created in large part by globalizing dynamics driven by big companies and money from outside the region and indeed from outside New Zealand (Haywood and Lewis 2008). The development of the region by these bigger players encouraged smaller, independent producers to set up wineries in the region too, leading to ever more plausible claims about it possessing a distinct *terroir*.

Terroir is (apparently) protected by legal apparatuses such as the French AOC, Spanish DO and Italian DOC(G) systems. But these tend to keep in check 'too much individuality on the part of a producer', because wines must exhibit the supposed 'typicity' of the area, and what counts as such is open to often controversial debate (Gade 2004: 855). Younger and sometimes more iconoclastic producers therefore today often prefer to avoid what they experience as constraining AOC rules and to sell their wines under less restrictive nomenclatures, a phenomenon also found in other countries such as Italy today. In Southern Europe, many of these newer producers are university-educated young professionals who have 'returned to the land', disillusioned with careers in global capitalism or unable to find graduate-level employment in recession-hit economies.

'Natural' concerns

A striking feature of wine today is the centrality of issues to do with 'nature', reflecting wider societal concerns to do with climate change and environmental degradation, both truly global problems. Climate change is already having major effects on wine production, and likely will have even more impact in the future.

Temperatures in Western Europe in the grape-growing season have risen on average by 3 degrees Fahrenheit from the mid-1980s to the 2010s (Lukacs 2012). This is having major consequences for many aspects of winemaking, from choosing which varietals to grow in warmer conditions, to harvests happening earlier, and weather conditions becoming more erratic. This means a consequent loss of human control over the winemaking process, the very objective that techno-science has been aiming at for decades. Changes in climate also affect *terroir*, which ultimately is a form of thinking and winemaking practice that strongly associates particular vines, grapes and winemaking methods with specific physical territories. As Pincus (2003: 87) argues, climate change, 'the fruit of the Industrial Revolution and continued population growth, is beginning to make decades of wine-making expertise irrelevant. In an increasingly warm world, the particular associations between wine and place will be difficult or impossible to maintain'.

Which types of wine have been made in particular locations, and how they have been made, has never been a matter simply of traditions stretching back to time immemorial. There has always been change, even if it was not thought much about or highlighted by those engaged in it. Yet the difference between the current period and earlier ones is the *rate* of change. In regions where there is a long history of winemaking, the totality of physical and natural endowments, coupled together with human labour, that has been given the name *terroir*, was born out of relatively slow adaptations of humans and vines to the environment around them, sometimes built up over centuries. The rate of adaptation sped up in some places from the later nineteenth century, and then almost everywhere after the Second World War, and especially in the last few decades of the twentieth century. Increasingly globalized markets upped the tempo for how winemakers, in adapting to new markets, adapt their practices as to how grapes are grown and how wine is made (Unwin 1991). The increased speed of change throughout the later twentieth century was primarily economically driven – that is, it was created by mostly human factors alone. But what makes the current period distinctive is that those factors are combined with climate change, which itself is the unintentional creation of human agency (McKibben 2006).

That combination, of human practices together with a thoroughly human-impacted 'nature', is rapidly accelerating the pace of change in the wine world today in historically unprecedented ways. If *terroir* was made possible by relatively slow human and plant adaptation to a relatively unchanging (or slowly changing) environment, then in a period when human life is subject to faster changes than ever before, and when the environment is changing in rapid ways that our ancestors could never have anticipated, it is no wonder that *terroir* is being unsettled in multiple manners today. As climate increases, it becomes possible to make richer, lusher wines almost everywhere where wine is made, even in classically 'cold climate' regions like Germany. By the same token, it is becoming too warm in some regions for some grapes and wine styles that require cooler climate conditions in order to flourish. In such areas, like Austria and Alsace, this will in future likely stimulate further moves to produce red grapes in locations that for centuries have only been able to support white varietals. This is a potentially radical disruption of what producers and consumers think of as the *terroir* of those regions. Such dynamics may speed up and radicalize trends to identify wines by grape varietal rather than by geographic origin, at least for mass-market wines (Hannah et al 2013).

Simultaneously, areas that were previously regarded as too cool for grape cultivation at all are being opened up to winemaking, such as the Netherlands and Denmark (Perkins 2004). The spectacular and rapid rise to prominence of English sparkling wine over the last fifteen years has been made possible by rising temperatures in the south of England, creating climatic conditions similar to Champagne (Field 2008: 14). This marks a return to the southern part of England of widespread grapevines, which flourished throughout the Middle Ages until the mini-Ice Age of the sixteenth and seventeenth centuries destroyed most English production. Even cold, damp Wales can now produce interesting white wines. As investors define climate change as both risk and opportunity, new patterns of ownership emerge, as in the case of large Champagne producers investing in England, in the hope of having a ready supply of sparkling wine for global markets should production in the home region falter due to environmental changes (Millan 2013). English producers have adopted the universal terminology of *terroir* to describe the environment around them and what they do to it and within it. This suggests that as growing areas change, *terroir* discourse will continue to be the way that producers, at least of higher-end wines, both make sense of what they are doing and sell their wines on global markets. Climate change may stimulate a proliferation of *terroir* ideas and practices, or mutations of them, rather than simply destroy them.

In terms of environmental degradation, as Hannickel (2013) points out, a lot of contemporary winemaking is just like other forms of industrialized agriculture. It involves such questionable practices as monocropping (which radically reduces biological diversity in the surrounding area) and the use of chemical pesticides, while the deployment of methyl bromide to sterilize soils prior to planting grapes contributes to the depletion of the ozone layer. As supplies of water become less available in many parts of the world, so too do less areas become available for the planting of new vines. For existing vineyards, water shortages are likely to become a more chronic problem, given that in already dry areas they rely on extensive irrigation, misting and sprinkling systems. Moreover, vineyards in higher areas can despoil delicate higher altitude ecosystems (Hannah et al 2013).

In such an increasingly fraught global environmental situation, it is not surprising that both producers and consumers, in line with broader trends in food consumption among wealthier groups in the Developed World, have turned more frequently over the last decade to wines that are apparently more environmentally sound and ethically virtuous. This has involved the rise of organically farmed grapes (which may or may not end up in fully 'organic' wines) and of biodynamic vineyard management, which promotes biodiversity among the vines (e.g. the presence of cows to produce fertilizer, the presence of insect-eating animals to reduce pest populations). Going beyond organic practices to embrace mystical ideas, first formulated by Rudolf Steiner, as to the vines needing to be in alignment with lunar and astral movements, biodynamic grape-farming challenges the idea of the vineyard as a self-enclosed plot of land, seeing it instead as intrinsically connected to the wider planet and cosmos. Despite the mystical elements, biodynamic winemaking still involves the use of soil science and careful research as to how elements in the total environment affect all the others (Lukacs 2012).

Recent years have also seen the rise of so-called 'natural' wines (Black 2013; Rothbaum 2006). These wines are presented as being made in as non-interventionist ways as possible, rejecting the techno-scientific trends of the later twentieth century in favour of something apparently more at one with Nature. Wild yeasts from the vineyard, claimed to be as much part of the *terroir* as the grapes and vines, are used, rather than the artificial ones industrialized winemaking deploys in the winery. Fermentation begins spontaneously, which may create very different wines each year, making vintages more distinctive, which is the opposite of the year-on-year consistency demanded by heavily techno-scientific winemaking. Sulphur is used sparingly or not at all, although this increases the risk of spoilage. The wine liquid may be moved by gravity rather than by artificial means like pumps. The use of enzymes, filtering and micro-filtration is avoided, creating wines that are often cloudy and full of sediment. These are taken to be 'natural' expressions of the 'real' wine of the *terroir*. These are wines that their advocates say are 'laughing at modernity' (Goldberg 2013; Rosenthal 2008: 202). Yet despite the strong emphasis on the hyper-locality of natural wines, they still must be sold in globalized markets. The selling of them stresses that very hyper-locality, while radicalizing long-standing *terroir*-based marketing that presents the winemaker as mere steward of the land, letting the natural endowments of the place come through with minimal actions on her part (Beverland and Luxton 2005). Natural and biodynamic wines are today being sold through the ambiguous means of a kind of anti-brand branding (Rothbaum 2006, Smith Maguire in this volume).

Natural winemakers for the most part genuinely believe that they are letting *terroir* 'speak for itself' in ways that more interventionist methods prevent. But this has created a tension between 'naturalists' and those winemakers who believe that *terroir* can only really be expressed if certain human interventions are deployed. The latter may well complain of the 'excessively conventional taste typical of sulphite-free wines' (Teil 2012: 483). As one French winemaker explained to Teil (2012: 483), natural wines 'lack identity ... you don't know if you're drinking a Cabernet, a Syrah, a Merlot'. For their critics, natural wines paradoxically betray *terroir*, as without certain interventions by humans, they may all tend to taste the same, wherever they happen to come from. This is a perverse and unintended form of homogenization of taste, the very phenomenon that mass market, techno-scientifically manipulated, 'globalized' wines are meant to involve. At a more institutional level, in the French case AOC panels can refuse to certify as typical of a *terroir* some natural wines because of their alleged 'non-typicity', even if formally they comply with the letter of the AOC rules. Such dynamics have heightened disputes over what 'typicity' in a *terroir* really means (Demossier 2010).

While the wines of other former Communist locations may have sometimes 'lost their accents' in the search for international markets, one possible way ahead for 'traditional' and 'natural' producers all over the world has been forged by winemakers in the Republic of Georgia (Feiring 2016). Georgia has claims to having the longest unbroken winemaking tradition in the world, extending over thousands of years, with some techniques used today being at least hundreds of years old (Feiring 2016). The Soviet Union engaged in its own particular type of homogenization of Georgian wine, forcing producers into both generic bulk production and a massive reduction of varietals in favour of a few high-yielding vine types that made crude table wine. Yet ancient grapes and methods survived through the Soviet period, and in the last decade or so have undergone a renaissance. The method of maturing wine made from distinctive regional varietals in clay *qvevri* containers buried under the ground was recognized in 2013 by UNESCO as part of the world's intangible cultural heritage, consecrating the practice as a 'living tradition', and thus rendering that style of winemaking as part of what that international body defines as 'world culture'. Recognizing and protecting 'heritage' is an important part of cultural globalization processes today, which runs in parallel with, and in some ways in opposition to, the commodification and branding of cultures by actors in the globalized neo-liberal capitalist economy (Elliott and Schmutz 2012).

Such recognition is a significant boost to producers who want to continue to do things in ways very different to standardized production for global markets, but who also wish to raise the profile of their wines in the high prestige, niche ends of globalized wine markets. Yet the growing transnational presence of *qvevri* wines also points to the changing tastes of retail wine buyers and their aspirations to cultivate the tastes of particular higher-end consumers. For the last several years, the UK supermarket Marks and Spencer has sold an entry-level *qvevri* wine, and this may herald broader attempts by supermarkets and other outlets to capture younger, hipper and more adventurous drinkers – exactly those people whose parents at first drove the development of New World consumption thirty years ago and more. The increased global profile of *qvevri* wines can be seen in the fact that small-scale winemakers in places from across the Old and New Worlds are today making wines in that manner, which then reach hip consumers in big cities, many of whose jobs involve servicing the global neo-liberal economy (Feiring 2016). Just as the latter is thoroughly implicated in the tendency towards massive amounts of homogeneous wine production, so too does it involve tendencies in apparently the opposite direction, namely the reactivation of ancient styles and the growing recognition by big city consumers of grape varietals hitherto hardly heard of outside of the region in which they have been grown (Smith Maguire in this volume).

Conclusion

It is one of the many ironies of wine globalization that, in its current phase, it seems to have come full circle – some of the hippest wines in the world currently are from that very region in the Caucasus where wine was probably first made, some 8,000 years ago. Indeed, the rise to prominence of Georgia as a source of fashionable wine, and of China as a location of both mass-market and in future possibly prestigious wines, problematizes the hitherto relatively stable classification of 'Old World' and 'New World'. Should China be called 'New New World' in wine terms, and should Georgia escape those labels altogether and be referred to as an 'Ancient World' producing area (Li et al 2018)?

It is perhaps these sorts of constant reinventions – taking place in radically different socio-historical and spatial contexts, and which have over history become ever more complicated and 'globalized' – which are ultimately most expressive of the nature of wine globalization processes, if and when these are considered in long-term perspective. It is a (wine) case of old wine in new bottles, new wine in old bottles, and new wine in new bottles. Understanding the processes that bring such mutations about is the task of the wine-oriented social scientist, and it is with more specific investigations of such matters that the rest of this book is concerned.

References

Alasuutari, P. (2009), 'The Domestication of Worldwide Policy Models', *Ethnologia Europaea*, 39(1):66–71.

Anderson, K., Norman, D., and Wittwer, G. (2004), 'The Global Picture', in Anderson, K. (ed.), *The World's Wine Markets: Globalization at Work*, Cheltenham: Edward Elgar, 14–58.

Asher, G. (2002), *The Pleasures of Wine*, London: Chronicle.

Beck, U. (2011), 'Cosmopolitanism as Imagined Communities of Global Risk', *American Behavioral Scientist*, 55(10):1346–61.

Beverland, M., and Luxton, S. (2005), 'Managing Integrated Marketing Communication (IMC) through Strategic Decoupling: How Luxury Wine Firms Retain Brand Leadership While Appearing to Be Wedded to the Past', *Journal of Advertising*, 34(4):103–16.

Black, R.E. (2013), '*Vino Naturale*: Tensions between Nature and Technology in the Glass', in Black, R.E., and Ulin, R.C. (eds), *Wine and Culture: Vineyard to Glass*, London: Bloomsbury, 279–94.

Bodnar, J. (2003), 'Roquefort vs Big Mac: Globalization and Its Others', *European Journal of Sociology*, 44(1):133–44.

Campbell, C. (2004), *Phylloxera: How Wine Was Saved for the World*, London: Harper Perennial.

Cinotto, S. (2012), *Soft Soil, Black Grapes: The Birth of Italian Wine-Making in California*, New York: New York University Press.

Colman, T. (2008), *Wine Politics*, Berkeley: University of California Press.

Colquhoun, K. (2007), *Taste: The Story of Britain Through Its Food*, London: Bloomsbury.

Corby, J.H.K. (2010), 'For Members and Markets: Neoliberalism and Cooperativism in Mendoza's Wine Industry', *Journal of Latin American Geography*, 9(2):27–47.

Curran, L., and Thorpe, M. (2014), 'Whose Terroir Is It Anyway? Comparing Chinese FDI in the French and Australian Wine Sector', AAWE Working Paper 168, https://www.wine-economics.org/aawe/wp-content/uploads/2014/09/AAWE_WP168.pdf

Dalby, A. (2000), *Empires of Pleasures: Luxury and Indulgence in the Roman World*, London: Routledge.

Demossier, M. (2010), *Wine Drinking Culture in France: A National Myth or a Modern Passion?*, Cardiff: University of Wales Press.

Dietler, M. (2006), 'Alcohol: Anthropological/Archaeological Perspectives', *Annual Review of Anthropology*, 35:229–49.

Dillon, P. (2004), *Gin: The Much-Lamented Death of Madam Geneva*, Boston: Justin, Charles & Co.

Dion, R. (1959), *Histoire de la Vigne et du Vin en france – Des Origines au XIXe Siècle*, Paris: Broche.

Elliott, M.A., and Schmutz, V. (2012), 'World Heritage: Constructing a Universal Cultural Order', *Poetics*, 40(3):256–77.

Ewert, J., and Du Toit, A. (2005), 'A Deepening Divide in the Countryside: Restructuring and Rural Livelihoods in the South African Wine Industry', *Journal of Southern African Studies*, 31(2):315–32.

Feiring, A. (2016), *For the Love of Wine*, Lincoln: University of Nebraska Press.

Field, M. (2008), 'Climate Change and the Future of Taste', *Gastronomica*, 8(4):14–20.

Gade, D.W. (2004), 'Tradition, Territory, and Terroir in French Viniculture: Cassis, France, and Appellation Contrôlée', *Annals of the Association of American Geographers*, 94(4):848–67.

Geraci, V.W. (2004), 'Fermenting a Twenty-first Century California Wine Industry', *Agricultural History*, 78(4):438–65.

Geraghty, R.M. (2007), 'The Impact of Globalization in the Roman Empire, 200 BC-AD 100', *The Journal of Economic History*, 67(4):1036–61.

Goldberg, K. (2013), 'First as Tragedy, then as Farce?: A Short Story about Natural Wine', http://www.larscarlberg.com/first-as-tragedy-then-as-farce-a-short-story-about-natural-wine/

Guy, K. (2003), *When Champagne Became French: Wine and the Making of a National Identity*, Baltimore: Johns Hopkins University Press.

Gwynne, R.N. (2008), 'UK Retail Concentration, Chilean Wine Producers and Value Chains', *The Geographical Journal*, 174(2):97–108.

Hancock, D. (1998), 'Commerce and Conversation in the Eighteenth-century Atlantic: The Invention of Madeira Wine', *The Journal of Interdisciplinary History*, 29(2):197–219.

Hancock, D. (2005), 'The Trouble with Networks: Managing the Scots' Early-modern Madeira Trade', *The Business History Review*, 79(3):467–91.

Hannah, L. et al (2013), 'Climate Change, Wine, and Conservation', *Proceedings of the National Academy of Sciences of the United States of America*, 110(17):6907–12.

Hannickel, E. (2013), *Empire of Vines: Wine Culture in America*, Philadelphia: University of Pennsylvania Press.

Harvey, D. (2014), *Seventeen Contradictions and the End of Capitalism*, Oxford: Oxford University Press.

Haywood, D., and Lewis, N. (2008), 'Regional Dynamics in the Globalising Wine Industry: The Case of Marlborough, New Zealand', *The Geographical Journal*, 174(2):124–37.

Held, D. et al (1999), *Global Transformations: Politics, Economics and Culture*, Cambridge: Polity.

Heller, C. (2007), 'Techne versus Technoscience: Divergent (and Ambiguous) Notions of Food "Quality" in the French Debate over GM Crops', *American Anthropologist*, 109(4): 603–15.

Hingley, R. (ed.) (2005), *Globalizing Roman Culture: Unity, Diversity and Empire*, London: Routledge.

Huber, T.P. (2011), *Wine: An American Provence*, Boulder: University Press of Colorado.

Hyams, E. (1965), *Dionysus: A Social History of the Wine Vine*, London: Thames and Hudson.

Inglis, D., and Robertson, R. (2008), 'The Elementary Forms of Globality: Durkheim and the Emergence and Nature of Global Life', *Journal of Classical Sociology*, 8(1):5–25.

Itcaina, X., Roger, A., and Smith, A. (2016), *Varietals of Capitalism: A Political Economy of the Changing Wine Industry*, Cornell: Cornell University Press.

Johnson, H. (1989), *Vintage: The Story of Wine*, New York: Simon and Schuster.

Jones, A. (2003), '"Power in Place": Viticultural Spatialities of Globalization and Community Empowerment in the Languedoc', *Transactions of the Institute of British Geographers*, 28(3):367–82.

Jung, Y. (2011), 'Parting the "Wine Lake": The Revival of the Bulgarian Wine Industry in the Age of CAP Reform', *Anthropological Journal of European Cultures*, 20(1):10–28.

Kassam, A., and Davis, N. (2017), 'Evidence of world's earliest winemaking uncovered by archaeologists', https://www.theguardian.com/science/2017/nov/13/evidence-of-worlds-earliest-winemaking-uncovered-by-archaeologists

Lagendijk, A. (2004), 'Global "Lifeworlds" versus Local "Systemworlds": How Flying Winemakers Produce Global Wines in Interconnected Locales', *Journal of Economic and Social Geography*, 95(5):511–26.

Li, H. et al (2018), 'The Worlds of Wine: Old, New and Ancient', *Wine Economics and Policy*, 7:178–82.

Lukacs, P. (2012), *Inventing Wine*, New York: W.W. Norton.

Macedo, M. (2011), 'Port Wine Landscape: Railroads, Phylloxera, and Agricultural Science', *Agricultural History*, 85(2):157–73.

Matthews, M.A. (2015), *Terroir and Other Myths of Winegrowing*, Berkeley: University of California Press.

McGovern, P. (2003), *Ancient Wine: The Search for the Origins of Viniculture*, Princeton: Princeton University Press.

McKibben, B. (2006), *The End of Nature*, New York: Random House.

Meneley, A. (2007), 'Like an Extra Virgin', *American Anthropologist*, 109(4):678–87.

Millon, M. (2013), *Wine: A Global History*, London: Reaktion.

Moran, W. (1993), 'The Wine Appellation as Territory in France and California', *Annals of the Association of American Geographers*, 83(4):694–717.

Murray, S. (2007), *Moveable Feasts: The Incredible Journeys of the Things We Eat*, London: Aurum.

Noev, N. (2007), 'Land, Wine and Trade: The Transition of the Romanian Wine Sector', *Eastern European Economics*, 45(3):76–114.

Nossiter, J. (2009), *Liquid Memory: Why Wine Matters*, London: Atlantic.
Peck, G. (2009), *The Prohibition Hangover: Alcohol in America from Demon Rum to Cult Cabernet*, New Brunswick: Rutgers University Press.
Perkins, S. (2004), 'Global Vineyard', *Science News*, 165(22):347–49.
Phillips, R. (2000), *A Short History of Wine*, London: HarperPerennial.
Pincus, R. (2003), 'Wine, Place, and Identity in a Changing Climate', *Gastronomica*, 3(2):87–93.
Pinilla, V., and Ayuda, M.-A. (2002), 'The Political Economy of the Wine Trade: Spanish Exports and the International Market, 1890–1935', *European Review of Economic History*, 6(1):51–85.
Pinney, T. (2005), *A History of Wine in America: From the Beginnings to Prohibition*, Los Angeles: University of California Press.
Pitte, J.-R. (2002), *French Gastronomy: The History and Geography of a Passion*, New York: Columbia University Press.
Pont, P.C.A.M., and Thomas, H. (2012), 'The Sociotechnical Alliance of Argentine Quality Wine: How Mendoza's Viticulture Functions between the Local and the Global', *Science, Technology, & Human Values*, 37(6):627–52.
Ritzer, G. (2007), *The McDonaldization of Society*, Los Angeles: Sage.
Roger, A. (2010), 'Scholarly Constructs and the Legitimization of European Policies: The Circulation of Knowledge on Wine and the Vine', *Revue Française de Science Politique*, 60(2):1–22.
Rosenthal, N.L. (2008), *Reflections of a Wine Merchant: On a Lifetime in the Vineyards and Cellars of France and Italy*, Berkeley: North Point Press.
Rothbaum, N. (2006), 'Old-school Wine', *Gastronomica*, 6(3):72–75.
Serventi, S., and Sabban, F. (2002), *Pasta: The Story of a Universal Food*, New York: Columbia University Press.
Simpson, J. (2011), *Creating Wine: The Emergence of a World Industry, 1840–1914*, Princeton: Princeton University Press.
Smith, D.E. et al (2013), *International Business of Wine*, Chengdu: Nordic International Management Institute Press.
Stening, S. et al (2004), 'The United Kingdom', in Anderson, K. (ed.), *The World's Wine Markets: Globalization at Work*, Cheltenham: Edward Elgar, 124–40.
Sternsdorff, N. (2013), 'Space and *Terroir* in the Chilean Wine Industry', in Black, R.E., and Ulin, R.C. (eds), *Wine and Culture: Vineyard to Glass*, London: Bloomsbury, 51–66.
Sweetman, R. J. (2007), 'Roman Knossos: The Nature of a Globalized City', *American Journal of Archaeology*, 111(1): 61–81.
Taber, G.M. (2005), *Judgment of Paris: California vs. France and the Historic 1976 Paris Tasting That Revolutionized Wine*, New York: Scribner.
Teil, G. (2012), 'No Such Thing as Terroir?: Objectivities and the Regimes of Existence of Objects', *Science, Technology, & Human Values*, 37(5):478–505.
Trubek, A.B., and Bowen, S. (2008), 'Creating the Taste of Place in the United States: Can We Learn from the French?', *GeoJournal*, 73(1):23–30.
Ulin, R.C. (2002), 'Work as Cultural Production: Labour and Self-identity among Southwest French Wine-growers', *Journal of the Royal Anthropological Institute*, 8(4):691–712.
Ulin, R.C. (2004), 'Globalization and Alternative Localities', *Anthropologica*, 46(2):153–64.

Unwin, T. (1991), *Wine and the Vine: An Historical Geography of Viticulture and the Wine Trade*, London: Routledge.
Veseth, M. (2012), *Wine Wars*, Lanham: Rowman and Littlefield.
Waters, S. (2010), 'Globalization, the *Confédération Paysanne*, and Symbolic Power', *French Politics, Culture & Society*, 28(2):96–117.
Whalen, P. (2009), '"Insofar as the Ruby Wine Seduces Them": Cultural Strategies for Selling Wine in Inter-war Burgundy', *Contemporary European History*, 18(1):67–98.

3 Reflexive *Imbrications*: Burgundy and the Globalization of *Terroir*

MARION DEMOSSIER

Snapshot 1

Burgundy: People with a passion for wine by Rudi Goldman
   https://www.youtube.com/watch?v=0vdniseVceY

Snapshot 2

On 4 July 2015 during the session of the 39th World Heritage committee[1] held in Bonn (Germany), the Climats de Bourgogne were unanimously recommended for addition to the UNESCO (the United Nations Educational, Scientific and Cultural Organization) World Heritage list as cultural landscape. Following the amendments proposed by Portugal and Vietnam to follow the ICOMOS (International Council on Monuments and Sites) recommendations to list it as a cultural landscape rather than a site, it was decided that the Climats de Bourgogne offered one of the best possible examples of cultural landscape, not just based on the visual dimension but because of the progressive construction of the knowledge and relationship between the people, the land and the soil. Their argument was that Burgundy fitted better this category than that of cultural site and there were precedents to classify it as such. Thanks to the convincing speeches of the Portuguese and Vietnamese delegates, the Climats de Bourgogne were eventually listed as a cultural landscape rather than a cultural site.[2] Most of the discussion focused on the protection of the site, especially in relation to the management plan set out by the *Association pour les climats de Bourgogne*.[3] The president of the association and co-owner of the Domaine de la Romanée Conti (known as DRC in the world of wine), Aubert de Villaine, concluded that 'the dossier reflects well French wine heritage which now becomes world heritage'.[4]

Introduction

Globalization has often been described by anthropologists in terms of a clash of cultures (Ong and Collier 2005; Tsing 2005) or as the result of the external forces created by sovereign rule, market rationality and regimes of citizenship which have had a profound impact on communities, nation states and social life. If anthropology, compared to other disciplines, has come late to the field of wine and globalization, it has often helped to conceptualize better the paradoxes inherent to local versus global economic and social processes of change, by bringing people back into the equation. Globalization is indeed about complex articulations of global, national and regional levels of phenomena (see the Introduction to this book), but the anthropological literature tends to emphasize the intensification of global interconnectedness, suggesting 'a world full of movement and mixture, contacts and linkages, and persistent cultural interaction and exchange' (Inda and Rosaldo 2002: 2). Recent research has sought to capture globalization in a more refined fashion using 'assemblages' (Ong and Collier 2005) or 'friction' (Tsing 2005) as metaphors to conceptualize the ways in which global forms have been articulated in specific contexts. Anthropological contributions have therefore helped to define more complex material, collective and discursive relationships to modernity. Yet they have largely focused on the negative impact of globalization, presenting either a rather gloomy picture of the forces at stake and their devastating consequences for local cultures, or a naive and romantic analysis of resistance to it. In this chapter, I seek to engage with this literature and that of the political economy of wine production and consumption, by developing a more positive and creative understanding of the complexities and nuances attached to these processes. I aim to place at the heart of my analysis the longer-term effects that globalization has on people and, more specifically, to understand how communities change and shape their worlds.

The two carefully selected snapshots in the preamble showcase different facets of the Burgundy story[5], and provide a compelling insight into the contemporary narrative of wine and globalization through the prism of locality. The Burgundy story refers to the global (in English) and local narratives (in French) which have consistently been deployed at different historical points: notably the interwar period and, more recently, during the campaign for the Climats de Bourgogne to be accorded UNESCO world heritage status. They will be used to illustrate the development of my argument around Burgundy and the globalization of *terroir*, proposed as windows to analyse what I have termed 'reflexive imbrication', which seeks to conceptualize better the increasing social, cultural, economic, political and spatial complexification across the planet, and how in that context Burgundy is made, distributed, drunk and what people think it means to them. *Imbrication* is used here in the French sense of the word, which originally comes from the Latin *imbricate* – 'covered with roof tiles' – and describes the arrangement of overlapping elements, a coating of imbricated scales, emanating from the same base and with a pattern going in one direction.[6]

Using the analogy of the Hôtel-Dieu of Beaune, with its iconic multicoloured tiled roof, which is seen as synonymous with the traditional values attached to Burgundy, this chapter seeks to assert how the *terroir* story responds to and shapes globalization. Through a study of the region's wine producers (principally the grands crus in the Côte d'Or[7]), analysed ethnographically over a twenty-five-year period, the argument focuses on concepts of 'place-making' (Gille and Ó Riain 2002: 277–9), 'being in location' (Escobar 2001) and the 'politics of scaling' (Demossier 2015), in order to propose a differentiated reading of globalization – that of reflexive *imbrications*. The choice of the term 'reflexive' underlines the tensions between structure and agency often discussed in theories of globalization and social movements. Agency is crucial to the understanding of why elites – here négociants (wine merchants), landowners and reputed winegrowers – are able to drive change, and is partially explained by their economic and social positioning.

Moreover, this chapter argues that the *terroir* story in Burgundy is presented as traditionally rooted and historically unchanged when, in fact, it achieves its powerful resonance from a close and reflexive (in the sense of carefully crafted) *imbrication* with the global wine world and its hierarchy of values (Demossier 2018). Burgundy as a region is a proxy for quality. Michael Hertzfeld (2004) defines the global hierarchy of values as representing the most comprehensive and globally ramified form of common sense which creates a sense of universal commonality. Here the local transcends the global by asserting itself reflexively in the new competitive wine world order. The same story is relentlessly being told, while progressive local adjustments overlap to make it more global. Local and global thus become obsolete analytical categories in the light of an ethnography of place which follows the commodity in its cultural, political and economic deployments (Appadurai 1990). This chapter seeks to engage with theories of globalization by shifting the ethnographic gaze back to the centre of our anthropological thinking, offering a more nuanced and complex understanding of place, product, locality and people.

Wine and globalization

The study of globalization offers an interesting insight into some of the major themes of anthropology, especially the ways in which anthropological thinking has had to face methodological and theoretical challenges. Wine as an anthropological object of scrutiny has not escaped these challenges. When, three decades ago, I started a doctoral thesis on Burgundian viticulture, it was expected that a traditional ethnographic research project would focus on a single defined and bounded site, clearly anthropologically conceptualized and with a strong emphasis on communities, techniques and material culture. Wine culture – the sphere of wine consumption and the ideas and values underlining it – as an object of study in European anthropology was still confined at the time within national boundaries, and formed part of a wider European cultural imperialistic project (Black and Ulin 2013: 2). The idea of culture was understood in national terms with an expectation of historical roots and of a stable territorialized existence (Clifford 1988: 338). Territorialization was thus a key ingredient of this long historical process, and wine communities featured prominently as part of both national and regional narratives about wine-producing regions. What characterized these regional and national imaginaries was a strong rootedness in the local soil of these communities. European wine regions still epitomize, to some extent, the romanticized traditional societies of an imagined pre-industrial era, which explains why investigation of them has often remained limited to the locality, which is continuously reactivated through the politics of place and a strong discourse against change, modernity and foreign influences.

For centuries, Burgundy's wines have been associated with broader historical, cultural, political and economic processes. Its commercial circulation and consumption followed the flows and networks of European elites, who sought to use quality wines as a commodity for exchange, pleasure, prestige and diplomacy. It was also central to Catholicism and urban political life. Historians, such as Roger Dion (1959), have charted the myriad connections established around wine, and how powerful they proved to be over time as part of the social and political fabric at national and transnational levels. Historians have, however, tended to remain limited in their ambitions, partly on account of the methodological challenges posed by access to sources and the use of foreign languages. Globalization remained difficult to analyse. Yet it was an intrinsic part of the circulation of the commodity, even if local consumption was often the rule. Similarly, the study of the political economy of wine has often been separated from other anthropological studies, despite a recent shift of attention towards phenomenology, commodification and reflexivity (Crenn 2015). American anthropology has only focused its attention on European wine-producing regions very recently, while European anthropology has traditionally given more legitimacy to the study of food rather than drink. It is tempting to conclude that the anthropological field of wine and globalization could still be described as embryonic, fragmented and lacking a solid theoretical basis, despite recent attempts to establish it, notably by the edited volume *Wine and Culture* (Black and Ulin 2013). Reconciling the anthropological project with the historical and economic study of globalization remains something of a challenge, which this volume partly seeks to address.

As the editors of this volume have suggested in their Introduction, it is useful to combine, transcend and intertwine insights and foci when analysing globalization and wine. Our two snapshots above illustrate both the *terroir* story and its constant adaptation to external pressures. Firstly, the globalization of wine necessarily entails an historical perspective to grasp the nature of viticultural history and the lessons to be learned. The anthropologist Friedman (1994) defines globalization as a set of processes that connect localities to the extent that the process contains specific logics of reproduction. The study of wine in Europe requires a historical perspective as it is intrinsically linked to the history of capitalism, power, religion, elites, politics and migration, but also localities and social change, all of which played a part in the development of wine-producing regions. It could be argued that the campaign for UNESCO world heritage status was another variation on a theme first played in the 1930s (Laferté 2006).[8] For Friedman, who believes in the importance of a global systemic perspective for our understanding of contemporary society, globalization is defined as a purely structural concept (Friedman 1995: 110). Yet even if the forces behind this new wave of globalization could be seen as more or less comparable to those of the interwar period, it is nevertheless clear that the context has changed both politically and economically, serving different purposes and with different effects.[9]

In order to further our analysis of wine and globalization, it is necessary to revisit some of the analytical obstacles attached to the study of this commodity. Another focus deployed in our snapshots which needs to be discussed is the use of analytical categories such as 'local' and 'global', which obscure the study of globalization and wine. As Kearney (1995: 550) argues, separating the local from the global is inherently problematic when one thoroughly infiltrates the other. These concepts have lost their epistemological validity in the light of contemporary ethnographic material. What is 'local' and what is 'global' for winegrowers? Some of my informants, who own a reputed vineyard, were not born into local families, they do not work the land any more, and their daily activities could be described as 'global', especially when they travel to promote their wines, exchange knowledge with producers in the New World, attend high-profile wine events in Italy and other countries, and sell to importers all over the world. Yet local discourses refer constantly to 'the ways of doing things here'. Over the past twenty years, the notion of 'local' as an ethnographic category has acquired a new salience, and has lost its rooted dimension, opening up new analytical avenues. The wine industry has built its system of values on these shifts in terms of meanings and representations, which have become customized, interpreted, translated and appropriated according to local conditions of reception (Appadurai 1995: 16). A convincing example of such a shift is that of the new environmental agenda (Demossier 2015, 2018) which is now deployed at local level in different marketing guises. Locality has become a fetish which disguises the globally dispersed forces that actually drive the production process (Appadurai 1990: 307). Several of my informants have temporarily left their *terroirs* to acquire other experiences abroad before coming back to their domain.

In Burgundy, for most of the producers and négociants, family business has become the defining feature of post-industrial capitalism, but it has also meant that the ways in which they are operating have changed drastically. These changes have not affected the social fabric in the same uniform way, as the value of wine has always depended upon a wide range of factors, and not everybody has been a winner in the Burgundy story. The creation of the Caves des Hautes-Côtes after the Second World War was crucial in enabling some of the poorer winegrowers of the region to survive, and in some cases, to acquire plots in nearby villages. The economic and social position of each winegrower is often based upon monopoly rent,[10] which could be defined as associated with their vineyards, and also the position of their wines within both the locality and the global hierarchy of wines. When defining monopoly rent, Chiffoleau and Laporte (2006) refer to the fact that firms are able to restrict supply and/or increase prices without fear of attracting competitors. A comprehensive approach to how wine producers in Burgundy determine their prices shows how the diversity of procedures used is related to the status of professional relationships. As Fourcade (2012: 536) argues, in these multiple ways 'the "rent" that [appellations generate is] capitalized into the value of the vineyard' so that 'the rent process is circular and self-sustaining over extended periods'. The areas with the highest rents per unit area are able to maintain the most demanding viticultural and winemaking practices over time.

For some domains, economic success has created a form of inertia and a refusal to countenance any form of change. It could be argued that the common local adage 'his son never leaves the cellar' is part of the cycle of social reproduction, but it also has implications for definitions of both local and global. 'Local' in this context has acquired a new resonance, with a pejorative twist attached to the description of those who have remained too attached to the locality: 'X is still very traditional, he is a *terroirist*, he does the same as his father', while economic success could paradoxically be seen as the way to be more rooted, because of the local economic impact it has on the community. Following globalization, these definitions have blurred, generating new tensions and conflicts (Demossier 2011, 2018). Some successful winegrowers have started to become négociants in their own rights.

Finally, another area of debate is the articulation between individual, group, community and the global hierarchy of values. In Burgundy, perhaps more than any other wine region, place still matters. This relationship to place and wine has materialized through a landscape, a system of interdependent parcels which idealize a model of viticultural art that has resisted historical changes, ruptures and crises. From *terroir* in the 1930s to UNESCO Climats in 2015,[11] the same story is perpetuated and relentlessly being told. This is presented as a stable historical social formation, like the tiled roof of the Hôtel-Dieu. The Burgundy story showcased in snapshot 1 foregrounds geology, history and geography at a time when, following the growth of the wine market and under the impact of generational changes and the development of wine education, more winegrowers want to show their independence by making their own wine, bottling it and selling it. Under this prevailing and comforting image of Burgundy as rooted in history, unchanged and untouched by external forces, hides much of the real story – that of a social struggle for emancipation from the grip of the local wine merchants and elites, of the progressive transformation of local peasants into economic entrepreneurs, and a qualitative engagement with the product. It is worth mentioning that most of the winegrowers I have worked with over the last three decades have defined themselves as peasants rather than business people, despite their increasingly active presence in the global wine market.

The *terroir* story

Burgundy and its high-quality wines have long benefitted from historical prestige, as well as the region being proclaimed as the birthplace of *terroir*. The region has been famous for nearly 2000 years and, superficially, Burgundy appears stable and unchanging, a region arrogantly proclaiming to be a 'terroir béni des Dieux' (soil blessed by God). This traditional narrative so well illustrated by the video presented in our first snapshot is nothing new; it relies on a story already articulated during the interwar period and analysed by Gilles Laferté (2006). In his study of Burgundy as a wine region, Laferté examines the transition of the image of Burgundian wine production from a traditional bourgeois representation to a more folkloric and peasant-based regional model, supported by the construction of Dijon as a gastronomic pole. He argues that the use of folklore, which was imposed by the local elites, négociants and landowners who held a dominant position in the regional landscape at a time of social conflict and frauds, played an important role in repositioning the region in international markets (Laferté 2006). During this period of economic upheaval, Burgundy wines had a more traditional image than other French vineyards, enjoying a privileged economic position which combined a long historical and commercial influence with a small volume of production characterized by a hierarchized landscape. The vineyards were principally owned by a large number of small landowners who acquired property following the phylloxera crisis of the late nineteenth century. This period was also characterized by the regulation and organization of the French wine market by wine professionals and landowners, to the detriment of the négociants who had previously dominated the market (Jacquet 2009). This reorganization took place against the background of the 1930s depression, characterized by economic crisis and acute frauds (Colman 2008).

Since the beginning of the twentieth century, Burgundy as a site of production has been constructed and marketed nationally and internationally. In the Burgundian imaginary, the same trope endures, with the terracotta tile covering the Hôtel-Dieu roof presented as a regional icon which incarnates the permanence of an impressive building dating back to the fifteenth century, tangible proof of *l'esprit bourguignon* or the spirit of the place (Bonnot 2002: 162). In reality, the famous tiles are the more recent product of the neighbouring region of Rhône-Alpes. As Burgundy was the site of Cluny and other great monastic settlements, the figure of the monk is another icon of the *terroir* story. The monastic trope was widely used during the campaign for UNESCO world heritage status, and is seen to prove the historical authenticity of the region and its long-lasting search for quality.[12] In Burgundy, history, religion and their ties to the soil have served as the hallmark of place and its reputation. In contrast to viticulture in the New World, history is used here to claim rootedness and uniqueness (Demossier 2018).

Another key ingredient in this construction is the relationship between man and nature. It is presented through the trope of the monk as embodying a mystic experience endorsing natural observation, the knowledge of the place, and the taste of the earth – the *goûts du terroir*. These themes are deployed at both local and international levels and are fundamental to the way in which Burgundy presents itself to the world. Burgundy could therefore be defined as a cultural formation across and over multiple sites of activities, underpinned by a global story with a strong resonance in regional, national and international terms. Nonetheless, like other reputed wine regions, the recent development of digital technology, the movements of information, symbols, capitals and commodities, have all facilitated the globalization of wine and the circulation of its associated regional imaginary.

A vintage crime: Trust, friendship and local knowledge

Burgundy wines were traditionally characterized by unreliability and heterogeneity in terms of the quality of wine production. A slow process of overlapping has progressively redefined the quality of the product through its increasingly complex and diverse transnational commodification, and through general progress in wine education. On the one hand, Burgundy wines have increasingly diversified to encompass both wine as a work of art (Domaine de la Romanée Conti, known as DRC, for example), and wine as a regional artisanal product, even, in some cases, as a mass consumed drink (Burgundy Pinot Noir and Chardonnay). On the other hand, Burgundy's strength lies in its diversity, both in terms of quality, price and the *typicité*[13] of the product within a small and limited space, while benefitting from the resonant and mythical global story of Burgundy. The value of wine today is produced simultaneously in multiple different locations and levels, and Burgundy with its hundred different AOCs (Appellations d'Origine Contrôlées) offers a perfect example of the complex value-mechanisms and processes at stake when discussing wine and globalization. In a world dominated by 'diverse mobilities of people, objects, images, information and tastes' (Urry 2000: 1), Burgundy seeks to offer a counterexample – that of isomorphism between place, culture, taste and people. Global changes have become progressively part of the *terroir* story, but they have become entangled within the social formation and within the 'place making' project (Demossier 2018).

As part of the place-making project, issues of authenticity and provenance have become part of the story. Wine frauds have always been part of the global wine political economy, but the nature of the frauds has changed following the increasing value of certain grands crus[14] and the rise of wealthy wine lovers across the world. In the 1930s, Burgundy wines were often blended with those from Algeria or other parts of France. They were intended first and foremost for local consumption in urban centres and neighbouring cities, and only a small number of the premium wines were destined for international or quality markets. One of the great achievements of the period prior to the 1930s was the regulation and organization of the wine market by the wine profession and landowners, to the detriment of the négociants, who had previously dominated the region. Progressively throughout the twentieth century, Burgundy wine acquired a more global status, due to better conditions of transportation and conservation and a fall in their costs. It was only in the 1980s and 1990s that wine came to be seen as an object of speculative investment.

Over the last two decades, and more specifically following the 2008 economic crisis, Burgundy has become established as an 'investible wine region', partly due to the volume of production, which is very small compared to Bordeaux or other reputed regions. Most of the wine investment companies offer recommendations and advice for those acquiring wines from specific highly rated producers, and their estimates are often the result of years of experience in the sector and of the local knowledge they have accumulated. One such example is that of the venerable wine company Berry Bros and Rudd, located in St James Street, London. Their website bbr.com sheds some light on the global phenomena of buying and selling globally to refined purchasers. I quote them:

> Investing in wine is by no means a new phenomenon – many years before fine wine became truly 'global' in the mid-1990s, wily buyers would often buy more than they intended to drink, selling the excess at a later date to fund subsequent purchases.

Their expertise relies mostly on the knowledge their local agent has accumulated over the last three decades.[15] The company has recently bought one of the rare British wine companies who had specialized in Burgundy, and their former co-owner has de facto become the buyer for Berry Bros and Rudd. Interestingly enough, their wine investment review document mentions both the 1990s and 2008 as boom periods, as well as the role of both the established fine wine market and a thriving auction market as the main drivers of the speculative system. Yet in Burgundy investment means a particular winegrower, a specific plot or *Climat*, and a particular vintage, pushing to the extreme the localization of the product as well as its vintage. The price of the grands crus in particular was constantly rising throughout the 1990s, as were the land values and the prestige attached to specific plots at the top of the scale (Demossier 2018: 63).

The Hospices de Beaune wine auction takes place each year on the third weekend of November, and confirms the astronomic rise of Burgundy wines over the last three decades and their status as a speculative investment. Burgundy wines were traditionally commercialized through direct contacts with consumers or through wine merchants, while only a handful of emblematic and economically innovative domains possessed their own commercial circuits and were able to sell through privileged contacts with wine companies or selected importers. For these winegrowers of high reputation, selling a small and stable quantity of their wines to the same buyer with whom they had established strong commercial bonds and personal trust was central to their strategy. For the most reputed domains, the seller allocated cases of wines, controlling literally where every bottle goes, relying on their buyers to maintain the same faithful clienteles. During my fieldwork, it soon became clear that any questions I had relating to the commercial dimension were likely to be met by the majority of my informants with an evasive answer or a vague statement. This was explained both by the general reticence to discuss financial matters publicly, and also by the varying degrees of economic knowledge available to local winegrowers. As one of my long-term informers explained: 'I organised a workshop on economic circuits and most of the producers attending had no idea about their production costs nor about the commercial strategy they wanted to pursue, can you believe that?'

Yet it was clear that both formal and informal circuits were coexisting, and that the wine economy in Burgundy was above all a matter of trust, confidence, vernacular knowledge and established friendships. When looking in the 1990s for an old vintage of *Pommard premier cru Clos des Epenots* 1961 for my husband's birthday, a friend put me immediately in contact with a négociant, 'a friend of a friend'. It took me a few minutes and only 25 French francs (around 25 pounds today) to acquire the 1961 bottle. Local knowledge and trust were keys to unlocking the parallel circuit through which specific wines could be acquired. Years later, when conducting interviews on the political economy of Burgundy wines, I had the opportunity of discussing with a wine investor how informal markets, which have emerged in the last ten to fifteen years through Facebook and other networks, have facilitated both the access to vintage Burgundy wines and exacerbated more dishonest practices. Fraudulent practices often rely on different knowledge geographies, with, for example, 'Indian and Chinese buyers not knowing well the local milieu'.

The recent Kurniawan[16] affair gives us an insight into the extent to which globalization provides a platform to multiply and, by the same token in this case, distort the value and the trust negotiated within closed circuits – friends of friends – around these few emblematic wines. When the Burgundian winegrower Alain Ponsot was contacted by one of his friends, an American lawyer, who informed him that some of his wines from 1945, 1949 and 1962 were being sold at an auction, Ponsot was shocked as the label did not exist before 1982. At the centre of the affair was the name of Rudy Kurniawan, who was convicted of fraud in 2013 and condemned to ten years imprisonment for counterfeiting. More than 4,700 bottles of wines were discovered next to some authentic grands crus. What is interesting about the case is the ways in which trust was established between Kurniawan and the auction house, as well as a circle of customers to whom he sold his precious bottles. Kurniawan presented himself as a wine lover and the collector of rare bottles, who started to buy some of the most prestigious wines regularly at high prices. He then started to sell them as well as other counterfeit bottles through the same network of auction houses, and some buyers trusted him sufficiently to pay up to one million US Dollars for the most precious vintages available. Building trust was clearly in this case a strategy, but one that was intended to support an elaborate fraud.

Several other examples of frauds affecting French vineyards could be cited.[17] It has, however, become easier for the producer to be able to trace his or her wines from production to consumption and to authenticate them. The Domaine de la Romanée Conti has developed ways of identifying each bottle, while control of the commercialization of their wines has also been one of their central strategies. Increasingly it could be said that the singularity of these wines is constructed through the reputation of the domain – which functions like a brand – and, in particular, the rarity of the vintage produced. Local knowledge is again central to the act of consumption. DRC even has the luxury of choosing not to sell its wines when the vintage is not thought to be good enough for its clients. Price formation relies on trust, confidence and expert knowledge, and this is a balance which is not always easy to maintain, unless you have access to the producer and locality. The balance therefore remains fragile and risky. As a wine investor informant put it: 'the more people invest in wine the more this market will behave like an investment'.

In his book on economic singularities, Karpik (2010) suggests that commodities like wine, which are unique, cannot be understood with the tools of neoclassical economics, in which supply and demand are said to determine prices. Judgement devices, he argues, are produced to help wine lovers to gauge the quality and authenticity of the product (Karpik 2010: 44–5). Both wine guides, reviews and personal contacts, such as friends and trusted wine professionals, characterize, as we have seen, the wine market. Yet these devices are also vulnerable to risk and counterfeit, as they rely on human activities and subjective evaluations. Moreover, wine, unlike any other commodity, is not a simple material product; it has social and symbolic qualities, as well as intoxicating virtues potentially clouding rational judgements.

Crafting authenticity and singularity

'Placelessness' has become the essential feature of the modern condition (Escobar 2001: 140). Yet the reassertion of place appears as an important arena for rethinking and reworking the reading of culture, capitalism and modernity. Reflecting on the geographical imagination, Harvey (1990) argues that both time and space are interrelated, playing a key role in processes of social reproduction, and have consequently become contested in the capitalistic mode of production. As part of those changes, wine production and consumption offer an interesting example of how time and space could be rearticulated to produce a story of singularity through the field of heritage, consumption, and the cultural production of place. The wine market is an extraordinary example of a market for singularities (Beckert, Rössel and Schenk 2014). Sociologists have recently turned their attention to wine (e.g. Beckert, Rössel and Schenk 2014; Fourcade 2012; Karpik 2010), arguing that its value stems largely from symbolic qualities ascribed to the products based on actors' interpretations. Variations in prices are therefore explained by social processes in which quality is constructed and contested. Moreover, differences reflect status differences among producers and consumers, and are thus socially constituted (Beckert, Rössel and Schenk 2014: 3). The picture becomes even more complex as the specific valuations of both producers and consumers are explained by the position of the respective actors in the socio-economic field, and are therefore socially contextualized (Beckert, Rössel and Schenk 2014: 4).

Moving from this sociological analysis, I would like to go back to people, community and place, to propose a more complex and differentiated reading of the cultural processes at stake. The Climats de Bourgogne are a very recent invention, designed in an attempt to renew the *terroir* ideology, while positioning Burgundian wines in the context of an ever more globalized market which has questioned the hierarchy attached to traditional wine regions (Demossier 2018). The Climats are presented as Burgundy's own recent translation of the word '*terroir*', taking on a different sense to that usually associated with geographical conditions. According to the Climats dossier,

> They are particular to Burgundy and designate a parcel of land dedicated to a precisely delineated vineyard, known by that name for hundreds of years, and therefore a precise plot, soil, subsoil, exposure and microclimate forming together within a vineyard characteristics that constitute a personality, unique to one terroir and one cru.[18]

For their advocates, Climats have been historically created, and constitute an exceptional mosaic of vineyards with a hierarchy of wines and an international reputation. Superficially, then, Burgundy might appear to be simply acquiring recognition for its unchanging landscape, tradition and culture. Yet in reality, for all the power of a rich local identity, folklore and culture broadcast to the world, underneath the comforting blanket of this seamless place untouched by economic change or social conflicts there hides a far more complex reality (Barrey and Teil 2011).

The Burgundy story has therefore been constructed on the foundations of *terroir* and its reputation as the birthplace of that concept, while a constant effort to craft this authenticity has been led at key historical points of juncture by different groups of actors and in a diverse range of ways. There are however fundamental social differences in both the construction and the consumption of the place. Indeed, the very act of naming geographical entities implies a power over them, and more particularly over the way in which places, their inhabitants and their social function are represented (Harvey 1990: 419). The act of representation is inscribed in the making and remaking of the place, and the Climats story adds another layer to the already rich and colourful veneer of the Burgundy story. This is about shifting the environmental agenda and positioning Burgundy in the new wine heritage landscape (Barrey and Teil 2011). By becoming a world heritage site and promoting a new reading of *terroir*, Burgundians make sure that they maintain their hegemonic position in the global hierarchy of wine, where place, taste and social experience still matter (Demossier 2015).

Yet at local level, in the Côte d'Or especially, ordinary winegrowers remain under the shadow of the elites and wine merchants, and the UNESCO status is another example of their exclusion, or at least passive acceptance. The Burgundy story is a powerful trope within the global hierarchy of wine, but it also anchored in the locality in a collective and shared belief that soil, history and *terroir* remain the sole determinants of the global value of its products. From *terroirs* to *climats*, the same story is perpetually constructed and deployed in different locations, passed from one generation to the next, and transmitted throughout the global wine economy, benefitting the whole community. This is where power lies in the endless anchoring that individuals, groups and communities in this part of the world continuously assess and reassess. This is a powerful story about hospitality, sociability and friendship, time, space and democratic values. As recalled by the New York sommelier Michael Madringale: 'There is something about this place in the world of wine that is unique, and it brings together the passionate people, the wine lovers of this world.' For the community, 'it is the true spirit of terroir, the spirit of the terroir of the wine makers, the roots of the vine and the spirit of Burgundy'. Experiencing Burgundian hospitality, characterized by simplicity, good food and generosity, clashes with the expensive reality of the local wines. This crafted self-reflexive imbrication relies therefore not only on the economic circulation of wines and financial profits, but also on the centrality of gift culture in Burgundian hospitality and the global wine economy. Friendship, gifts and trust are central to one's definition against the background of capitalist social relations.

Wine as a global commodity has a multifaceted social function, which goes deeper than other commodities due to its ethylic and pleasurable effects. It facilitates communication and social relations, and generates social memories of specific places, events, meetings and pleasures. It also ensures that social relations are constantly maintained through commensality, gastronomic discourse and the sharing of collective values. For the community this is not pure folklore. It is about being in location and 'sitting in a culture' – that is to say, being connected physically to a place. In the story about 'place making', the philosopher Edward S. Casey notes, 'to live is to live locally and to know is first of all to know the places one is in.'[19] Burgundy epitomizes this tie to a place, 'being in location', which has been preserved, nurtured and narrated for many generations. The deeply rooted social construction of *terroir* at the local level and its reflexive imbrication have been powerful and ubiquitous rhetorical devices employed by producers when asked about the highs and lows of the production and sale of wines. In this context, the concept of *terroir* presents a particular case of extreme localization, whereby three, four or five successive generations of the same family have established a working relationship with a particular milieu and a specific 'noble' plant, Chardonnay or Pinot Noir, in an ecological milieu which has been presented as unchanged despite being the subject of intense agrarian transformations and commercial expansion. These families have anchored themselves to a specific place and village and, consequently, they have accumulated a wealth of experience, albeit not one that was necessarily a synonym of 'quality'. As one female informant stated to me: 'It is not easy to move the goal posts here when belonging is counted in centuries.'

Conclusion

As a world-renowned wine region, Burgundy, like Beaune's emblematic Hôtel-Dieu roof, has assembled a coating of imbricated scales which have established the foundations for the *terroir* story. This is a story about the original and sometimes mythical links between place, culture and taste which has found a new resonance with the invention of Climats and the acquisition of world heritage status. New tiles have been added to anchor the Burgundy story in the global hierarchy of wine, by reiterating the original myth of *terroir* and by adding both the heritage and environmental varnish to the local politics of place. Both strategies are primarily led by elites, but they are also driven by local politicians and key regional actors, and are inscribed into the new competitive wine world order, which is going through a major global transition which can be described as a blurring of the divide between the Old World and the New (Overton, Murray and Banks 2012). More than ever, anchoring while adapting requires local elites to rethink the *terroir* story, while maintaining the hegemonic position of Burgundy and its grands crus in the world of wine.

Burgundy thus offers a unique illustration of how a resonant and historically rooted story of *terroir* provides a structure for the contemporary deployment of new stories about place. The application for UNESCO world heritage status, led since 2008 by the local elites, has reactivated under different guises the story of quality, soil, history and nature, while closely guaranteeing that communities, winegrowers, négociants and the local population engage with or, even more rarely, contest it. It is clear that the invention and promotion of the Climats story has been a resounding success. Yet in order to become more globally recognized, it will need to be embraced more widely, repeated, translated and passed on, as well as being constituted as a new category of perception locally, nationally and internationally. In the pursuit of such a strategy, the iconic image of both the roof and the vineyards provides an enduring symbol about place, with the diversity of tiles and plots embodying the emblematic and powerful Burgundian representation of *terroir*.

This kind of powerful construction, which is often underlined by a series of hegemonic discourses about locality, necessarily impacts upon a wide range of actors who contribute to the making of quality wine and to the sustainability of place in a rapidly changing economic context. It also has a huge economic impact and a growing potential for further speculation. Wine entrepreneurs in Burgundy do not seek necessarily to diversify and create multiple meanings of authenticity to accommodate, modify and at times resist the effects of globalization on local culture and economic life.[20] They paradoxically wish to engage, take control and master global forces by consolidating, reinforcing and perpetuating the story of their origins and authenticity, thus creating a differentiated engagement from other producers at local level. The heritagization of the site, as well as the environmental shifts, are far from collective and homogeneous processes, because all too often it is forgotten that they will benefit some but potentially harm others. This also opens the door to increasing divisions and growing contestation. Yet these consolidate the hegemonic position of Burgundy's wine in the global market.

The traditional collective values which were at the core of the Burgundian self-identity, such as hospitality, generosity and humbleness, have been progressively eroded by the impact of economic success and growing affluence, which have led to the transformation of the place. As one of the Dutch importers I met during a recent fieldtrip remarked: 'It is impossible to buy anything here, they have nothing to sell, I have to go South where good quality wines are still affordable.' The paradox between being a UNESCO site, and object of consumption and of distinction, as well as part of the heritage of humanity, is one of the most challenging issues that Burgundy will have to face. By focusing on the place, producers and interested commercial elites can present Burgundy as if it were accessible to all, part of the world's patrimony, conveniently forgetting that only a tiny minority will ever purchase a bottle of *Romanée Conti*. By investigating the development of the Burgundy story over the longue durée, we can obtain a fascinating insight into some of the fractures of modern society and the constant battle between different strategies. But it is also a crafted and enduring construction of place, assembling every piece into a seamless tapestry through historical junctures and elitist enterprise. It is the story of that complex *imbrication* that I have followed, not only through the window offered by the locality, but also through its powerful deployments in the face of globalization.

Notes

1. See http://en.unesco.org/events/39th-session-world-heritage-committee. Consulted on 02 February 2016.
2. See http://whc.unesco.org. WHC 15/39.COM.INF.19 English and French summary records. Consulted on 15 February 2016.
3. The *Association pour les Climats de Bourgogne* http://www.climats-bourgogne.com/. In Burgundy, a Climat is the name for a specific vineyard site combining vine plots, grape variety and know-how. Consulted on 22 March 2016.
4. My translation. See http://whc.unesco.org. WHC 15/39.COM.INF.19 English and French summary records, p.194. Consulted on 15 February 2016.
5. When I use the term 'Burgundy', I refer more specifically to the Côte d'Or and its hierarchy of wines. For more information, consult http://www.climats-bourgogne.com/
6. I would like to thank my colleague Dr. Tony Campbell for suggesting this idea of pattern.
7. The hundred or so official geographic origins for Burgundy wines fall into four hierarchically ordered levels: regional, 'village wines', premiers crus and grands crus. For the purposes of our argument, the focus will be on the premiers crus and grands crus. In Burgundy, grands crus represent 0.8 per cent of the region's production and 1.5 per cent of its appellations. There are about 100 appellations in Burgundy, as opposed to 57 in Bordeaux, even if Bordeaux is more than four times larger (Fourcade 2012: 541).
8. As I am writing, another local fraud scandal has hit the region. For more information, see http://www.bienpublic.com/edition-cote-de-beaune/2016/04/01/fraudes-sur-les-vins-perqui-sition-et-garde-a-vue-chez-bejot. Consulted on 07 April 2016.
9. See for more details Jonathan Friedman's YouTube video *Globalising Fantasies, Trenchant Realities*: https://www.youtube.com/watch?v=mlUu2p8LKGo. Consulted on 22 March 2016.
10. For more details, see Chiffoleau and Laporte (2006) and Fourcade (2012).
11. 'Climats' has been used as a new term coined to replace *terroir* in the Burgundian global strategy, and was the cornerstone of the application to UNESCO world heritage status (Demossier 2015). For more information, consult: http://www.climats-bourgogne.com/en/
12. For an example of the deployment of the Burgundy story as part of the UNESCO application for world heritage status (Climats de Bourgogne), watch: www.youtube.com/watch?v=VnFErwQlQtE. Consulted on 29 March 2016.
13. 'Typicité' is a term in wine-tasting used to describe the degree to which a wine reflects its varietal origins. The term is also used by the French wine profession when granting the AOC agreement to a specific wine. For more discussion about the concept, see Teil (2012).
14. Prices for grands crus oscillate between 20 Euros per bottle and 10,000 Euros or more. To give you an idea, one bottle of Domaine de la Romanée Conti has recently sold for 850 Euros, while older vintages could reach up to 12,000 Euros per bottle, and these wines are the object of intense speculation.

15. For more information, see Jasper Morris (2010) and watch the following video: www.youtube.com/watch?v=OPXGxb3lQQo. Consulted on 07 April 2016.
16. For more information, read http://nymag.com/news/features/rudy-kurniawan-wine-fraud-2012-5/index3.html. Consulted on 31 March 2016.
17. http://www.bienpublic.com/edition-cote-de-beaune/2016/04/01/fraudes-sur-les-vins-perqui-sition-et-garde-a-vue-chez-bejot. Consulted on 07 April 2016 (personal communication).
18. My own translation. See http://www.climats-bourgogne.com/fr/notre-dossier_17.html. Consulted on 2 February 2016.
19. Cited by the anthropologist Arturo Escobar (2001).
20. For a useful analysis of the social sources of authenticity, see Wherry (2006).

References

Appadurai, A. (1990), 'Disjuncture and Difference in the Global Cultural Economy', in Featherstone, M., Lash, S., and Robertson, R. (eds), *Global Modernities*, London: Sage, 109–33.

Appadurai, A. (1995), *Modernity at Large: Cultural Dimensions of Globalization*, London: Routledge.

Barrey, S., and Teil, G. (2011), 'Faire la preuve de l'« authenticité » du patrimoine alimentaire', *Anthropology of food*, http://aof.revues.org/6783. Consulted on 31 March 2016.

Beckert, J., Rössel, J., and Schenk, P. (2014), 'Wine as a Cultural Product: Symbolic Capital and Price Formation in the Wine Field', Max-Planck-Institut für Gesellschaftsforschung, Köln, discussion paper: 1–20. www.mpifg.de/pu/mpifg_dp/dp14-2.pdf. Consulted on 31 March 2016.

Black, R.E., and Ulin, R.C. (eds) (2013), *Wine and Culture: Vineyard to Glass*, London: Bloomsbury.

Bonnot, T. (2002), 'Des tuiles, des toits et des couleurs: de Beaune à Disneyland Paris, une tradition bourguignonne', *Terrain*, 38(March):153–62.

Chiffoleau, Y., and Laporte, C. (2006), 'Price Formation: The Case of the Burgundy Wine Market', *Revue française de sociologie*, 47(Supplement):157–82.

Clifford, J. (1988), *The Predicament of Culture. Twentieth-century Ethnography, Literature, and Art*, Harvard: Harvard University Press.

Colman, T. (2008), *Wine Politics. How Governments, Environmentalists, Mobsters and Critics Influence the Wine We Drink*, Berkeley: University of California Press.

Crenn, C. (2015), 'Le vin comme objet de recherche anthropologique', *Anthropology of Food*, http://aof.revues.org/7831. Consulted on 31 March 2016.

Demossier, M. (2018), *Burgundy: A Global Anthropology of Place and Taste*, New York and Oxford: Berghahn.

Demossier, M. (2015), 'The Politics of Heritage in the Land of Food and Wine', in Logan, W., Craith, M.N., and Kockel, U. (eds), *A Companion to Heritage Studies*, Chichester: Wiley-Blackwell Companions to Anthropology Series: 87–100.

Demossier, M. (2011), 'Beyond *Terroir*: Territorial Construction, Hegemonic Discourses and French Wine Culture', *Journal of the Royal Anthropological Institute*, 17(4):685–705.

Dion, R. (1959), *Histoire de la Vigne et du Vin en france – Des Origines au XIXe Siecle*, Paris: Broche.
Escobar, A. (2001), 'Culture Sits in Places: Reflections on Globalism and Subaltern Strategies of Localization', *Political Geography*, 20:139–74.
Fourcade, M. (2012), 'The Vile and the Noble', *The Sociological Quarterly*, 53:524–45.
Friedman, J. (1994), *Cultural Identity and Global Process*, London: Sage.
Friedman, J. (1995), 'Global System, Globalization and the Parameters of Modernity', in Featherstone, M., Lash, S., and Robertson, R. (eds), *Global Modernities*, London: Sage, 109–33.
Gille, Z., and O'Riain, S. (2002), 'Global Ethnography', *Annual Review of Sociology*, 28:271–95.
Harvey, D. (1990), 'Between Space and Time: Reflections on the Geographical Imagination', *Annals of the Association of American Geographers*, 80(3):418–34.
Herzfeld, M. (2004), *The Body Impolitic: Artisans and Artifice in the Global Hierarchy of Value*, Chicago: University of Chicago Press.
Inda, J.-X., and Rosaldo, R. (eds) (2002), *The Anthropology of Globalization*, Malden, MA: Blackwell.
Jacquet, O. (2009), *Un siècle de construction du vignoble bourguignon. Les organisations vitivinicoles de 1884 aux AOC*, Dijon, EUD: Coll. Sociétés.
Karpik, L. (2010), *Valuing the Unique. The Economics of Singularities*, Princeton, NJ: Princeton University Press.
Kearney, M. (1995), 'The Local and the Global: The Anthropology of Globalisation and Transnationalism', *Annual Review of Anthropology*, 24:547–65.
Laferté, G. (2006), *La Bourgogne et ses vins: image d'origine contrôlée*, Paris: Belin.
Morris, J. (2010), *Inside Burgundy. The Vineyards, the Wine & the People*, London: Berry Brothers & Rudd Press.
Ong, A., and Collier, S.-J. (2005), *Global Assemblages: Technology, Politics, and Ethics as Anthropological Problems*, Malden, MA, Oxford: Blackwell.
Overton, J., Murray, W.E. and Bank, G. (2012), 'The Race to the Bottom of the Glass? Wine, Geography, and Globalization', *Globalizations*, 9(2):273–87.
Teil, G., Hennion, A., Barrey, S., and Floux, P. (2012), *Le vin et l'environnement*, Paris: Presses des Mines.
Tsing, A.L. (2005), *Friction: An Ethnography of Global Connection*, Princeton: Princeton University Press.
Urry, J. (2000), *Sociology beyond Societies: Mobilities for the Twenty-first Century*, London: Routledge.
Wherry, F. (2006), 'The Social Sources of Authenticity in Global Handicraft Markets. Evidence from Northern Thailand', *Journal of Consumer Culture*, 6(1):5–32.

4 Building and Sustaining Legitimacy in an Emerging Wine Region: The Case of North Carolina, USA

IAN MALCOLM TAPLIN

Introduction

Wine is both a ubiquitous product that is an essential part of the gastronomy of many cultures, as well as being a reviled substance that is associated with moral depravity in others. In the former it is the sine qua non of eating a meal, as well as a pillar in many rural economies. In the latter it continues to be opposed by many in religious communities, whose invocation of scriptures justifies its banning. In cultures where religious conservatism is combined with traditions of often excessive alcohol consumption, wine has been tarnished with the same brush of degeneracy as hard liquor.

In previous chapters of this book we have seen how a product – wine – that was often specific to a particular location and met the taste preferences of a population therein became globalized, and according to some, increasingly homogenized. As a cultural product, however, wine consumption also reveals many of the contradictions and moral uncertainties noted above that confound those with omnivorous tastes. The greater awareness of wine following the onset of globalization, especially in regions where it was not previously a beverage of choice, has often resulted in challenges to extant norms regarding alcohol. But that same increased awareness of the product and the lifestyles associated with it have provided an impetus for producers to make wine and win over hitherto sceptical local consumers. This chapter attempts to disentangle these issues by focusing upon the growth of a wine region and wine culture in an area often seen as hostile to alcohol.

Understanding of recent developments in the global wine industry – which include the role of place (*terroir*), scientific and technical innovations in the making of wine, new distribution patterns, how experts confer legitimacy to certain wines, and how consumer demographics are changing – provides a useful background to an examination of an emerging wine region, in this case in the United States. More specifically, this enables us to examine the dissemination not just of wine per se, but the overall culture of wine drinking as a legitimate social activity and pastime. It also allows us to show how new wineries have used European varietals (of *Vitis vinifera*) to endow their product with appropriate cultural (and geographical) legitimacy. The wines might be 'locally' produced, but their heritage is essentially European – French, Spanish and Italian varietals being uppermost. The resulting discourse that emanates from increased product availability further substantiates the notion of wine fields and worlds (see Chapter 1), the contexts in which market interactions of supply and demand operate.

The sale and exchange of wine remains embedded, unlike many other agricultural products, in an often complex set of traditions and deep-rooted assumptions regarding its legitimacy. In this chapter I analyse the early struggles to establish a wine industry in North Carolina (NC), partly deriving from imperfect or inadequate viticultural knowledge, and partly because of entrenched opposition from religious and other groups who had concerns about wine's impact upon social life. I then move to a discussion of industry evolution in the past few decades, as attempts to manufacture cultural and economic legitimacy have solidified their hold in the local economy. Globalization is important here inasmuch as more of the local population have come to understand wine quality and types, and are willing to consume a local product that exemplifies broader international trends. By examining how resource-rich wineries play a de facto leadership role in upgrading operational performance and marketing in this emerging wine world, one can better understand how the product has come to be accepted as an appropriate beverage to a hitherto sceptical consumer population. Companies have been able to do this by emphasizing the distinctiveness of their product from other local beverages (including many of the traditional North American grapes that produce sweet wines), and by constructing an authentic identity for their product that resonates as a sophisticated beverage for a discerning educated (and globalized) consumer. I also point to the changing demographics in the area that have created a localized demand for wine, as well as to the birth of wine tourism, which has brought many people to wineries who otherwise might not be familiar with wine.

Much of the discussion on how this industry has grown focuses upon the dynamics of 'clusters' – dense groupings of similar firms in a geographical area, which are able to benefit from shared knowledge and similar operational facilities (Baptista 2000; Lazerson and Lorenzoni 1999; Maskell 2001). Such clusters, part of the wine worlds that structure the collective nature of wine production (see Chapter 1), effectively coordinate activities and provide incentives for specialized firms which service the sector and allow it to grow. The resulting spillovers in localized knowledge help foster innovation and make lower transaction costs for individual firms. This has been much discussed in studies of the Italian wine industry (Giuliani 2006), but has also been paramount in the evolution of Napa Valley, California, as an ultra-premium wine district (Taplin 2010). In the case of NC, the role of networking within an emerging cluster has been crucial in enabling the industry to overcome information and technical deficiencies that plagued earlier, failed efforts to establish itself (Breckenridge and Taplin 2005). But it is also the story of how a global(ized) product such as wine can emerge in areas without a tradition or history of wine drinking, and can overcome many of the liabilities that a new industry faces in a very short period by leveraging extant knowledge from more established wine regions.

A brief history of wine in NC

The first systematic evidence of wine consumption on a commercial scale in the state of NC (in the mid-Atlantic region of the United States) can be found in the records of Moravian immigrants who came to the area in the eighteenth century (Taplin 2011). Of mainly German origin, these immigrants used wine as an integral part of their religious services (communion), as well as in their taverns as a social beverage. They sought to import much of the wine they consumed, as growing it locally proved difficult. How pervasive wine consumption became is difficult to gauge, despite frequent references to problems in its supply contained in the various minutes of church leaders (Fries 1922). However, it does seem as if they managed at least to establish a local wine culture even though it was mediated through religious services.

Commercial wine production in the state occurred in the 1820s when a schoolteacher and preacher from New York named Sidney Weller bought a 400-acre derelict farm in Halifax County in the eastern part of the state (Adams 1973). What started as a nursery, then as a crop-yielding farm, eventually became a winery in 1835, which he named Medoc vineyard. With 6 acres of vines under cultivation, he sold his wine at between $1 and $6 a gallon to markets throughout the east coast. He subsequently became a strong advocate for winemaking in the region, arguing that it was a morally uplifting and culturally respectable activity, in addition to providing much-needed libations for a population used to local hard liquor (the ubiquitous 'moonshine'), as well as frequently non-potable water.

We know little of the quality of his wine, but the grapes that he grew were *muscadine*, locally known as scuppernong. Classified technically as *Vitis rotundifolia*, this grape is native to the area and was apparently noted by the first settlers in the state in the 1500s (Drew 2006; Ghodes 1982). The vines are huge, the grapes the size of cherries, and they grow in large clusters that have very high yields. When fermented the wine is often bitter tasting, hence the need for added sugar to tame the musky flavour. While this grape grew in abundance, and essentially organically, it was not initially the preferred taste for many. Unfortunately, numerous experiments at growing *Vitis vinifera* grapes (the type associated with European wine countries) had all failed, so if people wanted to make wine, then this was what was at their disposal (Morton 1985; Pinney 1989).

By the latter part of the nineteenth century, using money from their successful clothing business, the Garrett family bought Weller's Medoc vineyard upon his death, and embarked upon a plan to ratchet up production of *muscadine*, plus other native varietals such as Concord, at several additional vineyard sites in the area. Their production grew from 3000–5000 gallons in 1871 to 175,000 gallons twenty years later. One of the sons, named Paul, eventually left the company to form his own winery (Garrett and Company), and his skill at marketing, plus an ability to procure large amounts of grapes from many sites in the south-east, enabled him by the turn of the century to create one of the largest wine companies in the United States. His signature wine was called *Virginia Dare*, named after the first child born to settlers in the colony in the 1500s, and it became the most popular drink in the United States in the early 1900s.

Having seen grape-growing and winemaking eventually flourish in the decades after the civil war, bringing income stability to some farmers and modest economic development to rural areas, it all came to an abrupt end in 1909, when a state referendum of the previous year resulted in a majority of the population voting to prohibit the sale and manufacture of 'intoxicating' liquors. This foreshadowed nationwide prohibition (the Volstead National Prohibition Act of 1920) – the result of a growing national as well as regional temperance movement, designed to eradicate the supposed moral degeneracy associated with excessive alcohol consumption (Beliseau and Rouse 2010).

Opposition to alcohol had deep roots in the south, where it was seen as a moral abomination by some conservative religious groups, and an impediment to worker efficiency and productivity by secular foes (McGirr 2015). This was despite the presence of wine-drinking Moravians who settled central parts of the state, and whose cultural traditions were compatible with the beverage (as well as beer). Undoubtedly alcoholism, public drunkenness and family violence were all commonplace, thus rendering frequent steadfast efforts to root out the cause of the problem. But there was also a strong culture of home-made brewing, and such production was part of a thriving 'cottage' industry designed to slake the thirsts of a population struggling in poverty. The proverbial 'moonshine' was accompanied by many varieties of fruit brandies that were easily made by fermenting fruit from numerous orchards in the areas (peach seemed to be the most prolific fruit source in central NC) (Gohdes 1982; Watson 1973).

The culture of drinking was therefore a complicated mix of opposing interests: some saw it as an economic bedrock of marginal farmers, others campaigned against its socially disruptive consequences and still others associated it, often negatively, with immigrant groups. The latter is certainly consistent with wine consumption elsewhere in the country, particularly the north-east, where Italian immigrants brought their traditions that made it a requisite complement to any meal. As a consequence, attitudes towards wine were often conflated with negative stereotypes of immigrant populations. Displeasing some, wine nonetheless gained a foothold as the country saw a further surge in immigration by populations for whom it was an integral part of their culture.

Nationally Prohibition ended in 1933, but the North Carolina Assembly sanctioned local decision-making over alcohol sales and manufacture, so decisions were made on a county-by-county basis. While the eastern part of the state (where the original wineries were located) mainly voted to go wet, the rest of the state voted to stay dry. The former voters were encouraged by various State Department of Agriculture initiatives designed to alleviate rural poverty and stimulate agricultural diversification and growth (Mathia 1966; Mathia et al 1977). Many in this area were marginal tenant farmers with small plots and limited educational backgrounds. Undercapitalized and often far from viable markets and population centres, such groups had always struggled. However, even after the federal government reclassified wine as an article of food to distinguish its production from distilling activities, the prohibitionist sentiments remained paramount, thus limiting sales and consumption. This impasse would remain in effect until the 1980s.

Wine's resurgence

Several changes occurred in the last decades of the twentieth century that placed wine production and consumption back in the public eye, with resulting economic and cultural ramifications. Asheville is a small city, situated amidst the mountains in the western part of the state, and the home of Biltmore house, the largest private residence in the United States. Built by George Washington Vanderbilt between 1890 and 1895, and now home to the Cecil family (Vanderbilt's heirs), the 125,000-acre estate added a vineyard to its agricultural operations in 1971. The owners felt that a winery would complement the Gallic ambiance of the chateau-style architecture of the main house, and might also encourage further tourism to the house, which is open to the public all year round. Having planted hybrid vines as well as *vinifera*, they then hired a respected French winemaker, Philippe Jourdain, in 1979. It was always recognized that the location's altitude might not be ideal for many varietals, so imported grapes and juice from California to supplement local production were extensively used. This also guaranteed the desired quality that the owners wanted and which they were uncertain local grapes could consistently deliver – especially given the infancy of local winemaking in the region. After a number of near disastrous winter storms almost wiped out local production in 1985, the estate has gone on to be a major wine producer, annually selling 150,000 cases of wine, half of which are sold direct from the winery. Only 20 per cent of the wine is from locally made grapes, and much of that supply comes from local vineyards on a yearly contract basis. The remainder is harvested and bottled in California under the Biltmore label and shipped east to the winery for sale. Somewhat ironically, Biltmore has the distinction of being the most visited winery in the United States – an interesting accolade for a state not always easily associated with wine production.

In the eastern part of the state, a resurgence of *muscadine* occurred around the same time period, much of it initially focused upon one winery called Duplin Wine Cellars that opened in 1976 (Gohdes 1982; Morton 1985). Following encouragement by the North Carolina Agriculture Department, two brothers, Dan and David Fussell, had planted 10 acres of *muscadine* grapes in 1972 to supply the upstate New York market with these grapes. When the price per ton of these grapes fell by more than a half by 1974, they decided to make wine themselves for sale locally. They persisted in the face of lingering temperance sentiments and with no experience of winemaking, initially producing 225 bottles of 'drinkable' wine (their quote). They continued to expand production, 'learning by doing', but also with some tax credit help from state government and technical assistance from agriculture agencies, and by 1995 finally had a profitable year. They currently produce around 500,000 cases annually, making them by far the largest winery in the state, and among the top thirty biggest wineries in the United States. Several other *muscadine* growers in the eastern part of the state have also grown large, but the majority remain fairly small operations. Duplin's success and growth has been so great in the last decade that they are unable to grow all the grapes they need themselves, thus sourcing throughout the east coast (Williams 2007). This has stimulated the sort of agricultural growth that early exponents of winemaking had advocated in previous decades. In addition to making a wine that is rather sweet, and thus consistent with the beverage choice profile of a population used to sodas and sweet tea, their recent success can also be attributed to developments in the health sector.

Many have argued that moderate wine consumption can have significant health benefits, but a scientific study in 1995 reinforced this sentiment by showing that heart attacks and strokes could be reduced by a regular glass of wine. Furthermore, *muscadine* grapes have the highest levels of resveratrol and allergic acid: the former is a substance in red wine that is most beneficial to health, whereas the latter is a strong antioxidant that inhibits cancer. A further aspect of wine's global impact emerged when wine drinking was associated with the alleged benefits of a Mediterranean diet, thus fostering a unity between health and culture that could be used to counter the opposition of conservative religious groups who continued to stigmatize alcohol. Elevating wine consumption to a beneficial health product undoubtedly neutralized some opposition and made it culturally acceptable to others. Perhaps most importantly, it established it as a beverage that could be a natural complement to food. The fact that *muscadine* wine is relatively cheap to purchase ($7–10 per bottle) gave it access to a wide group of the population unused to large expenditures for beverages. In this respect wine lost some of its elitist connotations that had hindered earlier consumption by poorer segments of the population. Although *muscadine* grape-growing had become economically viable and the wine fairly easy to make, it was nonetheless a varietal that more established oenophiles did not particularly appreciate. For them, *vinifera* grapes were deemed the only legitimate ones for wine, but in the past all efforts to grow such varietals in the state had met with dismal failure. However, that was changing by the late 1970s.

In the central part of the state, in an area called the Piedmont, several pioneering individuals planted *vinifera* grapes, starting in the late 1970s (Taplin 2011). Wine lovers themselves, they believed that this was the sort of wine people who appreciated wine would want. As growers, they benefited from a corpus of viticulture knowledge that identified many of the problems that had beset earlier attempts to grow these grapes in the south. Initially agricultural programmes at Cornell University in upstate New York (with its own established wine industry) provided the requisite technical knowledge, but this was eventually supplanted by oenology and viticulture programmes at local community colleges in NC, principally one at Surry Community College, as well as an extension agricultural programme at NC State University. As it became increasingly clear that many French varietals and hybrids could be grown successfully if one understood ways of combatting the numerous diseases that afflicted the vines, more newcomers entered the industry. This was followed by winemakers coming from out of state to work with the new larger wineries, bringing valuable professional and experiential knowledge that allowed them to troubleshoot routine issues that plagued many vineyards. The state increasingly offered modest support for the industry, and in 1986 a legislative act established the North Carolina Grape Council, charged with funding viticulture research, stimulating winemaking knowledge, and underwriting promotional and marketing activities for the emerging industry. Further changes allowed excise tax collected from wine sales to be applied to oenology and viticulture research at key state colleges. Such institutional support would continue to buttress an industry still struggling to gain legitimacy and a collective identity. But many areas in the state still clung resolutely to their 'dry' sentiments, setting the stage for at least a muted continuation of the culture wars surrounding alcohol.

Growth in new wineries was gradual through the 1990s, but after the turn of the century it increased rapidly, and for the past decade at least one new winery a month has opened in the state (Ofori-Boadu et al 2011; Taplin 2011). This level of growth has been somewhat bifurcated: *muscadine* growing dominates the eastern part of the state, while *vinifera* is concentrated in the central and western parts. The lack of *vinifera* in the east is largely due to climatic factors, principally that *vinifera*-destroying Pearce's disease flourishes in the warmer and more humid eastern parts, while *muscadines* are a natural, vigorously growing product in the area. Duplin and several other *muscadine* producers have witnessed impressive growth and altered the perception of wine drinking as they built market share. But among wine aficionados, this wine was too sweet, lacked the proper flavour profiles, and was seen as pandering to a clientele lacking in sophistication.

While *muscadines* retain a powerful local following and have successfully tapped into a consumer base with a preference for sweetness, such wines are disdained by those whose palates are deemed more sophisticated and therefore more in accordance with what oenophiles define as proper wine. An intriguing feature of the industry's evolution in the state is the presence of local, 'unrefined' and often older consumers who cling to a sweet taste preference that is defined as distinctly un-cosmopolitan. This situation involves a symbolic and cultural struggle between 'cosmopolitans' (sophisticated wine drinkers) and 'locals' (who are deemed not to be such). Such distinctions are found globally across many product markets and are thus not distinctive to wine; their resonance here is that they are part of the same emerging industry and are shaping its evolution. Different parts of the industry attempt to cater to these very different markets, and even the official state wine growers' organization is bifurcated in this manner, with the two subgroups often finding it difficult to achieve a common growth strategy.

In spite of the popularity of *muscadines* among a segment of the population, arguably the industry's legitimacy is emerging around a new breed of *vinifera* growers. In the remaining part of this chapter, I concentrate on these growers, because it is here that many of the most intriguing aspects of a wine culture have occurred, particularly its globalized aspect. The majority of new wineries have been small, family-run operations with modest resources to manage limited production. A few, however, were more ambitious endeavours: wealthy individuals, passionate about wine, but with extensive resources and capabilities that permitted them to subsidize winery development and a longer-term profitability goal. In addition to these two groups who were responsible for forging an identity for the industry in the areas there was also a considerable number of grape growers who supplied the emerging industry. These individuals often used family land, sometimes as a diversified crop from other agricultural staples, in other cases as a part-time activity. Unwilling (or possibly unable, through lack of financial resources) to make wine themselves and to develop the necessary facilities, they have remained grape farmers. Often working in conjunction as contract suppliers for some of the bigger wineries when the latter were starting, they received valuable viticulture skills from professionals in such wineries that helped them improve the quality of their product. Their role has been crucial but often overlooked (not least because it is sometimes difficult to find out who is actually growing grapes, unless one has detailed contract information from wineries).

Clustering and knowledge brokering

Many of the small wineries that were started in the 1980s and 1990s were family owned and operated, self-funded, started by individuals seeking a new lifestyle occupation, and funded by resources from an earlier successful career. Annual production typically ran from approximately 500 to 2500 cases in these wineries, with most selling their wine direct from the winery. For some, earlier trips to France or Napa Valley in California had piqued an interest in winemaking; they chose NC for their winery because they already lived there and/or they had inherited land through family. They were not resource rich and their viticulture knowledge was scant, so they faced a steep learning curve, plus the financial resources to start a winery were considerable. Once vines are planted, it takes three to four years before yielding a proper harvest, during which time there is no revenue stream. Given that harvests are once a year, the process does not lend itself to a trial-and-error system of production – you have one chance annually to get it right! While some information was available through state agricultural cooperative agencies and universities, local operational knowledge was scant. To overcome this deficiency, newcomers relied upon each other to develop an informal cooperative structure that enabled collective learning. Seeking out others in the same situation, but with perhaps a year or so more experience, they were able gradually to develop site-specific knowledge which became crucial when combined with recommended techniques from specialists. Such cooperation effectively lowered the start-up costs and entry barriers for them and other newcomers. This pattern is consistent with the role played by clusters in other countries' wine industries. An informal, cooperative and largely trust-based structure emerged, in which collective organizational learning provides crucial tacit knowledge for new industry entrants. Key operational knowledge became embedded in the social relations between owners who could leverage this information in ways that fostered their own growth as well as the incipient industry's identity. This is consistent with findings from other studies of the interdependency of social capital and knowledge embeddedness within networks (Inkpen and Tsang 2005; Uzzi 1997).

While most of the new firms grew *vinifera*, some additionally planted *muscadines*. Recognizing that a wine culture in the region was still emerging and that many people still preferred sweet beverages, this was a pragmatic, financially-driven choice. *Muscadines* were easy to grow and the wine often easier to sell than *vinifera*. Many wineries had perhaps 10 per cent *muscadines*, yet even at a relatively low retail price (around $10 per bottle), these wines could account for 30–40 per cent of the sales volume.

In addition to the Duplin and Biltmore wineries that were referred to earlier, there have been half a dozen or so other large wineries that have been established. What distinguishes this group apart from their size (anywhere from 5000 to 35,000 case production) was the extensive resources their owners were able to bring to the venture. This meant professional vineyard managers and winemakers, an extensive tasting room staff, and local and regional distribution of wines. With the ability to sustain a longer-term profitability plan (often up to ten years prior to break even), these wineries were afforded capital resources and impressive facilities that firmly established winemaking as a physical presence in the area. Not only did this further the visibility of the product, the professional staff were able to produce a more consistent and better-quality wine, thus enhancing the industry's legitimacy.

During this time period there was considerable uncertainty as to which grape varietals would grow best in the area's soils and climate. This so-called *terroir* factor was difficult for many to grasp in the initial years, in part because of the American obsession with a scientific approach to problem-solving that often diminished more subtle and nuanced aspects of local conditions. Gradually more wineries, especially the larger, better-resourced ones, came to appreciate this Gallic phrase, in part because it captured the essence of location that shaped their authenticity. This is clearly in line with the transnational spread of *terroir* thinking that is increasingly influential in complementing the technical aspects of actual winemaking. But it also plays into the growing localism movement in food that is being embraced by many globally – the authenticity of things local that is increasingly a transnational phenomenon.

Smaller wineries lacked the resources to engage in this trial-and-error approach, and were more likely to plant four or five of the common varietals (Chardonnay, Cabernet Franc, Cabernet Sauvignon, Riesling, several Spanish and Italian varietals and Viognier – the latter because it had grown well in the climatically similar, adjacent state of Virginia) that were presumed to be suitable to the local *terroir*. The large wineries often planted up to ten or more varietals and then waited to see which flourished. This experimentation with European varietals is yet further evidence of the global being adopted locally – the idea that one not only try different grapes but should build a reputation on particular varietals (Spanish or Italian, for example) as a basis for one's own identity. In other words, a winery growing Italian varietals will emphasis Italian cultural traditions (food pairings, for example) and market a quasi-Italian heritage to differentiate themselves from others in the region.

As with most industries, a representative body emerged that was designed to provide a forum for the discussion of wine-growing ideas and support those interested in grape-growing and winemaking. The initial impetus came in the 1970s from *muscadine* growers who formed what is now the North Carolina Muscadine Growers Association. But since the early 1980s, attention has shifted to the growing of *vinifera* and hybrid grapes, first with the formation of the Piedmont Grape Growers Association, and then the North Carolina Wine Growers Association (NCWGA) which was formed in 1993. The latter has taken a more prominent role in the past decade as the industry has expanded. Tasked with education and information sharing about grape cultivation and winemaking practices, improved communication between members, and supporting viticulture and oenology research, plus marketing of NC wines, it has become a powerful forum to advance the collective interests of the industry. Its associational membership structure provides suggestions for changes but lacks any sanctioning power – hence ongoing debates about how to improve the overall consistency and quality of the wine produced. Nonetheless it has worked in conjunction with the State Department of Agriculture, and then of Commerce, to publicize the industry locally and regionally, particularly encouraging wine tourism and winery visits. Its annual meeting is also an opportunity for dialogue, networking and information gathering.

Developing an identity

For many wineries, growing grapes and making wine were the least of their problems. Selling their wine often proved the most daunting task, in part because there was little local familiarity with wine, or if there was, local price points were high compared with familiar wines in local stores (Bhadury and Troy 2008). Small output meant higher pricing that reflected higher per-unit production costs. Larger wineries could afford to keep retail prices lower by taking less revenue; smaller ones clearly could not. Among consumers, even those who were familiar with wine took time to understand that it could be made in the state, at least of the quality that they were used to. Admittedly some of the early wine produced in the late 1990s was clearly flawed, which confirmed consumer scepticism and diminished the overall credibility of the embryonic sector. Some culprits argued that this was merely a reflection of local *terroir*. Some probably did not recognize what they were making as problematic, but some might have known, yet lacked the resources to address the problem and were forced for financial reasons to continue marketing the wine. These are problems endemic to many new industries, and it generally takes time and experience to mitigate the flaws – providing one understands and has the capacity to rectify the problem eventually. Winemakers at the larger wineries have continually pushed to address this problem, as has the NCWGA through their promotion of a voluntary quality alliance programme started in 2012. But bereft of any clear sanctioning ability, both groups have been left with merely encouraging an informal benchmarking, with the hope that others can be 'shamed' into improvement.

For any new industry that depends upon local customers to thrive, there needs to be a sense of identity, especially when the product sold is essentially novel in that particular area. Developing a customer base for wine would always be difficult where 'dry' sentiments often prevailed. But NC has over the past two to three decades seen considerable in-migration, especially in the Piedmont area where the wineries are located. The newcomers, often from the north-eastern part of the United States and the West, were often well-educated professionals, many of whom liked wine. While they did not immediately rush out to buy the local product – in fact many were sceptical about it – they did eventually come to appreciate drinking it since it was not dissimilar to the growing popularity of the 'farm to table' movement in agriculture. In other words, a cultural change was occurring whereby the legitimacy of buying local often trumped the higher price points and variable product quality, and was more generally seen as supportive of small local producers. What applied to local farm produce similarly attracted many people to wineries.

Wineries were also astute in recognizing that there was a certain Arcadian charm to their often idyllic rural setting, with rows of vines stretching down hillsides with distant mountain views. It was, many people discovered, the perfect setting for a wedding or corporate event. With tasting rooms and an outdoor event area, a winery could quickly become a wedding site, charging for the facilities rental, plus having a guaranteed and captive audience for their wine. Many wineries have jumped on this bandwagon, often advertising their facilities for weddings more than they do for their wine (Taplin and Nguyen 2016). This mirrors similar trends in other countries' wine regions, where wineries recognized that the desirability of their location could be easily translated into cash flow while simultaneously promoting their brand (Kyuho 2016). As many local winery owners concluded, weddings and other paid events could subsidize what otherwise might be a loss-making winery operation. Unfortunately it has proved a disincentive for some to concentrate upon improving or even maintaining the quality of the wine, since visual aesthetics trump the beverage on offer.

As wineries became concentrated in certain areas, they realized that instead of seeing adjacent wineries as competitors, they could capitalize upon a growing area density and could develop wine trails to encourage visitors. Even established wine regions such as Bordeaux have begun to embrace this trend (Bouzedine-Chameeva et al 2016) that has become commonplace in parts of South Africa and Australia. This is part of a growing practice of wine tourism, where consumers spend a day or more visiting and tasting at various wineries in close proximity to each other (Kyuho 2016). Some professional tour companies have capitalized upon this trend and offer chauffeured vans and buses to take groups of people, thus obviating the need for the proverbial 'designated driver'. Such activities have increased visitation according to most local studies, thus improving revenue streams. Most people who visit, in addition to paying for the tasting (generally between $5 and $10 per person), will buy at least several bottles.

Commercially speaking, such cooperative affiliation might appear to contradict normal business practices where one attempts to limit competition rather than encourage it. Yet this is part of the communal framework that has developed in this embryonic industry: a distinct culture whereby many business practices are openly shared to promote the collective good. Winery owners have many times said that the more wineries in their area, the better it is, since they become a destination for visitors rather than just attracting passing-by traffic.

The final piece of the emerging identity picture has been the creation of American Viticultural Areas (AVAs) in NC. This is part of a broader trend in terms of legal and official recognition of *terroir* and supposed authenticity, that has its origins in the original Bordeaux classifications of the nineteenth century and the AOC and DOC designations in France and Italy. Such designations do not guarantee quality, as they are merely an indicator of common *terroir* specific to a particular area. But such specifications go beyond local growing characteristics and speak to a certain identity that characterizes wineries in the specified areas. They also further cement the institutional support for local specificity that is increasingly being adopted worldwide in wine regions. The affiliation benefits are such that by labelling a bottle with an AVA, one can claim a sense of place for the product. They are important for brand development, as anyone who appreciates Napa Valley, Bordeaux or Tuscan wines can attest to.

The first AVA was Yadkin Valley, established in 2003, largely through the efforts of two individuals, Ed and Charlie Shelton of Shelton vineyards, who owned one of the large wineries in the area (McRitchie 2003). In 2005 there were fourteen wineries in this AVA, but by 2015 that number had increased to forty-two. A sub-appellation of Yadkin Valley is Swan Creek, created in 2008 and now with seven wineries. What is interesting about this AVA is the presence of one large winery (Raffaldini) that has exclusively and successfully grown Italian varietals (Sangiovese, Montepulciano and Vermentino). The third AVA to be created was Haw River in 2009, and most recently a fourth one, Upper Hiwasse Highlands, was created in 2014. This AVA has twenty-six vineyards and is notable because of its western location in the foothills of the mountains.

Institutional support and leader firms

As with any market activity, supply of and demand for a particular product is shaped not only by cultural forces that we alluded to above, but also by institutional frameworks and the leadership role played by major industry actors within a cluster. The former can play a powerful role by externalizing certain costs that many individual firms are unable to absorb; the latter refers to ways in which certain large, professionally-run firms assume the mantle of leadership in informal governance.

Clusters develop heterogeneously with firms of different size plus varying resources and capabilities. Not surprisingly, asset-rich large firms frequently possess the professional attributes that enable them to exercise a leadership role within the cluster and to shape the industry's emerging identity. This is particularly the case with viticulture and oenology, since winemakers are geographically mobile, transmitting new ideas and techniques across regions and countries with remarkable ease as they move, and without the necessary proprietary limitations (Migone and Howlett 2010). As Visser and de Langen (2006) have argued in the case of wine cluster development in Chile, some large firms possess superior strategic insight, plus they have an ability to raise funds towards a collective investment in the sector's growth. Their professional staff (vineyard managers, experienced winemakers, marketing staff) allows them to codify extant practices, transform tacit local operating knowledge into formal procedures, and widely disseminate new operational logistics. Their prior industry knowledge enables them to inject a technocratic and scientific approach to grape-growing that was often lacking by other firms whose owners were new to the industry. That this was done in a shared way with other wineries is part of an ongoing collective organizational learning typical of wine regions in their formative years (see Taplin (2010) for discussion of this in the case of Napa, California). Individuals within these firms (and there are about five in the state) played a central role in developing and administering the NC Winegrowers Association. Because their output is greater than most firms, it was important for them at the outset to develop regional and even national markets for their wine. To do this, it was necessary continuously to upgrade the legitimacy of the industry, and they have been in the forefront of marketing attempts and promoted links with intermediaries in ways that benefit the region as a whole. They have contributed to the identity formation mentioned in the previous section, and have been a powerful 'voice' for the industry locally. More than most of the smaller wineries, they have been able consistently to make a quality product (at least after they had experimented with varietals to determine what grew best), and this has provided a de facto benchmark for others who lacked the resources for experimentation or the knowledge to minimize their product flaws.

Institutional support for the wine industry in the state has wavered from earlier relative indifference, to concerns over the alleviation of rural poverty, to the more recent realization that the industry has considerable economic impact upon the state through employment, tourism and sales taxes on wine. In recent decades the support has been more direct, underwriting the costs of new oenology positions at North Carolina State University, and a mobile testing laboratory at Appalachian State University that enables wineries to submit wine samples for evaluation (Corwin 2006). While there are various winemaking and viticulture classes at several area community colleges, the viticulture and oenology department at Surry County Community College provides systematic technical skill instruction via a two-year accredited degree programme. Started in 1999, the programme has evolved into the main vehicle for the dissemination of winemaking in the area, offering students full-time and part-time opportunities for study. In 2009 it moved into a custom-built centre (the Shelton-Badgett NC Center for Viticulture and Enology (SBVE)) that houses a state-of-the-art, commercially-bonded winery funded through a mix of NC General Assembly appropriations, NC Community College System grants, NC State bonds and private donations (McDavid 2005).

The above institution's physical presence and academic curriculum have provided a focus for the professional training of vineyard managers and winemakers. It enables the systematic transmission of expert knowledge, and has codified many of the local idiosyncrasies of grape-growing that plagued earlier viticulture efforts. But it also has an important symbolic presence in providing a legitimate focal point that has helped consolidate the industry's identity in the region. Most of the winery owners and many winemakers in the past decade have received their detailed training at this institution, accumulating valuable knowledge that continues to be shared with others in the embryonic industry. This has been an important part of the industry's growing identity, conferring an institutional dynamism and embedding routine winemaking activities under an umbrella of organizational efficiency similar to that of other global wine regions (Visser and De Langen 2006).

Attaining maturity

As the wine industry in NC has grown, it is clear that two issues remain uppermost in explaining this positive trajectory. One is the continued challenge of mediating cultural opposition among some groups to alcohol consumption, and thus firmly establishing a pervasive wine culture. The other relates to differential sets of resources that winery owners have been able to accumulate. The former has been mitigated somewhat in the last few years by the phenomenal growth of craft brewing in the western part of the state. Beer and wine consumption have often been seen as less fraught with moral degeneracy claims that are often associated with hard liquor. The appeal of craft beer, made by local producers, is considerable among younger Americans who are in the same demographic group as those who are often driving wine sales nationwide. The two beverages are often seen as complementary inasmuch as they are associated with a segment of the population not wedded to established brands and who are willing to experiment – especially if a product has a local identity. Several wineries have gone so far as to create a brewery on site. According to their owners, the rationale was to maximize revenue from fixed infrastructure costs (tasting room facilities and staff), and to provide a beverage that non-wine-drinking 'partners' could consume while the others tasted wine. Anecdotal evidence suggests that craft beers do not cannibalize wine sales; they merely provide a gendered alternative beverage for couples visiting wineries.

In terms of formal opposition to the sale of alcohol, this has legally diminished over the past fifteen years, as more and more counties voted to permit such sales of alcohol (wines in supermarkets, liquor in state-controlled stores). Since a winery could legally operate in a dry county – federal laws regulating the sale and distribution of alcohol have precedence over local policies – and as the majority of their sales were direct to the consumer out of the tasting room, they could flourish in spite of local denigration. Once certain regions were recognized as ideal locations for wineries, and winery density increased, local opposition gradually diminished. The economic benefits for state coffers and changing demographics also played a role in this transition. There remain local populations who vehemently oppose the consumption of alcohol, but these people appear to have been trumped by others who enthusiastically support the embryonic industry, voting both through their wallets and at the ballot boxes.

In terms of resources, it is important to note that different capabilities are required at different stages of an industry's evolution. With growing maturity, resource-rich firms are attracted to the sector given its demonstrable success in the past. Such firms bring additional capabilities that further reward innovation, but also penalize those firms which are operationally unable to minimize their internal resource weaknesses. Elsewhere, I have argued that the bundling of resources at different stages of the industry's evolution continues to benefit those firms that are resource rich and increase the operational liability of those that are resource scarce (West and Taplin 2016). While the mortality rate of wineries in the state over the past three decades has been minimal (perhaps half a dozen have closed) and some have been sold, it has become apparent that there are three types of firms in the industry: larger wineries with extensive resources; boutique wineries with more modest financial assets but which nonetheless are profitable within a short period of time and have built a loyal customer base; and a third group that encompass individuals who used inherited land to start a winery and whose enthusiasm often exceeded ability. The latter have modest production goals and have been the group most likely to embrace weddings as a way to guarantee revenue streams. As a consequence, they have often paid less attention to wine quality than the other two groups, in part because they lack the requisite resources and capabilities, and partly because they have found a viable alternative income source.

The success of the first two types of winery has been contingent upon their ability to leverage formal and informal resources and networks in systematic ways. The third type's inability or unwillingness to do this has left them exposed to quality issues for their wine. But their continued operation in what is essentially a tourist and event business provides a degree of immunity from financial concerns, and their physical existence does contribute to a growing regional identity. Their wine might not be good, but the setting is magnificent: after several glasses on a celebratory day, the overall experience overwhelms any reservations about what the customers drank!

Conclusion

In this chapter I have argued that wine is as much a cultural product as anything else, and its market success therefore depends on specific historic conditions, institutional frameworks, and demographic trends. In the narrative of globalization, Old World varietals have been adopted by New World producers and, in doing so, have invoked some distinctive cultural attributes of the Old World. For example, wineries in NC which sell only Italian varietals adopt a neo-Tuscan architecture and ambience. Similarly, those whose focus is on Spanish grapes invoke an Iberian atmosphere in the winery. This play on the cultural aspects of grapes is crucial in marketing to a customer base whose own globalist attitudes frame their choice of wines. It is also an integral part of the evolving wine culture in the region, as more people become aware of, and develop an interest in, the consumption of wine.

From the perspective of wine production, one can trace the subtle ways in which inroads occurred when entry barriers diminished (technological changes that allowed winemakers to mitigate diseases); land suitable for grape-growing became available and was relatively inexpensive; and institutional support increased when the local economic benefits were acknowledged. Regardless of how one operationalizes the concept of *terroir*, it took time for individuals to discover what soil and climatic conditions were most suited to the types of grapes they wished to grow. Through collective and cooperative efforts, individuals were able to understand better the technical challenges to attain requisite quality levels. This formalized the network structure that is vital for the emergence of a viable wine world, and it also provided an instrumental role for technical specialists. Finally, a steady supply of passionate individuals desirous of career changes or the status of owning a winery, plus a growing local population either familiar with wine or willing to try it, brought the supply and demand sides of the oenological equation together. In terms of the latter, demographic changes played an important role, as newcomers to the state with greater familiarity with wine, plus younger generations with alcohol preferences for wine, craft beer and spirits, drove local wine sales.

Once a cluster of wineries developed, it attracted others with greater resources whose skill sets resulted in improved wine quality and enhanced legitimacy for the industry. Such organizational growth continues to depend upon dense sets of relationships and norms of reciprocal obligation that bind individuals in different wineries together in ways that are mutually beneficial. In terms of production, there are now both large- and small-scale wineries operating within the same area. The former, however, have been more successful in building brand awareness that has enabled them to differentiate their product. But in doing so, they have reinforced the legitimacy of the area as one where quality wine is actively produced.

With a growing number of AVAs that denote the specificity of growing conditions, wine fields are nurtured and provide the cultural and institutional space for consumer engagement. That, and the growing consumer market for wine in the area, have combined to explain the recent successful growth of the industry when earlier attempts to develop it failed. When people drink NC wine they are nonetheless drinking a global(ized) product, with complex connotations of cultural specificity and taste preferences that to some extent have become globally standardized. Above all, this historical narrative suggests that events in NC are not dissimilar to those in other wine regions, even if individual circumstance might differ. The transformations include adopting cultural traits associated with otherwise country-specific grape varietals, seeking winemakers and vineyard managers who have gained experience overseas and who bring that knowledge to analyse local conditions, and furthering the commitment to local products as authentic expressions of a particular region. Even though some events in NC are atypical of broader trends, there are enough similarities to appreciate the universalism of both the product and the circumstances under which it becomes established in an area. Without suggesting path-dependent conformity in the wine industry's evolution in different regions, it is nonetheless intriguing to see how the industry manifests itself in a new region and displays similar attributes across regional contexts. The global in this case has truly become local.

References

Adams, L.D. (1973), *The Wines of America*, Boston: Houghton Mifflin.

Baptista, R. (2000), 'Do Innovations Diffuse Faster within Geographical Clusters?', *International Journal of Industrial Organization*, 18:515–35.

Beliveau, B.C., and Rouse, M.E. (2010), 'Prohibition and Repeal: A Short History of the Wine Industry's Regulation in the United States', *Journal of Wine Economics*, 5(1):53–68.

Bhadury, J., and Troy, S.P. (2008), 'Business Development Needs of the Wine Industry in the Yadkin Valley, Swan Creek, and Haw River Viticultural Areas', http://www.uncg.edu/bae/or

Bouzdine-Chameeva, T., Faugere, C., and Mora, P. (2016), 'Wine Tourism in Bordeaux', in Kyuho. L. (ed.), *Strategic Winery Tourism and Management*, Palm Bay, FL: CRC Press/Taylor Francis, 89–114.

Breckenridge, R.S., and Taplin, I.M. (2005), 'Entrepreneurship, Industrial Policy and Clusters: The Growth of the NC Wine Industry', in *Research in the Sociology of Work*, 209–30, Amsterdam: Elsevier.

Corwin, B. (2006), 'State Legislators Back Industry with New Laws', *On the Vine*, January–February, 19.

Drew, R. (2006), *The North Carolina Muscadine – A Historical Timeline*, Wilmington: Drew Image.com

Fries, A.L. (ed.) (1922), *Records of the Moravians in North Carolina*, vol 3, Raleigh, NC: Edwards and Broughton, 1922–69.

Giuliani, E. (2006), 'The Selective Nature of Knowledge Networks in Clusters: Evidence from the Wine Industry', *Journal of Economic Geography*, 7:139–68.

Gohdes, C. (1982), *Scuppernong: North Carolina's Grape and Its Wines*, Durham: Duke University Press.

Inkpen, A., and Tsang, E. (2005), 'Social Capital, Networks and Knowledge Transfer', *Academy of Management Review*, 30(1):146–65.

Kyuho, L. (ed.) (2016), *Strategic Winery Tourism and Management*, Palm Bay, FL: CRC Press/Taylor and Francis.

Lazerson, M.H., and Lorenzoni, G. (1999), 'The Firms Feed Industrial Districts: A Return to the Italian Source?', *Industrial and Corporate Change*, 8:235–66.

Maskell, P. (2001), 'Towards a Knowledge-based Theory of the Geographical Cluster', *Industrial and Corporate Change*, 10(4):921–43.

Mathia, G.A. (1966), *Economic Opportunities for Muscadine Grapes in North Carolina*. A.E. Information Series No.128, North Carolina State University at Raleigh.

Mathia, G.A., Beals, A., Miller, N.C., and Carroll, D.E. (1977), *Economic Opportunities for Profitable Winery Operations in North Carolina*. Economics Information Report no. 49, North Carolina State University at Raleigh, NC.

McDavid, S. (2005), 'State Legislature Fine Tuning Laws Related to Viticulture', *On the Vine*, July–October, 10–11.

McGirr, L. (2015), *The War on Alcohol*, New York: W.W. Norton.

McRitchie, P. (2003), 'Another First for North Carolina – But What's an Appellation?', *On the Vine*, Spring–Summer, 12–13.

Migone, A., and Howlett, M. (2010), 'Comparative Networks and Clusters in the Wine Industry'. American Association of Wine Economists, AAWE working paper no. 62.

Morton, L. (1985), *Winegrowing in Eastern America: An Illustrated Guide to Viticulture East of the Rockies*, Ithaca: Cornell University Press.

Ofori-Boadu, V., Osei-Agyeman, Y., Bhadury, J., Dobie, K., Troy, S.P., and Williamson, N.C. (2011), 'The Emergent Vinifera Wine Industry in North Carolina: A Descriptive Overview', *Local Economy*, 26:182–96.

Pinney, T. (1989), *History of Wine in America: From the Beginnings to Prohibition*, Berkeley: University of California Press.

Taplin, I.M. (2010), 'From Cooperation to Competition: Market Transformations amongst Elite Napa Valley Wine Producers', *International Journal of Wine Business Research*, 22(1):6–26.

Taplin, I.M. (2011), *The Modern American Wine Industry*, London: Pickering and Chatto.

Taplin, I.M., and Nguyen, M.-T.T. (2016), 'Wine versus Weddings: Wine Tourism in the Emerging North Carolina Wine industry', in Kyuho, L. (ed.), *Strategic Winery Tourism and Management*, CRC Press/Taylor and Francis, 69–88.

Uzzi, B. (1997), 'Social Structure and Competition in Interfirm Networks: The Paradox of Embeddedness', *Administrative Science Quarterly*, 42:35–67.

Visser, E.-J., and de Langen, P. (2006), 'The Importance and Quality of Governance in the Chilean Wine Industry', *GeoJournal*, 65:177–97.

Watson, A.D. (1973), 'Society and Economy in Colonial Edgecombe County', *North Carolina Historical Review*, 50:231–55.

West, P., and Taplin, I.M. (2016), 'Making Wine and Making Successful Wineries: Resource Development in New Ventures', *International Journal of Organizational Analysis*, 24(1): 123–44.

Williams, E. (2007), 'Duplin's Wild Ride', *On the Vine*, January–February, 4–5.

5 From Post-Socialist to Pre-EU: The Globalized Transformation of the Republic of Macedonia's Wine Industry

JUSTIN OTTEN

Introduction

A small, landlocked country, the Republic of Macedonia sits at the crossroads of culture and climate. Culturally, like the rest of the Balkan region, the country was a colourful melting pot during the Ottoman Empire, where the East and West met. A cosmopolitan place indeed, Christians, Muslims and Jews of all ethnic backgrounds conducted business and lived in the region's cities, towns and villages. In terms of climate, Macedonia is where the Continental meets the Mediterranean, and the rich soil and bright, southern European sun mean that agriculture is, and long has been, a significant part of the country's economy. Indeed, during the Ottoman era both the country as a whole and the particular region focused on in this chapter were producers of some of the empire's main products – cotton, poppies, and tobacco – which were subject in their own time to new and shifting international market demands. American cotton production, for example, posed significant competition to Ottoman markets in Europe (Issawi 1980). The complex internal and external forces of globalization have thus long been present in the country and wider region, leading to constant shifts in both production and the livelihoods of communities doing the producing, with the latter factors in turn affecting local politics and culture.

Home to the largest contiguous wine region in the Balkans – Tikveš – Macedonia produces nearly a quarter of the Balkan Non-Associated Countries[1] 2 per cent of global wine production (Noev and Swinnen 2004), making the country a small but steady player in the global wine marketplace. With wine being one of modern Macedonia's main agricultural products and exports (second only to tobacco), the recent globalization of the wine industry there has been significant and yet unique. This has been so because not only have the global wine world (production) and wine culture (consumption) changed in recent decades, but also in post-socialist countries such as those of the former Yugoslavia, there has been a breaking away from the shackles of Yugoslav socialist production strategies that typified the industry there for nearly half a century. In post-Communist countries, privatization happened rapidly in the early 1990s. Bartlett (2007: 204) however found that, while some privatization legislation was enacted in Macedonia in 1995, the 'financial deepening' of it was not evident until 2003. Furthermore, although Macedonia was spared from the conflicts, the violent dissolution of the Yugoslav Federation delayed privatization throughout the region, resulting in ongoing significant shifts in the 2000s.

In addition, as a European Union (EU) candidate country since 2005, Macedonia has been subject to the EU's Instrument for Pre-Accession Assistance (IPA), a preparatory instrument that in terms of agriculture is meant to prepare the country for regulation under the EU Common Agricultural Policy (CAP).[2] The combination of this transition to a global wine market and concurrent preparation for EU accession in the last decade, has created several challenges not just for everyone involved in the wine industry, but also for entire communities in the country's wine regions as well. Post-socialist states seem to have additional unique struggles in this regard.[3] Macedonia is thus attempting both to globalize as well as to participate in the EU's 'gastro-nationalism' (DeSoucey 2010), whereby the country promotes its specific regional origins, cultures and products in order to attract – mostly European – wine tourists. Yet like all small players in the global marketplace, the country must continuously adapt to ever-changing Western notions of wine quality and consumer preferences. As Borneman and Fowler (1997) have discussed, Europeanization is fundamentally about reorganizing territoriality and peoplehood, and thus production and commercialization too.

Based on ongoing ethnographic fieldwork – including participant observation and interviews – since 2010, which has utilized theories of neoliberalism[4] and investigated privatization and redevelopment of the country's premier wine region, Tikveš, this chapter analyses the changes made there and how they characterize the country's wine industry, as well as indicating where it is headed. The chapter discusses the following factors: (a) post-socialist social and economic change within the country generally, and in agriculture and viticulture more specifically; (b) the impact of the European Union's IPA and other pre-accession programmes and policies; and (c) rebranding, marketing and attempts to sell Macedonian wine to international audiences. In doing so, the chapter deals with the contradictions and controversies surrounding the globalization of wine, as well as discussing the rebranding of wine regions such as Tikveš, the re-creation of their value, and the individuals involved in this transformation.

Post-socialist social and economic change in Tikveš

The Tikveš wine region is a part of a rocky yet fertile stretch of land called Povardarie that runs south from the Macedonian capital, Skopje, along the Vardar River. Ending 55 km from the border with Greece in the south-central part of the country, Tikveš covers roughly 2,000 square kilometres, and has a distinctive Mediterranean micro-climate due to the Vardar River acting as a conduit: although the cold mountain water flows south through it, warmer air from the Aegean Sea heads north. Indeed, the region has hot dry summers and winters which are sunnier and warmer than elsewhere in the country.

Historically, the Tikveš region has undergone numerous transformations. Occupied since Neolithic times, and with a significant settlement – and now archaeological site – dating back millennia (Stobi[5]), the rich soil there has been used to grow grapes since at least Roman times. However, during the lengthy Ottoman period (fifteenth to twentieth centuries) grapes were not the primary crop. Instead, land was used to grow poppies, cotton and tobacco for international trade, as well as various fruits and vegetables for local consumption (Kamčevski 2007). After the demise of the Ottoman Empire, agricultural policy shifted when the Kingdom of Yugoslavia (1918–1941) conducted land reform, which resulted in small plots of 3 hectares on average being redistributed (Miljković 1996). Then, under the Socialist Yugoslav Law on Agrarian Reform and Resettlement of 1945, 1.6 million hectares of land were expropriated from large landowners. This land was both divided and redistributed to over 300,000 families, with the rest going to the creation of state farms and enterprises. Given the Yugoslav government's plan to see modern agriculture drive industrialization, in the 1960s the majority of the State-owned land was developed into vertically-integrated agricultural enterprises known as *kombinati* (in the plural). Each region had its own *kombinat* (singular), if not several of them, and they were used to produce a variety of jarred and bottled food and beverage products for the country's growing urban population.

These historical circumstances are worth mentioning because the role of both family-farmed vineyards and State-owned agricultural enterprises was significant in the Yugoslav Macedonian wine industry and remains so today: grape growers (*lozari*) grew the grapes that made the wine at the local *kombinati*. In the process, growers were assured of an annual income and the wineries of a significant crop to use in production. In some years, so many grapes were harvested that they were dumped in fields or local municipal swimming pools, and this method of production lasted beyond the breakup of Yugoslavia. With the *kombinati* not being privatized until the late 1990s and early 2000s, their large production capability meant that for a decade after the fall of socialism they could maintain similar production levels because they were State-owned. Yet in the past decade especially, these enterprises – all now privately owned and operated – have been forced to alter and significantly decrease such production, a reduction that has been the bane, if not grounds for the demise, of independent grape growers. The reason for such a shift in Macedonia's wine industry has been the contemporary global wine economy in all of its complexity.

During socialism (when Macedonia was the largest wine producer in Yugoslavia) and in the decade after, average wine with little outside competition was the norm in the country, and growers' grapes were simply mixed together and not tested for sugar content and thus quality level. Consequently, the wine coming from the *kombinati* was generally average at best, and if there were excess grapes produced, they were indeed taken by the *kombinat* for the sake of compensating the growers. Worth emphasizing is the effect of the recent globalized transition in the wine industry on families and their vineyards: with nearly all families in Tikveš producing grapes for their local *kombinat*, the reduction and shift in wine production has been devastating for many. Therefore, what distinguishes these growers' efforts today from the agricultural production of the past is privatization unravelling governmental inputs in the form of tractors, tools and guaranteed payment for crops, and thus overall support and security. Once market forces came into play, and the government detached itself from managing and supplying inputs to them, agricultural industries such as wine were forced to change and diversify.

Many in Tikveš lament this transition, calling it a 'catastrophe' (*katastrofa*), since it has resulted in the abandonment or replacement of numerous vineyards with various cash crops. For those who continue to grow grapes, the transition often leaves growers with an excess of grapes and accrued debts; now more than ever, families struggle to pay for the hired labour necessary at harvest time and the inputs required throughout the long growing season.[6] This shift to a capitalist, privatized wine industry along with Europeanization (Bache et al 2011) has resulted in numerous 'discontents' (Stiglitz 2002), and has meant not only that there is no longer guaranteed payment such as there was during the socialist period, but also that dishonest and illicit grape purchasing has become commonplace by wineries (*vinarii*) and grape-purchasing companies (*vizbi*), which purchase grapes directly from growers at rock-bottom prices and then sell them to wineries for a higher price or produce wine on their own. Although not a uniform phenomenon, as many wineries have contracts with certain growers or have taken to managing their own vineyards, nonetheless many grape-growing families have handed over their crop to both wineries and '*vizbi*' only to wait months if not a year or longer for payment.

While these pains are in fact typical in free markets and have been observed in other post-socialist countries undergoing Europeanization,[7] such delayed payments create capital constraints in the wine chain and thus instigate problems for the grape growers, including their ability to pay off debts and make investments in their vineyards, as well as just to survive and provide for their families. This reduction in capital then affects local communities and towns, hence the often-heard laments about the 'catastrophe of privatisation' and the region's post-socialist transition.[8] In fact, such terminology is widely used in local discourse about the wine industry, and the steady decline in individual family grape-growing has indeed encouraged a shift to the farming of other crops for self-sustenance and sale at local markets. Tensions resulting in protests and court cases have ensued as a result, yet what is increasingly clear to many in Tikveš is that there is no going back to the era of socialist production.

In an attempt to ameliorate the situation, around 2010 the Macedonian government began offering a variety of subsidies for the production, selling and purchasing of grapes. Yet given economic reforms such as privatization and reduced governmental inputs, along with reduced wine production, grape yields have declined since the 1990s in the country. For example, one problem with the reforms had been a lack of incentives to replace old vines, which affected the volume of grape production, since old vines yield fewer grapes and new vines generally take three years to bear fruit. A subsidy introduced around 2010 has allowed for the replacement of vines, yet the primary problem for grape growers since then has been the shift from State-run wineries purchasing their grapes to private wineries not necessarily doing so.

Thus with a decline in wine production, it makes no sense to replace old vines if there is no market for one's grape crop. Furthermore, large wineries have instituted formal contracts so that if they want to purchase a grower's grapes, they will contract with the grower in advance and impose strict standards on the crop, particularly with regard to sugar content levels (known as 'degrees Brix'). If such standards are not met, then the grapes may be refused. Alongside this trend, after 2010 wineries began consolidating vineyards in order to better regulate grape and wine production, and to cut out the need to deal with individual grape growers and the various costs of sourcing from them. This follows the global standard in mass wine production, as small, family-run vineyards such as those in Tikveš are generally very labour-intensive and require varying investments in human capital, equipment and technology, all the while producing grapes that may differ from those in the adjacent vineyard (even if they are of the same grape variety). Indeed, with different farming techniques, such fragmented grape production has been seen as a problem for the investors in, and owners of, wineries, who have concerns about inconsistent and unconsolidated grape sourcing.

Therefore the transition has presented challenges to both grape growers and wine producers, with the wine industry struggling to orient itself to the global wine market. But it is not alone in this regard. Macedonia is part of what Noev and Swinnen (2004) refer to as the Balkan Non-Associated Countries (BNAC). Wine production in the BNAC has been significantly affected by the political and economic reforms of the last few decades. Given the violent dissolution of the Yugoslav federation, as well as Albania's economic collapse, by the late 1990s wine output in the BNAC declined at least 25 per cent compared to the height of production in the early 1980s. This is a number consistent with estimates of the industry's decline in Macedonia. Production continued to decline in the new millennium, particularly in Macedonia, where the ethno-nationalist conflicts in Serbia, Bosnia and Kosovo took a toll on the country's former markets, and where privatization, consolidation of vineyards, and a growing preference for beer began to radically alter the wine industry. Indeed, wine consumption per capita today is less than ten litres in Macedonia (which is a quarter of that of central and eastern European countries), and it has steadily declined as wine has become both more expensive and just one of many beverage options available for purchase.[9]

A prime example of the Macedonian wine industry's transformation is the 2004 privatization of the largest former State-owned winery and *kombinat*, AK Tikveš. Now known as the Tikveš Winery, the key feature of it during socialism was that it only maintained 10 per cent of the town's vineyards, as they were a part of the *kombinat*. Otherwise it sourced its grapes during the late summer harvest from over 2,000 of the Tikveš region's growers and their families. When it was bought out by a large conglomerate in the Macedonian capital, the winery's production levels, methods of sourcing grapes, and both the types and quality of wine produced, were all radically altered. In short, wine production levels were drastically reduced, leaving many independent grape growers with a crop surplus. Contracts and quality testing methods were implemented; marketing and administration shifted to the capital, and the price, variety and quality of wines increased. Indeed, in adapting to market pressures, the winery rebranded itself, began focusing more on quality than quantity, and has continuously conducted savvy marketing campaigns at home and abroad to promote its wines, penetrating markets as far away as the United States. One of their red wines was even recommended in the November 2014 Food Section of the *New York Times*, in a 'Top Five' list of wines to consider pairing with the American Thanksgiving holiday meal. While it is arguably an excellent wine, this mention is evidence of an effective corporate-style marketing and public relations apparatus at work. As a reimagined private company with great influence, the Tikveš Winery is representative of the style of companies driving the global wine market's production and consumption. As Veseth (2012) has found, these companies are not just engaging in the world's markets, but are indeed creating and reimagining the consumer tastes which typify them.

Foreign direct investment (FDI) in the Macedonian wine industry has been hindered by a number of factors. Being a small and poor country, concerns range from low domestic demand for wine, particularly of higher quality and price; the continuation of restrictive State controls within the industry; corruption and a lack of transparency; and economic and political uncertainty, as well as regional instability in the Balkans. Privatization has therefore been conducted largely by Macedonians within the country, resulting in diverse ownership structures in the wine industry: from incumbent managers taking over formerly State-owned wineries (*kombinati*), to new enterprises that range from small, family-run wineries to large multi-million-Dollar facilities funded by well-off business people. Given the Yugoslav structure of grape sourcing, there has been a diversification in terms of where wineries get their grapes from. Some continue to have contracts with independent grape growers, who tend to harvest their crop on their own terms, while other wineries have bought or leased multiple vineyards and are strictly managing grape production and thus quality levels as per global norms. In adapting to the restructuring of wine production and the global marketplace, there have been opportunities for new boutique wineries to arise. Privatization has therefore caused both disruptions and restructuring to the previous industry configuration, affecting suppliers, producers and consumers. How that and various other factors affect the industry's performance in the EU and elsewhere is discussed in the following section.

The impact of EU agricultural policies on redevelopment of the wine industry

As a European Union candidate country since 2005, wineries in Macedonia have been cognizant of, and already subject to, EU regulations, including those limiting both the number of hectares of new vineyards allowed, wine production standards, and the quantity of wine that can be exported to the EU. Additionally, with the EU's Common Agricultural Policy (CAP)[10] in mind, European policies seek to boost the competitiveness of European agriculture, and through the Instrument for Pre-accession Assistance (IPA),[11] to develop rural economies beyond their production of crops by stimulating rural industry and tourism. Yet this transition presents numerous challenges to the region and its inhabitants, from securing the capital required for IPA projects, when many small businesses have already accrued debts, to a lack of strategic agricultural policy and goals by the State. There are thus contradictions and confusions in Tikveš, and with little support or clear understanding of what is needed nationally, it is difficult for the individual farming family to plan and invest in their land with the confidence that they will receive income for their labour.

It is the combination of EU with domestic policies that has wrought further confusion and difficulties for the industry. For example, while government subsidies to replace vineyards exist for both families and firms, the country cannot increase its total amount of vineyards due to EU accession restrictions. Furthermore, set quotas on Macedonian wine exports to the EU, separated into a quota for bulk wine and another quota for bottled wine, are a particularly contentious issue due to the fact that the annual export limit for bulk wine is often reached by Spring of each year, leaving surplus wine in Macedonian cellars that cannot be offered to EU consumers. This is problematic because bulk wine has long represented a significant portion of Macedonian wine exports and sales, both within the former Yugoslavia and outside it. There are sales of bulk wine to bottlers and distributors in Slovenia and Serbia, and more significantly to Germany, where *Mazedonischen wein* continues to be known as a decent, cheap option at the bottom of the wine section shelf. Bulk wine is arguably what has sustained the Macedonian wine industry through its post-socialist transformation, yet in being shipped in bulk and bottled elsewhere, it is not a highly profitable endeavour for wineries, and its eradication is actually the goal of many large ones (with the more profitable bottled wine taking its place). That said, despite a decrease in the number of vineyards in the country, wine production in Macedonia is relatively cheap due to the surplus, and thus below average market price, of grapes, which sell at a much lower cost than the average European price of approximately half a Euro per kilogram.[12] Furthermore, the CAP's fixed minimum pricing of grapes per hectare, which was implemented in other pre-EU, post-socialist countries, has not been applied in Macedonia. Whereas Slovenia, for example, set 294 Euros per hectare as a minimum price for grapes in the year 2000, Macedonian grapes are bought by either local wineries or the *vizbi* middlemen for the lowest price possible, sometimes for as little as eight to ten Macedonian Denari, or €0.13–0.16 per kilogram, and usually for no more than €0.25–0.30 per kilogram.[13] The result is that bulk wine remains profitable and even smaller wineries export their wine in such a manner. Yet in being subject to the IPA in preparation for the CAP, while continuing to sell wine in bulk, the Macedonian wine industry has had to juggle transforming itself for a global marketplace, while adapting to what many see as overly bureaucratic EU regulations and restrictions. But with EU and other European countries being the most convenient markets, not to mention Macedonia's candidate status to enter the EU, wine producers must comply.

Other obstacles facing the wine industry include increasing EU wine imports into the country alongside strict preconditions to sell Macedonian wines in terms of quality and certified hygienic production methods. There is also the name issue with Greece[14]. This has affected how wineries are supposed to bottle the wine and present the country of origin of their product, as well as (and perhaps more significantly) how German and Slovenian bottlers of Macedonian bulk wine label it. Some have conformed to Greek demands by writing 'former Yugoslav' in small italics above the name Republic of Macedonia on the label, but this issue incenses Macedonians, who are attempting to establish a clear geographical domain for their wine. Additionally, a notable problem which has arisen is that while on the one hand Macedonia is addressing structural changes through its distribution of subsidies, on the other hand the situation can be characterized as a seeming aiding and abetting of the elitist element behind privatization in the wine industry and the country overall. Indeed, the government has been subsidizing not only grape production and growers, but also wine producers, by giving subsidies to *vizbi* and wineries when buying grapes, thereby subsidizing wine production and the profits of producers as well. In fact, for several years until its 'bankruptcy', one notorious *vizba* (which was coincidentally owned by the brother of a Macedonian MP) was first place in taking the majority of subventions given to those purchasing grapes, bringing in over half a million Euros in subsidies annually. At the same time, wineries are consolidating land holdings and reorganizing business operations, in order to ensure a higher level of wine quality for export, and to meet those international and European standards that are increasingly seen as central to the new industry's success.

What individuals and their families in the Tikveš region are doing to survive this transition is the focus of the EU's IPA for Rural Development (IPARD) programme. The IPARD's objective is to 'support implementation of policies to promote competitive and sustainable agriculture; develop strong and sustainable communities, and a diverse and sustainable rural environment' (Delegation of the European Union, Fact Sheet 2010/03). Overall, the IPARD is designed to 'improve the technological and market infrastructure of commercial agricultural holdings and the food processing industry, aiming to increase the added value of agri-food products and achieve compliance with EU quality, health, food safety and environmental standards, whilst at the same time assuring the quality of life of the rural population, increasing rural incomes and creating new employment opportunities'. The IPARD programme is thus significant for a predominantly agricultural country such as Macedonia, as its clearly stated aims are to transform not only the agricultural industry there, but also the communities involved in that industry, for the purposes of global market engagement. Yet such reorientation of production is difficult, as rural producers are rarely capable of generating the required capital needed for change themselves, particularly such capital as the IPARD calls for. Furthermore, the EU's policies reflecting the 'free-market' seek to incorporate Macedonian agriculture into a globalized, international financial system that is still seen as foreign, particularly by local, small-plot farmers. Macedonian agriculture had until recently looked more like the European policy of several decades ago: protected by government price setting, supported by and for government-owned industrial production, and not meant to be competitive. This has all changed with the selling off of state-owned wineries and the laissez-faire approach taken by the State, yet this process has occurred with great speed only in the past decade and a half. As David Kideckel (1995) observed in Romania's post-socialist transition, agriculture is a unique branch of industry because land is a fixed and limited resource and influenced by local customs and conditions which growers cannot quickly adjust to external demands such as those imposed by market-development priorities. Nor are the growers usually aware of what those external forces are. As some in Tikveš are slowly realizing, their local customs and cuisine are providing opportunities for rural, 'slow-food' tourism, yet developing this cottage industry is challenging.

In the meantime, many grape growers, citizens and even some local governments have called foul on the wealthy business people and politicians[15] behind the wine industry's significant transition in Macedonia, individuals who comprise the increasingly common hybrid nature of post-socialist, capitalist *cum* semi-authoritarian governance in Eastern Europe (Levitsky and Way 2010). Furthermore, a Law on Wine passed in 2013 to help the struggling grape growers receive a fair price for their crop was struck down by the country's Constitutional Court, which considered it interference in the market. Indeed, the ongoing transition in the Macedonian wine industry is a neo-liberal game of chance with few rules, and an international affair whereby most grape growers and small wineries are anything but confident in the future of their livelihoods and ability to compete in the externally-influenced markets within and outside of the country. They continually ask whether there will be demand for their grapes or wine in the future and, despite developing according to EU standards such as the IPA addresses, they wonder whether the country will ever even join the EU. In fact, it is only a minority of growers and wineries who consider EU membership in terms of market opportunities, as the EU is a saturated wine market and so-called Euro-scepticism runs high, with the Europe of a decade ago (when the country acquired candidate status) an increasingly distant utopian ideal.[16] Moreover, neo-liberal, austerity-type measures have been factored into agricultural support for current EU candidate countries, and have resulted in a decoupling and reduction of support compared to that provided to post-socialist countries which entered the EU previously. Because the EU's agricultural policy has traditionally rewarded farmers who produce more, larger farms (of which there are few in Tikveš) benefit more from subsidies than smaller ones, such as the family-labour holdings of Macedonia (OECD 2010). Therefore, a wine region such as Tikveš is in constant transition, yet the blueprint for the region's future may not be the most compatible with EU demands, nor be viable for the country's wine industry. High unemployment and out-migration are not helping improve the situation of the wine region or the country more generally, and many businesses survive only via reconfigured social relationships and exchange (Otten 2015).

For both wineries and grape growers, hope in the region lies in the wine industry finding new markets for its products and thus wine production increasing. However, farmers will also become more competitive and increase their net income if the government assists in better strategizing its agricultural production policies, thus reducing farming costs and recovering lost productivity. At present, the country's development plan, including the IPARD, is attempting to modify Macedonia's agricultural sector and to make it conform to EU standards, but in doing so may be, to borrow from the Macedonian saying, trying to 'plant the vine and drink the wine'.[17] This is a saying used to describe those expecting too much, too fast. The EU and government may be guilty of not only aiming too high but also missing the mark in terms of understanding what needs reforming in rural regions such as Tikveš. For it is not just the agricultural sector but the culture of bribery and corruption at the governmental, bureaucratic and judicial levels that need attention and better regulation too. Addressing these issues will not only help ensure agriculturalists in Tikveš and elsewhere enjoy a more equitable livelihood and future, but more transparency, fair play and self-promotion will improve the performance of the wine region's numerous industries, from wine production through to tourism.

Branding and the international market for Macedonian wine

Although the transformation of the Macedonian wine industry has been the source of much discontent, pressure on, and desire by, the wineries to find new markets and increase their profits has led to the rebranding of, and new marketing strategies for, Macedonian wine. While the government has improved somewhat in helping promote the country's wine industry at trade fairs abroad, the maintenance of current markets and the development of new ones have been threatened by the increase in availability of both Old and New World wines in the local and European market, and there has in fact been much complaint about the lack of strategic State support for wine promotion. In consideration of EU regulations, along with the inundation of wines from other European producers and New World wines, Macedonia's wine industry therefore faces a continuous uphill battle in gaining ground and profitable market share. Yet just as elsewhere in Eastern Europe, investments in the retailing system – which can assist in the promotion of wine to the domestic market – have increased in the last decade, with distribution systems becoming more demand-driven. There have also been savvy rebranding and marketing campaigns at home and abroad, penetrating markets as far away as the United States and China. For example, a Tikveš Winery television commercial which aired in Macedonia and the former Yugoslav region, had a scantily clad woman in a Paris apartment (with the Eiffel Tower in the background) enjoying a bottle of Tikveš wine, with the narration entirely in French yet with local subtitles. Such advertising catered to those seeking the exotic and foreign in their wine consumption (not to mention the connection to one of Europe's most well-known wine-producing countries), and the commercial was likely cost-effective as well, requiring only the altering of the sub-titled translation for another national market's primary language.

Rebranding has primarily consisted of new logos, imagery, labels and product line identification. The Tikveš Winery, for example, modified its logo and used it on all wine labels, and also created new product lines with their own set of standard bottle labels. This included the blends (red and white), basic varietal wines (e.g. Chardonnay, Cabernet Sauvignon, etc.) and special selections (from a particular Tikveš vineyard). Other wineries have similarly sought to create brand recognition and gain market share. However, given the outrage over the Tikveš Winery's privatization, its owners have also had to try to quell the Macedonian market and demonstrate that despite the rupture to socialist wine production (which has received significant media attention in the country), it was for good reasons and now there is a better product to show for it. With the shift to beer consumption in the country, gaining an audience for their wines has been, and remains, a challenge for Macedonian wineries. What the industry has done is to focus on its native grape and wine types as well as blends of them. These include white grape types such as *Smederevka, Temjanika* and the increasingly popular *R'katsiteli*[18], and red grape types including *Kratošija, Stanušina, Kardinal* and *Vranec* in particular. Indeed, *Vranec* is Macedonia's premier varietal and constitutes the majority of Macedonian red wine. It is the primary grape in the recently introduced red '*cuvee*' blends (available through many wineries), and is seen as the industry's most unique and thus marketable wine, with winery owners boasting that it can compete with an Italian Sangiovese or Spanish Rioja. Dark and full-bodied, *Vranec* is a cousin to Zinfandel and grows well in the long, hot and sunny summer days in Tikveš. *Vranec* is perceived to be such a quality grape not only because of the dark red wine it produces, but also because its sugar content levels (degrees Brix) are extremely high. Overall, the quality of it and other Macedonian wines is the result of the region's *terroir*, the natural environment (soil, climate, location, etc.) from which the grapes come, which in the case of Tikveš is the combined influence of the Mediterranean and continental climates on largely clay soil, together with hot summer days, cooler nights and sufficient rain.

Although the word has only recently been adopted in the local wine lexicon (*teroar*), there is a move towards *terroir* understandings and practices, and the industry is well aware of the importance this plays in marketing.[19] For while knowledge of geographical origin (*poteklo*), and its importance in determining the wine's overall quality, is nothing new, the competitive global wine market and wider trends in the industry have meant that wineries must adopt particular discourses and consumer preferences in order to promote not just their name but also the vineyards from which particular types of grapes come. Therefore the Tikveš Winery now has an entire range of wines from their 'Barovo' vineyards (which sell for two to three times the average price of a bottle of wine), and other wineries have followed suit.

In addition to this, the wine industry has faced a sort of *inter-nationalist* competition: due to Greece's ongoing opposition over use of the name 'Macedonia', a new label for Macedonia's Povardarie (Vardar River region – where numerous wineries exist) wines was adopted in 2013, through collaboration among the 'Wines from Macedonia' trade association. The association had been working with the United Nations Food and Agriculture Organisation (FAO) and the European Bank for Reconstruction and Development (EBRD) to help resolve not just Greek opposition to the name Macedonia, but also Greek government threats to European (e.g. Slovenia, Germany) importers of wine, such that they could end up in court for purchasing and selling Macedonian wine. The association therefore developed the new moniker and claims that the label 'Vardar Valley' wines (which pinpoints the geographic origin of the wine, rather than its country of origin) will boost its value and ideally allow Macedonian wines to compete worldwide. It remains for the wine producers to accept, use and promote this tool. Wineries have been reluctant to use this moniker, as many disagree with such a seeming capitulation to the 'name issue' with Greece.

Furthermore, except for countries and states such as France and California, where particular wine regions are well known globally, the country of origin is very important to a wine industry seeking to gain more recognition. As a representative from a local wine consortium, *MakVino*, explained, this among other factors affects the wine industry's competitiveness and potential for wine tourism, whose promotion has been a goal of the region and country. Although it is not well known internationally, Macedonia secured a name for itself in the former Yugoslavia as a significant wine producer under its constitutional name. No one will have heard of the Vardar River valley, but they are much more likely to know a country's location and perhaps something historical about it. This cultural knowledge and interest is important because it lends wine consumers interest in visiting the source of a product, which for Tikveš and Macedonia is precisely the sort of wine tourism they hope to develop more. For better or for worse, complaints about lack of a unified tourism strategy at the State level have been countered by international development organizations which have sought to alleviate the burden of this transition by working with local municipalities in promoting tourism. For example, the US Agency for International Development (USAID) helped set up a wine region information centre in the Tikveš town of Negotino and an accompanying website, and took several wine producers to California for oenology training at the University of California-Davis. Additionally, European IPARD funds have led to the creation of numerous small, family-run wineries, though none have been well developed for significant levels of tourism in terms of capacity and facilities.

The cultural and historical production of wine is indeed a big draw in the global marketplace, and the government funded a number of 'Macedonian Timeless' commercials on CNN International and other news outlets, which promote the country's long history. The commercial focusing on wine heritage[20] showed Macedonians of antiquity joyfully gathering and stomping on grapes, and archaeologists uncovering a jug of that ancient wine and imbibing it, before switching to a late nineteenth-century scene of wine producers, and then to the present day, with a sophisticated-looking couple enjoying a glass of wine. What was noticeably absent was any representation of the socialist era in this minute-long promotion.

Despite this government promotion, there have been complaints from both sides of the wine industry, both the grape farmers and wine producers, that the government has failed to participate in the country's wine marketing and promotion. As the aforementioned *MakVino* representative stated, 'The promotion of the wine sector is the final link [after subsidies, other support of the industry, etc.] which is missing. It is good to support agriculture, but they must target sales appropriately'.[21] Combining this with her concern about the name issue with Greece, she added that

> foreigners don't know much about Macedonia let alone its wines, so if there's a tasting by one winery in the centre of London once every few years it's useless, because the market is so challenging and competitive. We must work together as a country.

But as the owner of an agricultural supply shop (*zemjodelska apteka*) explained, knowing what to work on together is the main challenge for the industry. As he stated:

> Business requires a positive regulated atmosphere, with a clean slate and little worry about past dues and future production. That is not what exists here. Growers here aren't paid for two to three years sometimes, they owe us and other shops money, and they're not certain to what end they're growing the crop they are at present, many digging their grapes up and planting other crops. Why would they work together when they don't know what they're working together on? An overall agricultural strategy is what's needed here, and that can only come from the government, not the 'free-market' and competing producers.[22]

While the larger wineries would like greater assistance from the Macedonian government, several have been forging ahead on their own. Being owned by wealthy business people or investment firms which allocate resources to marketing and public relations, the Tikveš Winery now sells its wines in some American restaurants and wine shops. The Stobi Winery – named after a local archaeological site in Tikveš – has successfully penetrated the UK market, selling in the large retail store Marks & Spencer and setting up a website for sales in the country. Both wineries, among numerous others in the country, have also secured top accolades in the wine world, ranging from awards and recognition by famous sommeliers, to being written about in the *Washington Post, New York Times, The Guardian*, and other media, and to increasing their presence on upscale restaurant wine lists. While penetrating new and less saturated markets is a goal of Macedonian wineries, doing so is not only a matter of finding a market and figuring out retail and logistical distribution, but in many potential large markets also involves making business connections and paying bribes or additional fees to 'set up shop'. In particular, the latter is applicable in the sought-after markets of Russia and China, where channels for distribution are much less clear than in some other countries.

As in many wine regions around the world, one strategy to boost the country's wine industry is the continued development of domestic wine tourism.[23] Wine tourism, which did not exist as an industry during socialism, has begun in the sense that wineries have built restaurants and tasting rooms within their facilities, and some have implemented regular tastings and tours of their cellars. The most successful winery in terms of tourism in the region has been the Popova Kula Winery in the Tikveš town of Demir Kapija. Based on a Napa Valley-style winery, its founder built it upon returning home from a career in the United States. Sitting atop a hill overlooking the town, the winery is tastefully designed for visitors to tour, taste and stay in. It has numerous wine-themed hotel rooms, a tasting room in the tower (*kula*) part of it, and a full-service restaurant with an outdoor terrace overlooking vineyards. It is seen by many as the gold standard in terms of local wine tourism, and its owner has been politically active in the region, trying to push the entire industry to shift its sales from bulk to bottled wine, particularly if it can be sold in restaurants and wineries where its sale price will be double or triple its retail price.

While larger wineries have seen some success in marketing their wines, accessing capital has been a challenge for newer, often small, wineries. Furthermore, once such wineries acquire capital, the combination of lack of a market for their products, combined with high interest rates and debts, has prevented their growth, and some wineries have already gone out of business. As one informant, whose family winery closed down because of competition from larger wineries, explained, it is the wine industry's lack of regulation and its consequent high level of competitiveness that left her family's winery unable to compete. Larger wineries with more money are able to reach further, market more, and even pay restaurants and servers to sell their wines, using incentives and bonuses.

As for the future and what the industry's strategy should be, wine producers must continue their production because of the potential opportunities, but the government and EU should assist them. The EU could do so by increasing the quota for Macedonian wine exports in order for the grapes (and wine) to be bought, and through some form of regulation growers could be assured of fair and timely compensation for their grapes. A long-term strategy that covers both representation of the wine industry at wine fairs abroad and the associated tourism industry needs to be implemented and realized. Present conditions – including a fractured national promotion strategy, uncertainly in wine regions over both EU entry and the future of wine production and tourism, and too many vineyards but limited ways to get the grapes and wine to market – amount to a clear loss for the industry. Progress will only be made when the government is able to negotiate the raising of the EU bulk wine quota, as well as – and perhaps better yet – stimulating bottled wine sales, the annual quota of which goes unfulfilled.

Conclusion

The Macedonian wine industry is a small but significant player in the south-east European wine world and increasingly elsewhere around the globe. To compare its main wine region, Tikveš, to Bordeaux or even Napa Valley, would misrepresent it. Tikveš is a significant wine-producing region because it has the right climate and was actively made into one during the socialist Yugoslav era. Since the end of socialism, the combination of privatization and globalization has created numerous challenges for the Macedonian wine industry, as it wrangles socialist production methods with EU and global wine market integration. As Waters (1995) found, globalization entails an 'organisational ecumenism': a single idealization of appropriate organizational behaviour that includes generic management skills, quantified performance targets, devolution and the use of private sector practices such as corporate plans, monetary incentives and flexible labour practices.

It is a combination of external and internal forces which are augmenting the political, economic and cultural landscape around the land and the industry which grow the grapes and produce the wine in Macedonia today. On the one hand, it could be argued that there is a seeming *'terroir-isation'*[24] occurring in Tikveš. Growers are falling victim to modern wine standards, and a government and privatized industry intent on seeing such standards bear fruit as the country undergoes a neo-liberal transformation and moves towards the EU wine market, a most challenging foe for old-style businesses. As illustrated in a photo-essay on the region (Otten 2013), it is through both the post-socialist privatization project, and then more recently the EU's pre-accession measures, that the industry has been subject to a variety of regulations and limitations on the names of its wine, on how much of it can be exported, and most of all, on how the country's industry operates. Alongside EU measures are the profit-seeking practices of oligarchs and other business people, who have either acquired formerly State-owned wineries or have branded entirely new ones. They support a consolidation of capital among the already well-connected local elite, which is a double-edged sword for the growers who work their own small plots of land in order to supply the wineries.

Yet on the other hand, even if the country never joins the EU, the upside of European integration for Macedonia is the opening of borders and trade, and availability of grants through the EU's IPARD scheme. Although the grants require capital investments from those receiving funds (making it challenging for some with the interest to participate), the grants have provided assistance to the agricultural sector and rural communities such as those in wine regions, allowing them to adapt better to the economic transitions occurring around them. Thus small wineries and tourism-related initiatives have received a boost from IPARD funding, which has supported the purchase of new technology, equipment and the construction of new facilities. Furthermore, in conjunction with a greater understanding of wine tourism, a Slow Food movement has begun in the country. In Tikveš, its objectives have been to preserve the local culture surrounding wine production and consumption (including gastronomy), including detailing what these customs and methods are precisely, educating others in them, and trademarking food products and wine varieties.

In modern Macedonia, wine and consumers are travelling to engage with one another in ways previously unseen in the country, as concepts of *terroir*, geographical domain and wine and food culture attract a new clientele to and within the country. These factors are what attract wine consumers looking for unique aspects of the wine they are drinking, not the often hidden fact that global wine production within the wineries is increasingly standardized and characterized by the use of sophisticated technology. But the end goal is the same, and in line with what the 2006 EU wine policy shift has sought to attain: a more competitive wine industry across the continent, in order to counter the rise of New World wines.

Thinking about Macedonia as a microcosm of the contemporary global order – individuals reacting to internationally-induced changes, and creating opportunities in order to help their families – one can say that only now is the dissolution of socialism really being played out. What the country has today is a new generation born after the breakup of Yugoslavia, who know no guaranteed employment and accompanying benefits, and who are engaging with wine commerce in new and different ways, and increasingly commanding it too. They only know that they have to do what their forefathers did, which is to work hard and follow the rainbow to 'the pot of gold' on the other side. Incidentally, rainbow in Macedonian is *vinozito*: wine (coloured) grain.

Notes

1. The BNAC includes all of the former Yugoslav republics except for Slovenia, as well as Albania.
2. This has brought the European Bank for Reconstruction and Development (EBRD) into the fold, which has provided capital for the wine sector's development (Coretchi 2009).
3. Research has shown that while the CAP only slightly decreased production and increased costs in the traditional EU-15 countries upon its introduction, the predominantly post-Communist ten new members (NMS) who entered in 2004 saw substantial increases in costs with various changes in production – often an increase in production for export, but with an overall decrease in domestic consumption (Beghin et al 2007). Even among post-Communist countries, varying economic factors and structures have resulted in a diverse array of challenges (Hartell and Swinnen 2000).
4. For more on neo-liberalism, see Chomsky (1998), Collier (2011), England and Ward (2007), Hann (2006), Harvey (2005), MacEwan (1999), Petras and Veltmeyer (2011), Plehwe et al (2005), Saad-Filho and Johnston (2005), etc.
5. This is also the name and location of one of the more successful new wine ventures, the Stobi Winery. It was built from scratch by a wealthy investor in 2011, has received stellar ratings for some of its wines, and has already penetrated the UK, among other foreign markets.
6. The growing season begins after mid-February with the first pruning of the vines, and lasts until September or October, depending on the grape type.
7. See Creed (1998), Hann (2006), Kideckel (1995), for commentary on post-socialist rural transition and European integration in other countries of central and eastern Europe.
8. As Verdery and Burawoy state in their book *Uncertain Transitions* (1999), since the fall of socialism there has been a breaking down of macro-level structures, such as the administered economies of most formerly socialist states. This has allowed the creation of space for 'micro worlds', resulting in a reversion to old ways of constantly struggling to maintain a level of subsistence. This is similar to what Creed was told by a villager upon commencing his fieldwork in Bulgaria: the country is 'always in transition' (1998: 1).

9. According to Anderson and Norma (2003), wine accounted for 26 per cent of alcohol consumption in the region in the 1970s, 22 per cent in the 1980s, 16 per cent in the 1990s, and 14 per cent after 2000–2001. However, the undocumented amount of home wine production is not accounted for here, and it has likely increased with the surplus of grapes not being sold to wineries. That said, given the technical aspects of wine production, most families in Tikveš choose to make the much easier to produce *rakija* brandy with their grapes – a product that is used for many things besides drinking, and which can be more easily transported around the country and sold to earn extra income.
10. The CAP is the overarching European policy for agriculture, which once a country joins the EU they are thenceforth subject to.
11. Through the IPA the Macedonian government has received over half a billion Euros since 2007 for five components, from institution building to rural development.
12. This is surely an advantage for the wine industry compared to other countries in the region, where vineyards are fewer and agricultural labour is either more expensive and/or non-existent (such as in Albania and Bulgaria, where emigration has depleted the countryside of young men), and ensures it will continue to grow for the time being.
13. In comparison with the European average of €0.50/kg.
14. Until 2019, Greece did not recognize Macedonia by its constitutional name, claiming that Macedonia (also the name of the north-central region of Greece) is historically Greek and thus the name cannot be used by another country. Greek policy therefore mandated that Macedonia be referred to as the Former Yugoslav Republic of Macedonia (FYROM), or often just *Skopia*, given the Macedonian capital city of Skopje. However, in June 2018 the two countries came to an agreement to rename the country as the Republic of North Macedonia, despite fierce opposition and protests within both Greece and Macedonia. How the name change will affect the wine industry remains to be seen.
15. Referred to as 'wine mafia' (*vinska mafija*).
16. This is due to several reasons: the crisis in the EU and neighbouring Greece, Brexit, Brussels itself expressing doubts that it can afford to take on new member states, anecdotal evidence from EU member neighbours of the decline in their standard of living (often heard when travelling through Bulgaria and Greece), and last but not least, the Greek government's staunch opposition up until 2019 to the Republic of Macedonia's right to self-determination and use of the name Macedonia, including for its wine labels.
17. *Bucni prčka, pij vino.*
18. R'katsiteli has become a cult wine for Georgian producers in particular, and is now widely sold to hipsters in Western Europe and North America.
19. For more on *terroir* from a cultural and anthropological perspective, see the first section of Ulin and Black (2013) – 'Re-thinking *terroir*' – as well as Trubek (2009).
20. Available at https://www.youtube.com/watch?v=O-C0BcZ_D8c
21. Interview conducted in person, June 2011.
22. Interview conducted in person, April 2011.

23. There has been a good deal of recent research into wine tourism, from California to Chile. From their sustainable development to the tourists and the tastes they are after, see Gmelch and Gmelch (2011) and Kunc (2010).
24. Borrowed from Mike Veseth's (2012) use of 'terroirists'.

References

Anderson, K., and Norman, D. (2003), *Global Wine Production, Consumption, and Trade, 1961 to 2001: A Statistical Compendium*, Adelaide: Centre for International Economic Studies.

Bache, I., Andreou, G., Atanasova, G., and Tomsic, D. (2011), 'Europeanisation and Multi-level Governance in South-east Europe: The Domestic Impact of EU Cohesion Policy and Pre-accession Aid', *JEPP*, 18(1):122–41.

Bartlett, W. (2007), 'The Western Balkans', in Lane, D., and Myant, M. (eds), *Varieties of Capitalism in Post-Communist Countries*, New York, NY: Palgrave Macmillan, 201–20.

Beghin, J. et al (2007), 'The Impact of the European Enlargement and CAP Reforms on Agricultural Markets. Much Ado about Nothing?', in Beghin, J., and Fuller, F. (eds), *European Agriculture: Enlargement, Structural Change, CAP Reform and Trade Liberalisation*, Hauppauge, NY: Nova Science Publishers, 51–63.

Black, R.E., and Ulin, R.C. (eds) (2013), *Wine and Culture: Vineyard to Glass*, London: Bloomsbury.

Borneman, J., and Fowler, N. (1997), 'Europeanization', *Annual Review of Anthropology*, 26:487–514.

Burawoy, M., and Verdery, K. (eds) (1999), *Uncertain Transition: Ethnographies of Change in the Postsocialist World*, Lanham, MD: Rowman & Littlefield Publishers.

Chomsky, N. (1998), *Profit over People: Neoliberalism & Global Order*, London: Seven Stories.

Collier, S. (2011), *Post-Soviet Social: Neoliberalism, Social Modernity, Biopolitics*, Princeton, NJ: Princeton University Press.

Coretchi, I. (2009), *EBRD Provides Further Support to Develop Macedonian Wine Sector*, European Bank for Reconstruction and Development, http://www.ebrd.com/pages/news/press/2009/090623c.shtml

Creed, G. (1998), *Domesticating Revolution: From Socialist Reform to Ambivalent Transition in a Bulgarian Village*, University Park, PA: Pennsylvania State University Press.

Delegation of the European Union, Fact Sheet 2010/03.

DeSoucey, M. (2010), 'Gastronationalism: Food Traditions and Authenticity Politics in the European Union', *American Sociological Review*, 75(3):432–55.

England, K., and Ward K. (2007), *Neoliberalization: States, Networks, Peoples*, Malden, MA: Blackwell Publishing.

Gmelch, G., and Gmelch, S. (2011), *Tasting the Good Life: Wine Tourism in the Napa Valley*, Bloomington, IN: Indiana University Press.

Hann, C. (2006), *'Not the Horse We Wanted!' Postsocialism, Neoliberalism and Eurasia*, Münster: Lit Verlag.

Hartell, J.G., and Swinnen, J. (eds) (2000), *Agriculture and European East-west Integration*, Burlington, VT: Ashgate.

Harvey, D. (2005), *A Brief History of Neoliberalism*, Oxford: Oxford University Press.

Issawi, C. (1980), *The Economic History of Turkey 1800–1914*, Chicago: University Press.
Kamčevski, P. (2007), *Lozarstvoto i vinarstvoto vo Tikvešijata niz istorijata*, Skopje, https://www.isbns.com.co/isbn/9789989243288/
Kideckel, D. (ed.) (1995), *East European Communities: The Struggle for Balance in Turbulent Times*, Boulder, CO: Westview Publishers.
Kunc, M. (2010), 'Wine Tourism: A Review of the Chilean Case', *International Journal of Tourism Policy*, 3(1):51–61.
Levitsky, S., and Way, L. (2010), *Competitive Authoritarianism: Hybrid Regimes after the Cold War*, Cambridge: Cambridge University Press.
MacEwan, A. (1999), *Neo-liberalism or Democracy? Economic Strategy, Markets, and Alternatives for the 21st Century*, New York: Zed Books.
Miljković, D. (1996), *Effects of Economic Transition Policies on Yugoslavia's Agricultural Sector: A Quantitative Approach*, PhD Thesis, University of Illinois at Champagne-Urbana.
Noev, N., and Swinnen, J. (2004), 'Eastern Europe and the Former Soviet Union', in Anderson, K. (ed.), *The Worlds Wine Markets*, London: Edward Elgar, 161–86.
Organisation for Economic Co-operation and Development (OECD) (2010), *The Doha Development Round of Trade Negotiations: Understanding the Issues*, http://www.oecd.org/document/45/0,2340,en_2649_201185_35738477_1_1_1_1,00.html
Otten, J. (2013), 'Neo-liberalism Illustrated: Privatization in the Republic of Macedonia's Tikveš Wine region', *Student Anthropologist*, 4(1):85–106.
Otten, J. (2015), 'Accession and Association: The Effects of European Integration and Neoliberalism on Rising Inequality and Kin-neighbor Reciprocity in the Republic of Macedonia', *Economic Anthropology*, 2(2):359–70.
Petras, J., and Veltmeyer, H. (2011), *Beyond Neoliberalism: A World to Win*, Surrey: Ashgate.
Plehwe, D., Walpen, B., and Neunhoffer, G. (eds) (2005), *Neoliberal Hegemony: A Global Critique*, New York: Routledge, 1–24.
Saad-Filho, A., and Johnston, D. (eds) (2005), *Neoliberalism: A Critical Reader*, Ann Arbor, MI: Pluto Press.
Stiglitz, J. (2002), *Globalisation and Its Discontents*, London: Penguin.
Trubek, A. (2009), *The Taste of Place: A Cultural Journey into Terroir*, Oakland, CA: University of California Press.
Veseth, M. (2012), *Wine Wars: The Curse of the Blue Nun, the Miracle of Two Buck Chuck and the Revenge of the Terroir-ists*, Lanham, MD: Rowman & Littlefield Publishers.
Waters, M. (1995), *Globalisation*, London: Routledge.

6 Globalization and Reputation Dynamics: The Case of Bordeaux Wines

PIERRE-MARIE CHAUVIN

Introduction

Associating 'globalization' with Bordeaux wines usually fosters two immediate reactions: on the one hand, one may acknowledge that globalization has done a lot to enhance the Bordeaux wine world and its products for several centuries; on the other hand, globalization can arouse local fears of losing control of Bordeaux wines' production and taste. Hence globalization is usually seen as a market opportunity or a threat to Bordeaux production identity. Rather than thinking of globalization as a threat or an opportunity, one can highlight through a multi-scaled approach the way globalization, combined with national and local factors (Smith 2008), has formed and changed the 'reputation system' (Chauvin 2010a) that organizes the allocation of reputation and status in this community. In this chapter, I will present how and why this 'reputation system' has been built and transformed, and what kind of role globalization has played in this process.[1]

This system is based upon four types of evaluations: classifications, grades, prices and informal categories or labels (such as winemakers' signatures and product categories). Economic actors try to manage the reputation of their wines by playing with institutional affiliations, numeric values and informal categorizations. Thus, I identify four arenas in which these specific reputational outputs are produced: the *institutional arena* (in which classifications are built and revised), the *media arena* (in which grades are formed and displayed), the *merchant arena* (in which prices are set up and spread) and the *productive arena* (in which names are associated with products, especially through winemakers' signatures). The productive arena is the specific productive part of what Inglis and Almila in Chapter 1 call the *wine world*. The merchant arena also belongs to the *wine world*, but thanks to the frequent interactions between merchants and consumers, this subpart of the wine world is obviously closer to wine consumption and it can be considered as crossing into the *wine culture*. The institutional and the media arenas can be considered as two subspaces of the *wine field* (as defined in Chapter 1). In these spheres, people are mostly professionals, but they can also include serious amateurs who shape wine discourses and values.

This systemic approach leads me to conclude that these different arenas are not independent spheres: in order to explain one specific output, one has to study the links between the different arenas. Instead of considering globalization as a fifth 'arena', we can consider it as a transversal phenomenon that has impacted upon each of the four main reputation arenas.

Globalization in the institutional arena: Bordeaux wine classifications, a cross-cultural construction?

The classifications of wines are among the most analysed cases of classifications in the social world. Three reasons can explain this focus: first, because the wine world is a very institutionalized economic sector in which the classifications are various and visible; second, because there are some obvious contrasts between different types of classifications within the wine world, especially through the opposition between the criteria of the 'grape' (*vins de cépage*) and the criteria of the origin (*the appellation*), which highlights the potential competition and friction between different classifications (Douglas 1986; Garcia-Parpet 2009); third, because the classifications of the wine industry are very helpful in showing the vertical hierarchies that classifications may foster (Chauvin 2010a; Podolny 2005; Zhao 2005). In other words, status and reputations depend to a large extent on classifications. The Bordeaux wine world is the best example of these status hierarchies, partly because of the variety of rankings concerning its different territories (Médoc, Graves, Saint-Émilion), but also because of the persistence and the exceptional inertia of some specific rankings.

The so-called '1855' classification is the most striking example of such inertia. It has globally been stable since 1855, except the small upgrade of Château Mouton-Rothschild in 1973, after years of active lobbying and innovative economic actions led by Baron Philippe de Rothschild and his team (Chauvin 2010a). Today, this classification constitutes the most commented, the most celebrated and the most criticized institution not just from the Bordeaux wine region but from all wine regions in the world, because of the economic and the symbolic influence of Bordeaux within the wine world. We will not present the exhaustive history of the emergence of the classification, which was well documented by Markham (1997), but we want to raise one specific argument about the *cross-national* origin of such a classification. This argument helps to understand how 'globalization' has participated in the dynamics of Bordeaux wine's culture and industry, not just in the past thirty years but also in the previous several centuries.

Where does the 1855 classification come from? The traditional way of presenting this classification consists in highlighting the role of local professionals (the so-called *courtiers*) who proposed a classification based on past transaction prices between producers and merchants. One may amend this bottom-up version by putting forward the role of national political actors (such as Emperor Napoleon III) who asked the Bordeaux professionals to produce a selection of their best growths in order to represent French excellence at the Universal Exhibition of 1855. But these overly

French-centred perspectives fail to identify the role of different international actors in this institutional creation. There are at least three reasons for considering this classification as a *cross-national* cultural construction.

First, the 1855 classification was the by-product of a long tradition of wine evaluations, elaborated by a large variety of personalities who produced their personal rankings and/or ratings. Among these personalities there are some important professionals, such as Guillaume Lawton, William Johnston and William Franck (Markham 1997), and some major political actors, such as Thomas Jefferson, who published in 1787 a classification together with comments about Bordeaux growths (Ginestet 1996), even though Jefferson wrote his reviews based upon previous professional ones. This is a good illustration of how the wine field (see Chapter 1), through one of its most famous and prescriptive parts – celebrities – can shape the wine world. Indeed, wine rankings, which are often categorized in the wine world and field as 'professional rankings', are also shaped by charismatic and visible amateurs, such as political celebrities.

Second, this classification was largely influenced by merchants, and above all by English merchants, who had a real effect on prices and reputations. Some merchants produced their own classifications, and all of them promoted and valorized Bordeaux wines on their domestic market.

Third, the 1855 Universal Exhibition was obviously not just a national event. It must be linked to the international cultural, political and economic competition between England and France. The prices observed by the local courtiers were partly based on the demand and the symbolic attraction for their wines by the English monarchy and aristocracy, English merchants, and other foreign merchants throughout Europe.

Hence, if one extends the temporal scope of the analysis, from a short-term eventful perspective (focused on 1855) to a long-term institutionalist approach, one must also move from a narrow French perspective to a cross-national one. Far from being an ex nihilo creation that occurred in 1855, the ranking is the product of a progressive crystallization. The previous classifications gave to the 1855 classification its three main characteristics: its territoriality (Médoc and Sauternes), its criterion of hierarchy (prices, which were supposed to synthesize such information as quality of wines and status of 'terroirs'), and its structure in five classes (1er Cru Classé, 2nd Cru Classé etc.). The criterion, the territorial target and the formal structure of the ranking are the products of an accumulation of small classificatory steps made by public authorities, professionals and amateurs. This highlights more generally how wine institutions are processual and social products which are shaped in plural arenas. If the final and official locus of rankings is the 'institutional' arena (considered as a sub-part of the *wine world*), the *wine culture* and *wine field* are engaged in the progressive dynamics that build the form and the structure of such hierarchies.

The stability of this classification has not prevented local and international actors from criticizing its validity. The participation of the *wine field* in the institutions of the *wine world* does not only consist in a positive and active construction during the period of their historical origins; it is also present during 'the social life' of the rankings, through the expression of critical comments and the imagining of alternative institutions. Many merchants, journalists and, more recently, some wine critics, have tried to propose more accurate and modern classifications of Bordeaux wines all through the twentieth century. For example, the journalist Franck Prial expresses the viewpoint of many professionals and amateurs when he writes in *The New York Times*:

> The list remains immutable, but the wine properties certainly have not. Many of the chateaux have been sold, many have been exploited by avaricious owners, and others have been ignored by indifferent ones. And, of course, many have improved. The sacrosanct 1855 classification, of course, reflects none of this. There are fourth and fifth growths that should be seconds and thirds; alternatively, there are highly rated properties that should be demoted. What's more, many properties that were ignored in 1855, and not just the famous ones, have made themselves eligible for classification, in some cases making wine better than chateaux already on the list.[2]

Like many Anglo-Saxon observers, Prial is particularly likely to consider the 1855 classification as an old-fashioned remnant, an archaic monument and a symbol of a vinous aristocracy bound to income from its land. How could such a stable institution survive without almost any change for more than a century? That is how Robert Parker presents this classification, and more generally the hierarchy of Bordeaux wines, in the film *Mondovino* (2004) made by Jonathan Nossiter.[3] However, this critical vision is also present within the Bordeaux wine world itself, especially among the owners who feel their growth deserves a better position than their official position on the basis of their market reputation, their price and the grades given by influential wine critics.

Globalization in the media arena: Bordeaux wines' grades, the rise of the international critics

The American critic Robert Parker is one of the most influential sources of reputation for the Bordeaux premium wine market. Econometric research has proved beyond doubt the link between Parker's ratings and prices of 'en primeur' wines (Hadj Ali et al 2008), and sociological inquiries has given precise insights into the effects of his ratings on the strategies of producers and merchants (Chauvin 2011b). Some journalistic investigation has also portrayed this special character of the wine market (McCoy 2005).

While Parker is often considered as an agent of globalization and an enemy of traditional hierarchies, we agree with Colin Hay's highlighting of a more complex interaction between Parker's scores and official classifications:

> Parker's ratings are more influential, and prices more sensitive to his en primeur scores, where – as in Saint-Emilion – the official system of classification is more flexible and less prestigious. But it also suggests how Parker scores may play a crucial role, alongside well-established and highly respected classification

systems (as for instance in the Médoc), in building up and, in particular, restoring the reputations of châteaux generally regarded to have fallen below their official place in the classification. In this respect, rather than overturning local classificatory schema, Parker's external influence may well work in parallel with them. (Hay 2007: 20)

Robert Parker has definitely become the only wine critic to have such effects on the economic wine world, and he strikingly embodies the way the *wine field* can penetrate and shape both the *wine culture* and the *wine world*. The story often told about the relationships between Parker and Bordeaux, and that is for example displayed in *Mondovino*, is that the taste of Bordeaux wines has changed tremendously because of the influence of Parker on them. This story is not totally false, because some producers effectively identified a so-called 'Parkerized' style of wines, and tried to make wines in conformity with this style, that is to say, powerful, oaky and inky red wines. But it would be excessive to consider that all Bordeaux wines have followed this trend. Most producers explain that they want to make fine and elegant wines, in the classic Bordeaux style, and that 'Parkerized wines' represent a minority of the Bordeaux production world. Most local actors recognize that Parker's influence – among other critics, but in a more striking way – has been a great incentive for quality improvement in the Bordeaux wine world. Most of them also underline the positive role of Parker towards Bordeaux wines, generally speaking, as the American critic has done a lot for the Bordeaux region in terms of visibility and international recognition. Parker has been a great intermediary between Bordeaux and the North American market, but he also facilitated access to other markets, such as the Asian ones. More recently, the appearance of new critics and new forms of evaluation on the internet may have transformed the wine field into a less monopolistic one: Parker is not eternal, and most economic actors wonder what happens when he stops his activity. Will we observe a more pluralistic critic world, or will one major critic emerge from the international scene? The years of the 2020s will be decisive in this process.

Globalization in the market arena: The international dynamics of Bordeaux wines' prices

The Bordeaux wine world is characterized by a high level of interaction and mutual observation. It seems that professionals usually make their decisions without real attempts to analyse the demand side. In this sense, the wine market is close to the market modelled by White (1981): as producers cannot observe the behaviours of consumers, they look at each other before launching their products. But it would be an error to deny the constant informal exchanges between the demand side and the production side, through the role of intermediaries such as local négociants and courtiers on the one hand, and international merchants and importers on the other. The flow of information concerning stocks, prices and demand coming from such intermediaries on the various markets, is decisive for local actors in generating their strategies. This information is important for producers when they set up their 'en primeur' release prices, but it is also useful for négociants when they determine their buying strategies, and for courtiers when they assess the 'market fluidity' of certain wines before advising wine estates and négociants on their pricing and market strategies. Hence, the market arena can be seen as a multi-territorial scene in which many international actors take some positions and influence the local release prices. It is also a strategic space in which the international *wine culture* and *wine field* are interacting with and infusing the discrete but central Bordeaux *wine world*.

Some marketplaces are obviously more influential than others. In recent years, the Chinese market has become the most important in terms of value and reputation dynamics for Bordeaux wines. Some wine producers have been able to raise their prices tremendously, thanks to upper-upper-class Chinese consumers. Chateau Lafite-Rothschild is the most striking example of this trend (Maguire and Lim 2014), as it is often seen as the favourite Bordeaux red wine of serious Chinese amateurs.

Apart from the Chinese market, the English marketplace is historically the most important market for Bordeaux wines' reputation dynamics, especially through lead merchants such as Berry Bros. & Rudd and Farr Vintners, but also through some more recent intermediaries such as Liv-ex, which offers many data services for merchants and funds. Such merchants participate in the work of reputation building. Their feedback concerning stocks and prices are important variables that producers take into account while they elaborate their release prices.

The easy diffusion of prices and rates within the wine world during 'en primeur' campaigns exerts a form of social control over producers before and after the release of their wines. Before the release, the memory of their previous prices and the rates allocated to their wines play a key role in the decision-making about prices. After the release of their wines, the reactions of the commercial part of the wine world to the prices lead them to adapt or moderate their strategy for their next campaigns. Building a new status through prices is not a short-term enterprise. Pricing is not only a question of costs; it notably requires a dynamic of positive judgements by the main value-makers of the market. In other words, they take into account the reputation of vintages and wines fostered by the main 'third-parties' (Sauder 2006) of the market.

The release prices are not the only devices that reflect the international dynamics in the market arena. The activity of reselling on different second-hand marketplaces (including the so-called 'Place de Bordeaux') implies other types of prices, such as 'prix de place' (Chauvin 2011a). 'Prix de place' are conventional prices defined by the courtiers on the basis of the supply displayed by the wine estates and the 'négoce' at a certain moment. According to the supply loaded in the courtiers' databases, there could be some slight differences between the 'Prix de place' defined by the different courtiers. Most of the courtiers have developed or used some technological software to update these prices and to make them as accurate as possible. How do they synthesize the different wine offers that circulate on the Bordeaux place market? The négociants regularly send their prices to the courtiers, while the courtiers regularly check if these offers are still valid.

The reselling activity can have effects on '*prix de place*' if it involves large quantities of wine. Moreover, merchants can display some qualitative information that contributes to building the singularity of wine offers and which has a positive effect on prices. This complementary information includes the origin of the wine ('*ex-château*' for example, if it comes directly from the producer without navigating through international markets), the nature of the storage, and the quantity offered, apart from the reputational information relative to the wine offered (Parker's grades, etc.). A merchant takes into account these different parameters when he or she has to make a decision about buying. The observation of prices and transaction volumes is today increasing with the use of the internet and computerized databases. The CEO of one of the biggest wine merchants in England (buying and reselling on several markets) explained how the techniques of publicization of prices have recently transformed the market. According to 'Johnny' (a pseudonym), the new information technologies have had two main consequences for his activity regarding wine exchanges: they have contributed to reducing the gap between the merchants' offers, and they have created a generalized observation arena in which everyone constantly watches everyone else so as to know the prices offered by the competitors. During our face-to-face interview in his office, Johnny showed me his computer screen on which were displayed the different offers of a specific wine (in a specific vintage) displayed in England. This list was displayed on www.winesearcher.com, a website allowing the user to check the state of offers (name of the wine, vintage, location of the seller, currency, etc.) in different marketplaces. Among the offers displayed on the screen, Johnny noticed a batch from his own company and said:

> You see, we have to permanently watch competitors' prices … Here, for example, prices are around £20,000 the case of 12, with more or less expensive wines depending on their origins. This £19,000 offer is the least expensive one because it concerns wine labels for the American market. In relation to that price, we have to be around £20,000 the case.

Merchants do not only observe each other by watching their competitors to check if they change their prices; they are also likely to set up prices just lower than the competitors they consider as relevant points of reference. Hence Johnny tells me how one of his competitors keeps on setting up prices at a slightly lower level than his own offers:

> One day, I offer a wine online and during the day the company X changes its price by setting it up at £3 less than my own price. Then I decide to change my price by decreasing it [by] £2 and by saying to my collaborators, you'll see next morning it will be £2 less … bingo, the day after it was at £2 less.

This narration refers to a form of competition on pricing strategy, limited by at least two kinds of mechanisms.

First, merchants select the actions of their competitor by analysing different criteria, and decide to react (or not) to certain actions according to these criteria. The principal selection criteria are the perceived identity of the competitor and the position one chooses to adopt towards it. Johnny's company is obviously an economic actor whose perceived identity is strong according to its competitors, such that it represents a permanent point of reference for some competitors.

The second kind of mechanism limiting the competition on prices is a kind of non-price competition founded on the qualitative heterogeneity of the offers made by the different merchants, including for similar wines (same wine estate, same vintage). The offers differentiate themselves by the origin of bottles, which are sometimes displayed through mentions such as 'US strip labels' or 'ex-château'. These give different values to the different wines. The mention of 'ex-château' indicates that the batch comes from the estate, and that it has not suffered from damaging transportation or storage.

The effect of the product's career on its estimated value follows a somewhat simple economic law: the estimated value is inversely proportional to the number of transactions it endures, and it is proportional to the degree of proximity from the estate. Thus the label 'ex-château', which guarantees that the wine comes directly from the estate's cellar, allows the merchant to display a superior price than the indication 'US label', which indicates that the wine has made at least one return flight between Europe and the United States. The economic law linking the wine's value and the story of transactions relies on the collective belief pertaining to the effects of transportation on the wine's organoleptic qualities. While in certain historical periods transport – especially maritime transport – was considered as a source of improving the quality of the product, today it is viewed as one of the main sources of alteration of the product. Hence, one of the recent innovations within the premium wine industry is the organization of traceability in the wine supply chain, by introducing electronic devices that collect data about temperature and humidity. Such technology systems allow producers to control the conditions under which their wines are transported.

Globalization in the productive arena: Flying winemakers and their signature

More often than not, producers' attachment to their wine takes the shape of a visceral link. This link became a threatened paternity when the exogenous figure of the wine consultant recently came into the foreground (Chauvin 2010b). The signature of wines by external 'winemakers' is a recent phenomenon in French vineyards, which has developed since the 1980s and 1990s in the New World countries (Lagendijk 2004; Williams 1995). If they are, in their role as production consultants, insiders of the *wine world*, their public and media visibility make them important characters of the *wine field*, and even sometimes of the *wine culture* too. This is a potential source of friction, especially in the Bordeaux region, where the division of labour was traditionally organized *within* the winery, and where the name of the growth used to override the name of the individuals who made the wine.

There are some elective affinities between the development of consultancy activities in the wine world and the capitalistic transformations of Bordeaux wine estates.

Many family-owned growths have been sold during the last thirty years. These transactions have had some effects on the organization and strategies of producers. New investors coming from banks, insurance and financial groups, as well as some successful entrepreneurs, sportspeople and top-level executives, came to acquire some wine estates without any deep knowledge of the sector and, above all, without skills in viticulture management. Hence they often hire consultants to improve the technical work and the external communication.

Before the appearance of such consultants, the only name that was put forward apart from the name of the wine or the estate, was the name of the owner, in order to celebrate the prestige and the continuity of the winemaking family. Nowadays the signature has become the target of a symbolic and economic struggle between the different actors involved in the wine world. The names of the producer, the consultant and even sometimes the name of a famous 'sommelier' recommending the wine, can be displayed on wine labels, but this sort of public signal does not concern the most prestigious wines. The ranked growths, whose status has long been closely linked to the institutions and professional structures of the Bordeaux wine world, do not need such explicit external reputation sponsors. It does not mean that flying winemakers do not intervene in such wine estates, but the communication is much more discreet about their actions, and more often than not their signature is not mentioned in public. In this case, it is more a question of technical improvement of the winemaking than of being a communication tool.

One may consider flying winemakers as 'entrepreneurs of reputation' (Fine 1996) for middle-range wine estates: they enhance the reputation of the growth by associating their name with the product. The winemaker's 'signature' represents a rising source of reputation for wines and growths. However, instead of putting into question the role of 'terroir' and official rankings in the building of prestige, the professional reputation of winemakers themselves is closely linked to the status of the château they work for. The consultant's signature, while a source of reputation that can be transferred to producer organizations, is an asset that consultants have difficulty assuming, because of the importance of the soil and vintage in the making of reputations in the wine industry.

There are a few spectacular cases of some winemakers who entered the wine market without any symbolic or economic capital and who succeeded in becoming a term of reference for the wine community, both through their products and their own names. These successful entrepreneurs combine different kinds of reputation sources, from the most traditional to the most innovative ones, and are not pure revolutionary actors trying to undermine the old hierarchies and traditions. They systematically aspire to have among their wine estates a 'portfolio' of some ranked growths, both for economic and symbolic reasons. Economically speaking, apart from the obvious financial issue (how much can the organization pay for their services?), there is a potential chain of interdependencies that this type of contract can facilitate: managers from other lower-status wine estates can interpret this kind of high-status connection as a good signal for choosing one consultant instead of another. The constant observation that we described concerning the pricing strategy is also relevant for productive decisions. Once a consultant is well implanted within the premium wine community, there is a kind of cumulative attention and demand towards his services. One may notice the sexual and age division of labour in this activity: famous consultants are mostly men, whereas women and young consultants often work backstage, allowing the 'signature' of the senior consultant to be displayed on the frontstage.

Stephane Derenoncourt is one of those famous flying winemakers, and the narration of his biographical story can help understand the way that the 'globalization of signature' has been a key element of Bordeaux's transformations in recent years. Derenoncourt does not come from the establishment of the Bordeaux wine region. He grew up in the North of France in a working-class family, and discovered the wine industry while harvesting wine grapes in Bordeaux during the 1980s. This seasonal job was followed by a short education in viticulture and by a first job as a worker in a small vineyard near Saint-Emilion. His local reputation was at this time ambivalent: his lifestyle was quite different from both the local bourgeoisie *and* the working class. His long hair, associated with smoking pot, led people to see him as the local 'beatnik'. But his first viticultural experiences turned out to be good and were noticed by some local producers. That is how Derenoncourt was recruited by the owner of Château Pavie-Macquin, a famous growth from Saint-Emilion, when the cellar master left the property. He stayed six years in this wine estate, and his work started to draw the attention of other local producers, as well as critics.

One of them, Stephan von Neipperg, Count of the Holy Roman Empire, used to give him a lift while driving his 4x4 to the nearby town of Libourne. He asked Derenoncourt to manage one of his finest estates, Château Canon-Lagafellière, and created a 'micro-cuvée' called La Mondotte. This wine got huge media attention, not only because of its impressive organoleptic characteristics but also thanks to the singular story of its birth (involving an interdiction by local authorities). Despite (or thanks to) the very low-volume production, the visibility gained by the wine rapidly became high, especially after the good ratings given by Robert Parker. This spectacular and quick success was a new tipping point in Derenoncourt's career. Many local and foreign producers started to ask him to work for their estates. His employer, the Count von Neipperg, advised him to start a consulting career.

This is how Derenoncourt has become one of the leading characters of the global flying winemaker scene, being hired by estates in the Middle East, Spain, Italy, the United States and other places. The fact that he has kept on doing his local activity, both as a consultant and as a producer (he bought a small vineyard in the Côtes de Castillon region and created a wine called 'Domaine de l'A'), while intervening worldwide in many different vineyards, helps us understand how the Bordeaux production scene has been globalized in novel ways in recent years. What some call the 'globalization of taste' is closely linked to the actions of such actors, as they act with the same technical style in different regions of the globe. However, consultants often underline the way they take into account the specific properties of local *terroirs*, and the specific demands of local owners, before choosing the right way to make wine.

This is another illustration of the way objective 'terroir' and winemaking styles are combined into a kind of cultural hybridization. Moreover, these cases show that wine professionals are ever more likely to import and export technical tools and skills, while their own careers are increasingly linked to multiple affiliations and territories. For these reasons, the wine industry can be seen as a social laboratory for observing the ways techniques, careers and cultures are increasingly globalized.

Conclusion

Raising the question of globalization as it pertains to the Bordeaux wine world necessitates avoiding three widespread ideas. First, globalization is not a radically new dynamic concerning an old and eternally preserved market. It has developed for centuries through the dynamics of classifications, evaluations, prices and signatures. Second, globalization is not an external force affecting a 'local' economy bounded to its territory. It has been a system of interactions and interdependencies between many economic actors, whose activities have involved multi-territorial approaches and strategies. Third, globalization is neither a threat nor an opportunity for the Bordeaux wine world; it is instead a *dimension* of Bordeaux wine identity which relies on the 'reputation system' that organizes the allocation of reputation and status in this community. Recent phenomena in the production scene, such as the development of 'winemakers' signatures', not only tend to make the 'old' reputation system (based on *terroirs* and rankings) more complex. They also are a potential source of a certain kind of qualitative globalization, namely the globalization of taste occurring through production techniques and decision-making criteria. But this sort of globalization cannot be seen as mere homogenization and simplification, as consultants generally try to highlight local identities while developing their own styles. How do widespread personal styles ('griffes') and more or less well-known local identities create hybrid singularities? This is an empirical question that further research may answer.

Notes

1. This chapter is based upon 100 interviews with wine professionals (local actors such as producers, 'courtiers' and négociants, as well as international merchants such as big English importers), and short periods of observation at various professional places (including trading rooms of local courtiers, London merchants' offices, Bordeaux cellars and vineyards during the harvest, etc.).
2. http://www.nytimes.com/1989/08/20/magazine/wine-the-battle-of-1855.html
3. It would be quite easy to give many quotes of this type. For example, 'virtually preserved in amber, the classification, at 150 this year, embodies France's love affair with rigid systems that perpetuate its notions of culinary – indeed cultural – superiority. Think Appellation Contrôlée. Think Michelin restaurant ratings. Think Académie Française, which has guarded the purity of the French language against invasive barbarisms – virtually any foreign words – since 1635.' ('Dusting off the 1855 debate', Howard G. Goldberg, http://www.thewinenews.com/)

References

Chauvin, P.-M. (2010a), *Le marché des réputations. Une sociologie du monde des vins de Bordeaux*, Bordeaux: Editions Féret.

Chauvin, P.-M. (2010b), 'La signature oenologique. Frontières et transferts de réputation sur le marché des consultants bordelais', *Sociologie du Travail*, 52(4):461–79.

Chauvin P.-M. (2011a), 'Architecture des prix et morphologie sociale du marché. Le cas des Grands crus de Bordeaux', *Revue française de sociologie*, 52(2):277–309.

Chauvin, P.-M. (2011b), 'Extension du domaine de la note. Robert Parker comme saillance du marché des Grands Crus de Bordeaux', in François, P. (eds), *Vie et mort des institutions marchandes*, Paris: Presses de Sciences Po, 79–107.

Douglas, M. (1986), *How Institutions Think*, New York: Syracuse University Press.

Fine, G. (1996), 'Reputational Entrepreneurs and the Memory of Incompetence: Melting Supporters, Partisan Warriors, and Images of President Harding', *American Journal of Sociology*, 101(5):1159–93.

Garcia-Parpet, M.-F. (2009), *Le marché de l'excellence. Les Grands Crus à l'épreuve de la mondialisation*, Paris: Seuil.

Ginestet, B. (1996), *Thomas Jefferson à Bordeaux*, Bordeaux: Mollat.

Hadj, A.H., Lecocq, S., and Visser, M. (2008), 'The Impact of Gurus: Parker Grades and "En Primeur" Wine Prices', *Economic Journal, Royal Economic Society*, 118(529):158–73.

Hay, C. (2007), 'Globalisation and the Institutional Re-embedding of Markets: The Political Economy of Price-formation in the Bordeaux *En Primeur* Market', *New Political Economy*, 12(2):185–210.

Lagendijk, A. (2004), '"Global Lifeworlds" versus "Local Systemworlds": How Flying Winemakers Produce Global Wines in Interconnected Locals', *Tijdschrift voor Economische en Sociale Geografie*, 95(5):511–26.

Markham, D. (1997), *1855. Histoire d'un classement des vins de Bordeaux*, Bordeaux: Féret.

McCoy, E. (2005), *The Emperor of Wine*, New York: Ecco/Harper Collins.

Podolny, J. (2005), *Status Signals. A Sociological Study of Market Competition*, Princeton: Princeton University Press.

Sauder, M. (2006), 'Third Parties and Status Position: How the Characteristics of Status Systems Matter', *Theory and Society*, 35(3):299–321.

Smith, A. (2008), 'Globalization within the European Wine Industry: Commercial Challenges But Producer Domination', in Jullien, B., and Smith, A. (eds), *Industries and Globalization: The Political Causality of Difference*, London: Palgrave, 65–91.

Smith Maguire, J., and Lim, M. (2014), 'Lafite in China. Media Representations of "Wine Culture" in New Markets', *Journal of Macromarketing*, 35(2):229–42.

White, H. (1981), 'Where Do Markets Come from?', *American Journal of Sociology*, 87(3):517–47.

Williams, A. (1995), *Flying Winemakers: The New World of Wine*, Adelaide: Winetitles.

Zhao, W. (2005), 'Understanding Classifications: Empirical Evidence from the American and French Wine Industries', *Poetics*, 33(3–4):179–200.

7 Fluid Modernity: Wine in China

BJÖRN KJELLGREN

Introduction

The rapid development of the wine scene in China during the last few decades, intimately linked both to domestic changes and globalizing processes, has sent ripples across the wine world. The numbers are staggering. From negligible production, consumption and international trade at the beginning of the reform period thirty-five years ago, China is today the world's largest growth market for wine. It was in 2015 the world's largest producer of grapes, the fourth biggest consumer of wine, the fifth biggest importer of wine in terms of volume, and the fourth biggest importer in terms of value, with imports worth slightly more than 2 billion USD. The anti-corruption campaign and austerity policy initiated by China's president Xi Jinping in 2013 may have put an end to demand for top-quality Bordeaux wine for public consumption, but this has been more or less balanced by a steady demand for more moderately priced labels, and as long as wine drinking is officially endorsed, the long-term prospects for wine in China look bright.[1]

As in the rest of the world, globalization in the Chinese context refers to an intensified transnational circulation of capital, goods, images, ideas and people, and wine is certainly part of this process. Looking at food, which of course has its own parameters, one can well argue that the process of 'globalization' has been with us since time immemorial – the spread of the Eurasian grape throughout the world is but one example. However, it is not only the content, speed and bulk of these flows – made possible by technical innovations, as much as by the worldwide capitalist system itself – which justifies us calling today's situation a genuinely new epoch. The ideational baggage that travels together with the material products is also of a new kind. Although as a rule always linked to the new and foreign, never before have these food flows been so explicitly associated with the ideas of the global and the modern, thus to an unprecedented degree nurturing also the cognate ideas of the local and the traditional.

In China, a Sino-Western dichotomy has been the pivot of ideological debates and political programmes pertaining to modernity since the second half of the nineteenth century, while the contemporary process of food globalization – as opposed to the Columbian Exchange, which altered the profile of Chinese agriculture and cuisine much earlier – has coincided with the political programme of 'openings and reforms' decided upon in 1978. This has made wine and other 'new' culinary articles – including also previously only locally available Chinese foodstuffs – intimately associated with China's post-Maoist modernizations and re-emergence as a major world power. Chronologically, spatially and socially, this new abundance of raw and cooked alternatives, this *modernité mangée*, has also followed the reform programme, making its presence felt first in the urban eastern parts of China, and there first among those who earliest managed to heed the battle cry of the reformers – 'to get rich is glorious'.[2]

In the standard narrative of China's modern history, the country's international humiliation in the late nineteenth century at the hands of British and Japanese colonizers forced it into a violent process of modernization that came complete with the unambiguous denial of domestic traditions. This sudden rupture seemed to reverberate to all corners of society, from the abolishment of the dynastic tradition and the introduction of modern European-modelled education and language policies, down to the substitution of traditional garments and buildings for Western-style ones (e.g. Spence 1999).

Modernization of the agricultural sector was not surprisingly one of the major focal points for the nation, and following the establishment of the People's Republic in 1949, the forms and methods of food production have continued to be an area of dispute and disaster (Becker 1996). Interestingly, while modern nutritional regimes were a topic for the national ethnic minorities, there was, however, little effort put into changing or 'modernizing' the culinary practice of the Han majority (Anderson 1988; Chang 1977). Even as language – together with food the primary icon of ethnic and sub-ethnic identity in China – was moulded into a national form and popularized, food could continue to fill a function as a link to China's pre-modern past, without getting stigmatized, criticized or simply abandoned the way numerous other vehicles of tradition had been (Xu Jieshu 1997).

Indeed, it was only with the advent of the market economy, and the cultural imagery that came in the wake of China's opening to the West that the culinary patterns of China started to merge with those of the industrialized West, in terms of food balance sheets as well as on the levels of dinner patterns and recipes. This, however, is a process that has not gone unnoticed or without criticism. On the contrary, the national pride taken in the domestic food culture, and the potential to turn this tradition into something both patriotic and profitable, has sent advocates of China's traditional cuisine to the barricades. Wine, however, with its claim to a double lineage – both ancient Chinese, and new and foreign – seems to be the perfect drink to accompany the emergence of a distinctly Chinese modernity that, in its apparent willingness to embrace the new and foreign, supersedes the hitherto predominant Sino-Western dichotomy (Yan 2002).

The development of the Chinese wine scene corresponds to numerous others, globally and locally, ranging from Foreign Direct Investment (FDI) flows, agricultural policies and trade disputes, to labour conditions, nutritional indicators and culinary creativity. The reasons why the present development in China influences the dreamscape of growers, brokers, merchants and other stakeholders in the international wine industry, as well as corresponding stakeholders in China, may then seem obvious.

However, in as much as wine in China is 'the stuff dreams are made of', there seems to be some rather clear-cut differences between dreams made by, on the one hand, producers and traders of wine outside of China, and, on the other hand, politicians and consumers in China. Outside China, dreams of wine, and of the new and rapidly increasing Chinese thirst for it, fall basically into one of two categories, both century old: the dream of the wealth potentially to be made off the gigantic Chinese market, and the ghastly dream that the Chinese themselves could take over the market, and not only that market but other markets and existing power structures as well; a 'yellow peril redux', as it were.[3] In China, the dreams, although they have equally real economic consequences, are arguably more political than economic in nature. On the individual level, drinking wine may be the dream of living – and displaying – the 'moderately prosperous' (*xiaokang*) life that the reform policy initiated in the late 1970s promised, but in the grand order of things, the proliferation of grape wine is part of the even older dream of a Chinese renaissance, a return to an 'old' world order with China as a major global power. To the Chinese leaders, the realization of what is indeed also officially labelled the 'Chinese Dream' is crucial, for in the balance is nothing less than the legitimacy of the Communist Party to rule China.

In this chapter, wine will be seen as a manifest but highly symbolic harbinger of this New World order – the fluid fulfilment of the Chinese Dream, to speak in the terms of the present Chinese regime. To understand this dream better, we will look into the different ways to remember China's wine history and the country's part in the age-old story of the globalization of the drink.

Wine and legitimacy

To appreciate the role of the Chinese wine industry of today, it is crucial to understand the ideological significance of the present market economy, which may well be more important than its economic significance, although the two, as we shall see, are closely related. This appears clearly if we apply Weber's (1914) power legitimacy typology to the last century of Chinese history – excusing the fact that this analysis of necessity also simplifies a complex and less linear reality. The dynastic institution, a traditional source of authority using the flexible principle of the Heavenly Mandate to keep revolutions and invasions within a given protocol of power, while claiming universal legitimacy for 'all under Heaven', had – following a series of humiliating wars between 1839 and 1900 – become untenable. It was replaced in 1912 by Sun Yat-sen's modern and legalistic republic, based on the American constitution. On paper, that is, since the first half of the last century saw little of power based on authority, with Nationalists, Communists, Chinese warlords and Japanese invaders all scrambling for power. Like the Nationalists, the Communists had as their foremost goal the reconstruction and re-establishment of China's lost glory, in the form of a united country with unyielding borders and a sense of community. To what extent it was necessary to get rid of the traditional Confucian ideology and embrace complete Westernization, *quanpan xihua*, in order to accomplish national revival, had early on been a major topic of disagreement. Both Nationalists and Communists had rejected culturally conservative nativism, *benweizhuyi*, but the debate would continue to smoulder, living on in the postcolonial predicament that followed the decision to dispose of indigenous traditions. Victorious, and partly for this reason seen as the more reliable alternative even among dedicated non-Communists, the Communists proclaimed the People's Republic in 1949. Taiwan's and – until 1997 – Hong Kong's existence as entities outside of the regime's control has also greatly contributed towards upholding the actuality of the theme of 'unification of the Motherland' – as also have external examples, especially the falling apart of the Soviet Union.

The rational ground for the Communists was augmented by the marketed charisma of Mao Zedong himself, who, making use of his and the party's Leninist ideology of power, as well as the propaganda culture of the Soviet Union, further strengthened this kind of charismatic legitimacy. Mao's charisma also shed welcome lustre over the Party and its government. Thus, even after the disastrous Great Leap campaign in 1958–59, and the chairman's de facto retreat to the so-called second line of control, the Party continued to boost its legitimacy with his ever more inflated charisma. Nonetheless, the Cultural Revolution in 1966–76, when Mao used his personalized power to crush his opponents within the Party, thereby throwing the country into chaos, eventually shattered popular belief in Mao, the regime and its ideology. With the death of Mao Zedong in 1976, legitimacy of the charismatic type became something of the recent but irrevocable past, and attention passed from ideological orthodoxy to economic pragmatism. The Party now depicted itself as the stabilizing force rescuing the country from the extremist political force the Party itself had incarnated – while still claiming credit for saving China during the wars of the 1930s and 1940s. The relative success of this operation can partly be said to be the side-effect of the regime's legitimacy having been so tightly tied to persons: the blame for mistakes and outrages could then be directed at certain individuals, thus leaving the system relatively unquestioned. But it was also done – as before and as today – by maintaining a firm grip over mass media and the activities of the general public. The crucial component of this repositioning was the substitution of the worn-out charismatic legitimacy by the rational kind. However, without a democratic election system to channel resentment that might arise, economic growth has become the sine qua non for the Party state's existence, and it is logical that the two major national crises for the government since the onset of the reforms – the popular support for the student movement in 1989, and the appeal of Falungong in the late 1990s – both were related to economic quandaries.

The modernization process also brought new attention to an old quandary, with many fearing a definite loss of cultural distinctiveness in the wake of the country's opening up. The debates on the future of Chinese culture and society during the 1980s and early 1990s in many ways echoed the debate of the May Fourth Movement in the early 1920s, and, as in the early twentieth century, the government seemed to opt for Westernization in nationalistic disguise. Nevertheless, the debate, and especially the calls for indigenization, clearly showed how sensitive the question of national identity became in these times of rapid change.

The link between a strong market economy and the advent of democracy has long been something of an axiom in liberal quarters, and when one contrasts the ideological hegemony and utterly politicized everyday life of the 1960s and 1970s with the de facto individual freedom of today's China, the argument seems intuitively well founded (Kjellgren 2003). However, this freedom is only valid for those who follow the logic of the Party state, and the possibility for exercising that freedom correlates directly to economic resources. For political dissidents and the economically disenfranchised, the seemingly won freedom appears considerably less. Failing to see how the market reforms in fact have strengthened the regime's position rather than weakened it, has made many, like Goldman and MacFarquhar (1999: 16), see 'an expanding, dynamic economy' as 'undermin[ing] the authority of the political leaders who made it possible'. Looking at the present situation, however, a dichotomy between Party state and market is not so conveniently detected. Not only is the open market economy the brainchild and construction of the Party state, it is also as strictly as possible controlled for unintended consequences and unsolicited influences. Although this may not be as unique to China as he tacitly implies, Yan (2002) has appropriately called the situation a 'managed globalization', and we can take the wine industry as a case in point. The Party state has not only laid down the goals and rules for production, distribution and politically correct advertisement, but also, through the China National Cereals, Oils and Foodstuffs Import and Export Corporation established in 1983, somewhat rigged the game. The company is responsible for the import and export of wine, while simultaneously managing the Great Wall, one of the top domestic wine brands and the biggest exporter. The wine industry is furthermore a highly welcomed aid in the recent efforts to level some of the economic gap between the affluent eastern provinces and China's underdeveloped western inland. China's old wineries are all situated in the north-eastern part of the country, but with preferential policies, promises of cheap labour and low taxes, labour-intensive wineries are now established in Xinjiang and Yunnan, giving evidence to the fact that politics are as important as climate in this business. Or perhaps it is more correct to say that politics *is* business. China's late president, Jiang Zemin, himself went so far in stressing the preponderance of economic development as to almost redefine the very word 'politics' as 'economic growth' (Jiang 1996). Nevertheless, it seemed almost a parody when Suntime – then a black horse on the winery scene, founded in 1998, with one of the world's largest vineyards, planted in the desert of Xinjiang – in 2002 declared that it would strive for 'Four Represents', thereby outnumbering Jiang Zemin's own so-called theoretical contribution to Chinese socialism, the 'Three Represents' of the Communist Party (Liu 2002). The fact that since 2009 Suntime has been a brand owned by Citic Guo'an Investment Group (Zhongxin Guoan) – a state-controlled company started in 1979 by Rong Yiren, 'the red capitalist', as a means to facilitate Deng Xiaoping's politico-economic agenda – perhaps hints at the non-joking nature of this declaration.

While the industry's think tank had outlined a shift in the nation's drinking habits towards fruit wine already in 1987, the public official blessing came in 1996, when then Premier Li Peng during Spring Festival celebrations went public with the same message. There should be no doubt that it is the Party state rather than the industry or the consumers that has decided China become a wine-drinking nation. The state, 'under the leadership of the Communist Party of China and the guidance of Marxism-Leninism, Mao Zedong Thought and Deng Xiaoping Theory and the important thought of Three Represents', as the Constitution (2004) puts it, 'guides, supervises and administers individual and private economies'.

Three trajectories of Chinese wine

There is nothing uniquely different about the ideological significance of wine in contemporary China. On the contrary, it is typicality that makes wine useful as an example of how also seemingly innocent parts of a country's culinary repertoire may be imbued with meanings only noticeable in the light of a broader historical and political analysis. However, as for example Wang Renxiang (1993) reminds us, China is also a country where alcoholic beverages have long been at the very heart of the food system, which is arguably in itself the single strongest source of cultural identity. For this reason, the importance of wine, with its ostensibly foreign character, cannot be measured in terms of money or volume alone. Most public associations that wine comes with today can be found by recalling Chinese wine history, three periods of which the country can be said to possess. The first winds its roots back thousands of years, the second starts in 1892, and the third traces its beginning no further back than to the Third Plenum of the Chinese Communist Party's 11th Central Committee meeting in December 1978, taking us back again to contemporary politics. As is usually the case with history telling, the seemingly old is always an interpretation made in and for the present, thus arguably revealing the present more than the past. With this in mind, let us start looking for wine in Chinese antiquity.[4]

Locating the indigenous roots

Today, China follows the rest of the world in relying almost exclusively on varieties of the Eurasian grape species, *Vitis vinifera*, for its wine production, and it is usually understood (e.g. McGovern et al 2004) that the ancient Chinese, like the peoples of North America, made no significant use of the many local wild grapes available to them, at least not before they had already mastered vine cultivation and wine-making techniques as those were imported from Central Asia in the seventh century CE (Schafer 1977: 121–2). This Chinese winelessness is, however, increasingly being questioned in Chinese narratives. Wu Hongguang (2001: 264–307), a mainland authority on domestic drink and food technology, argues that grapes from wild domestic species such as *V. thunbergii*, *V. flexuosa* and *V. amurensis* must reasonably have been used to produce wine in China well before the time when evidence of this is found in any written sources, that is, long before the Zhou dynasty (circa 1100–256 BCE) during which indigenous vines are mentioned as being cultivated in royal gardens.[5] In internal presentation material, China's oldest and most prestigious winery, Changyu (2010), boldly declares that there is 'universal recognition' of China having a wine history of 9000 years, and of being the place of origin of both grapes and grape wine. Leaving the 'universal recognition' aside, an ancient history is perhaps not too unlikely a claim: as an Anglophone authority on Chinese fermentation technology, Huang Hsing-Tsung (2000: 153), puts it, the 'making of wine from grapes [...] needs no inventiveness. It is, in fact, practically unavoidable'. Huang, however, assumes that grape wine in China – at least before the Tang dynasty – was produced with the same indigenous *qu* (ferment cake) technique that was used for making grain wine, something which 'could have done considerable violence to the taste of the final product', and in itself may have been a reason for grape wine's relative unpopularity in ancient China (Huang 2000: 243). While *qu* is rarely or never mentioned on Chinese websites dedicated to wine, the ancient domestic roots are usually mentioned as merely stating the basic facts.

Disregarding the question of *what* 'grape wine' was produced, and focusing more on archaeological evidence that substantiates the claim that grapes *were* early on used for winemaking, grape wine has now become one of the oldest and most authentically native of Chinese beverages. While scientists claim that grape wine was made in China at least three thousand years ago, more popular writers to be found on various Chinese wine sites usually posit that wine made from wild grapes was produced in China between six and seven thousand years ago.

Ungrounded in hard evidence as these claims still may be, they are well in line with the more general argument that China has not only 'one of the longest histories in the world', as the Preamble to the Chinese Constitution (2004) politely puts it, but *the* longest culinary history in the world. In what appears as one of the literature's greatest understatements, Li Tingzhi's culinary dictionary (2003: 3) states that 'Chinese cooking started relatively early'. It then goes on to date the advent of the national cuisine to about 550,000 years ago and the use of fire by the Peking Man. Other culinary authorities (e.g. Nie 1999: 12; Xiong and Tang 1998: 267) give the same starting point, while some food historians (e.g. Tao 1983: 1) even refer back to the misty time before fire, making the claims about domestic wine's ancient roots seem highly modest. The search for native roots for what is today by most Chinese perceived as quintessentially Western and non-Chinese, follows a beaten track summed up in the phrase *gu yi you zhi*, 'it was there [in China] already in antiquity'.

Since many things and institutions in China *do* come with a long and relatively well-known pedigree (e.g. fermented beverages – McGovern et al 2004), it seems sensible to pursue the suggestion of Chinese anthropology's *doyen*, Fei Xiaotong (2000), who in 2000 declared that all modern phenomena have local roots ready to be discovered. In China this sentiment for time, which historically has taken the form of a nostalgic longing for a Golden Age, is limited neither to the Communist regime nor to the present age. But, using history as a spell with which to bind the monster of modernity, whether this comes in the shape of crime, loose morals, demands for democracy, or the vain striving for other alien things, is of course more needed in times of rapid change and massive global influences. Wine may seem a trivial example when put next to democracy and human rights, but it is the same labelling mechanism of work. To the defenders of Chineseness, unwanted ideas and practices are never native to the Chinese tradition – even when they, like the America-inspired Republican constitution, at some point in time have been the theoretical pillars of the nation. On the other hand, their search for native roots to things liked and endorsed always ends either in success or in truly domestic hybrids, such as the presently enacted 'socialism with Chinese characteristics'.

Going back to the historical documents, we find, as stated, vine cultivation hinted at in Zhou dynasty records like the *Book of Songs* (*Shijing*) and the *Book of Rites* (*Liji*). But the first documented contact with Eurasian vines, and Western wine technology, is found in Sima Qian's first-century BCE history book, *Shiji*. Sima's annals tell us how Han dynasty emperor Wu's envoy from 138 to 119 BCE to the countries beyond the newly colonized western regions (i.e. from what is now Xinjiang province in China to the Fergana valley in today's Uzbekistan), General Zhang Qian, saw 'grapes that were used to make wine. The wealthy could have well over 10,000 *shi* – roughly 200,000 litres – of wine in store, and the oldest was kept several decades without getting spoilt' (Sima, 1965, *Shiji*, Dayuan liezhuan). Obviously impressed, Zhang Qian took with him both vines and oenological expertise to the Han court, and soon Chinese vineyards sporting Eurasian grapes were established at the heart of the Han Empire, producing grapes that were turned into wine for the emperor. This episode establishes some basic associations still upheld now. Wine is imported luxury, from the West, for the elite to drink, but soon also produced in China. The image of Xinjiang as China's traditional wine region is of course not forgotten by those who grow grapes there now. The already mentioned Suntime, and its sister brand Xi Yu – Western Regions – have several wine labels portraying pre-Islamic Central Asian noblemen, several with the brand name written in mock Arabic style. Dragon Seal has a wine featuring a camel caravan moving through soft sand dunes, evoking all the romanticism of the Silk Road. With Xinjiang's Uighurs, whose 'autonomous region' Xinjiang officially is, being Muslims for centuries, while the Han Chinese owners of Suntime and Dragon Seal have their head-offices in metropolitan Shanghai and Beijing respectively, as far away from the desert as they possibly can be, one cannot but recall something of Barthes' (1957) critique of French wine interests in Algeria.[6] With fundamentalist separatists in Xinjiang being the Chinese regime's own internal terrorists against which to wage war, east-coast companies planting vine in the desert are naturally highly welcome and also, as already stated, a way of substantiating the official long-standing policy of 'developing the west'.

Returning to history, the western regions were lost during the short-lived reign of Wang Mang (9–23 CE), but were recaptured during the following Eastern Han dynasty. However, wine remained a rare treat in the central parts of the country, and in a recorded case (*Sanguozhi*) a certain Meng Ta managed to secure a high office by bestowing a *hu* of grape wine – approximately 20 litres – on the right person. This episode is candidly referred to by Li Hua (2002: 148) as 'the first time an office was bought with wine', and one is reminded of the contemporary practice to lubricate officials with expensive drinks, imported cognac being the favourite (a practice which, however, is becoming increasingly uncommon, replaced as it is by the more substantial 'gift' of money). When the Eastern Han dynasty collapsed in 184 CE, China was once again cut off from the wine-producing western regions, and cultivation seems to have ceased in the war-ridden central parts of the divided country. Wine here becomes a natural sign of China's strength and flourishing trade with the outside world, its absence a sign of domestic crisis and regression. However, written sources inform us that wine and vines were reintroduced a number of times. When the Tang dynasty was established in 626 CE, grape wine was uncommon, although sometimes sent as a tribute to the capital. Providentially, the new dynasty soon turned its economic, military and cultural interests westwards. Within a short time, stocks with Horse Nipple grapes were brought from the state of Qocho (present day Turfan in Xinjiang, conquered in 640 CE) and replanted. Their fruits were made into wine for the Taizong emperor. Gradually the use of grape wine spread to other groups, and officially immortal poets such as Bai Juyi and Li Bai sang the drink's praise, while new wine houses opened in Chang'an, the capital. Tang poetry is among the finest ever produced in China and – free from copyright restrictions as it is – frequently used in advertisement. Dragon Seal even has a whole series of wines named 'the luminous jade cup' (Yeguangbei), after a line in a famous wine poem by Wang Han. Many of China's websites dedicated to wine today have photos of Western wine experts out among the vines, very akin to the depictions of central Asians in the Tang capital. A metropolitan China was attracting international talents then as it is today. Despite the presence of these international experts, grape wine, however, continued to play a minor role on the drinking scene as a whole. The seasonality of the grapes and the easily disturbed winemaking process mean that grape wine could never compete with 'wine' (*jiu*) made of rice and/or other grains and fermented with special ferment cakes, *qu*, the process typical for Chinese grain wine. The impact of this practice is evident in Zhu Gong's wine manual from the Northern Song dynasty (1117 CE), where grapes are peeled and rid of their pips (thus inhibiting natural fermentation), mixed with grain and then fermented with the help of added *qu* (Zhu 1999). With contemporary China's wine industry striving to meet international (i.e. OIV – International Organisation of Vine and Wine) standards, this last story is today held up mostly as a warning, but so-called half-grape wine, with only 50 per cent grape juice, was taken off store shelves only in June 2004, and the mixing of expensive imported wine and soft drinks was *comme il faut* in restaurants and bars only a few years ago.

Returning once more to history, the Mongols, traditionally intoxicating themselves with the help of koumiss – fermented horse milk – perhaps seem unlikely patrons of grape wine, but their conquests had by the late thirteenth century taken them through Central Asia all the way to the Persian Gulf and the Black Sea. When Genghis Khan's empire broke up following his death in 1227, the newly acquired taste for grape wine had spread among his followers. During the Yuan dynasty (1271–1368) – the

Chinese khanate, as it were – grape wine, according to the *Xin Yuanshi* (Ke 1920), was offered to the imperial forefathers alongside the traditional milk wine. Marco Polo (Polo, 1903, Book II, XXXVII), as well as Chinese contemporary sources, tells us that there were wine-producing vineyards around Taiyuan in present day Shanxi province and elsewhere, even as the majority of the population preferred other beverages. On common grain wine and its newly popularized distilled versions, a 25 per cent sales tax was levied, but grape wine 'that requires neither grain nor *qu*' and its distilled versions were only taxed between 3.3 and 6 per cent. Despite this preferential policy, grain wine kept its position as the number-one alcoholic beverage. This again was a history retold as it was repeated. Li Peng, the premier who in 1996 urged the people as well as the country's leaders to drink less grain-based spirits and more fruit wine, was also, so the story goes, concerned about the vast quantities of grains turned into alcohol. Moreover, four hundred years after the Yuan dynasty, alcohol-related illness was also an issue, as more and more citizens found themselves without public health care at a time when reports praising the health effects of red wine were everywhere to be read.[7] Consumption of about half a bottle a day, writes Li Hua (2002: 17), referring to an unnamed French study, would be a good way to avoid heart problems. If everyone heeded this call, it would mean an annual consumption increased about three hundred times. But, needless to say, those who cannot afford their hospital bills hardly have the means to support such a beneficial habit.

The recent past remembered

The first direct import of wine from Europe is likely to have occurred during the Ming dynasty (1368–1644), when Spanish and Portuguese traders found their way to South China. But by the end of the next and last imperial dynasty, when the Great Qing had been forcefully opened for foreign interests following the Opium War (1839–42), the needs of a growing number of expatriates and their churches had made the time ripe for modern, Western-style wineries in China. This, the second of the three wine history periods, begins in 1892, and the hero is a 'patriotic returned Overseas Chinese', Zhang Bishi. Born poor in Meizhou, Guangdong province, he had, like many around him, migrated to Southeast Asia, where he, unlike many around him, made a fortune. He returned in glory, fulfilling the dream of most sojourners abroad, and set up a number of industries in China. Zhang decided to set up a modern vineyard in Yantai, Shandong, having heard from a French army officer that men in his troop had recognized first-class *terroir* when on an expedition there. Thus, the first modern wine plant, Changyu, was established in China. In the process, Zhang Bishi introduced more than thirty grape varieties from Europe, such as Cabernet Sauvignon, Cabernet Franc, Merlot, Petit Verdot, Traminer, Italian Riesling, White Riesling and Sauvignon Blanc. Unaware of the danger, he also 'introduced' the phylloxera disease, but, with no existing vineyards to ruin, the damage was limited. His first wine was officially presented in 1914, three years after the abdication of the last Manchu emperor, and the following year Changyu's wine brought home China's first international recognition for wine, in the form of a gold medal from the International Pacific Panama Exhibition.[8]

During the Republican era, a small number of other wineries established themselves. Most of these, like Changyu, also produced brandy and other kinds of alcoholic beverages. They included La Shangyi Cave de Pékin (after nationalization, renamed the Beijing Winery in 1953), which was established in 1910 by the Catholic convent in Beijing to serve the needs of the Church and the foreign embassies, curiously by turning a graveyard into a wine cave; the Qingdao Winery, later renamed Melcher & Co., which was established by Germans in 1914; and the Tong Hua Winery, which was established in the by-then Japanese-occupied north-eastern province of Jilin in 1938. In fact, of the seven modern wineries established before the Communist takeover in 1949 and still operating today, only two were established and run by Chinese: Changyu in Yantai, and the less successful Qingxu Winery in Shanxi province.

This early foreign dominance is today remembered in a two-fold way. On the one hand, Changyu can brag – and does brag – about its pure-blood origins, and the fact that most wine today comes from Chinese companies is seen as a source of pride and as a sign of China's regained power of self-determination. There is a reason why statesmen from Sun Yat-sen to Jiang Zemin have visited Changyu and bestowed their calligraphy and praise on this particular winery. At the same time, however, wine is today very much sold on its association with the modern and sophisticated foreign, and so it becomes symbolically important that Changyu's founder Zhang Bishi got his revelation from a Frenchman. Dragon Seal, a brand that often on labels and in advertisements flirts with China's imperial past – in contrast to the smartly dressed young and beautiful urbanites that otherwise represent the industry's standard imagery – is the reorganized Beijing Winery, with its roots in the French friars' wine cellar, something which gives an air of authenticity to the company as strong as its modern French oenological expertise. Indeed, French roots can even be conjured by new-founded companies, like Yunnan Highland Wine, whose labels – otherwise decorated with exotically depicted minority women in a style typical for the province – claim that 'two hundred years ago, French missionaries discovered this unique highland for growing excellent wine grapes'. This text, incidentally, comes only in English, as do many label texts on most bottles. Bordeaux is still the image model for most wineries today, but English is the language of the international, and of the well-to-do Chinese of the twenty-first century.

It can be noted that a similar strategy of selective historical memory is also used by the much larger Chinese beer industry. Stress is on the one hand put on the fact that China since 2001 is the biggest producing country in the world, and the highest praise for a beer is being labelled as 'national banquet beer'. On the other hand, it is always 'right' to claim German roots. That the leading domestic brand, Tsingtao, was founded by Germans is never forgotten, while the Teutonic ancestry of the Qingdao Winery is seldom remembered, German wines not enjoying the same status as French wines. Given complex, at times outright hostile, feelings among Chinese consumers about Japan, the 1930s Japanese roots of the Tong Hua Winery are on the other hand hardly ever alluded to. Instead, the Tong Hua Winery's use of indigenous stocks and grapes from North East China's Changbai mountain range is the brand's unique selling proposition.

Going back in time again, some attempts were made in terms of upgrading the wine industry in the years following the Communist victory as part of the larger plan to rebuild the country. The 156 most important industry projects in the first five-year plan of 1954 included the establishment of a new winery outside Beijing, and vines were replanted in old vineyards from Xinjiang in the north-west to Jilin in the northeast, while ten new vineyards were established in Shanxi, Shaanxi, Henan, Hebei, Anhui and Jiangsu. New and old grape varieties were imported from Hungary, Bulgaria and the Soviet Union, while research was carried out to explore the potential of domestic grapes.[9] The disastrous Great Leap campaign in 1958, which together with the organization of rural China into People's Communes resulted in the greatest famine in China's known history, of course stopped the process, and the break with the Soviet Union in the early 1960s also meant the end to fraternal expertise coming from wine-producing countries loyal to the Soviet Union.

In the 1970s, new vineyards were set up in Xinjiang, Gansu, Ningxia, Hubei, Guangxi, Yunnan and Tianjin. The country's total wine production, which has been estimated to less than 100 tonnes in 1949, had in 1978 risen to around 15,000 tonnes, and around 100 wineries were spread across the country.

The ascent of a reformed industry

The latest chapter in the history of wine starts with the Third Plenum of the Chinese Communist Party's 11th Central Committee meeting in December 1978, when Deng Xiaoping's political programme, known as 'Reform and Opening', was chosen as China's and the Communist Party's salvation. The plans were to be kept at the macro-level, but on the micro-level the market system was to be implemented, private ownership encouraged, and overseas investments were once again welcomed in the Middle Kingdom.

The early 1980s saw the emergence of the triad of wineries that still dominates the market today, with a combined total of more than 50 per cent market share. These were Dynasty, a Sino-French joint-venture established in 1980 with what is today called Rémy-Cointreau on the French side of the enterprise; Great Wall, established in 1983 by the already mentioned China National Cereals, Oils and Foodstuffs Import and Export Corporation; and the pioneering Changyu, now Asia's largest wine company, of late in partnership with French company Castel for its wine production and marketing, and with huge ambitions already referred to. The early 1980s also saw the establishment of a simple but functional national wine standard, and work soon began to prepare shifts from sweet to dry wine, from white to red, and from parochial to international. In 1987, the National Work Meeting for Alcoholic Beverages, a planning body for the industry, scheduled four changes to come, of which the shift from distilled drinks to non-distilled, and the shift from grain-based drinks to fruit-based ones, constituted a vintner's dream. In 1988 a record output of over 308,000 tonnes of wine was recorded, but the market then fell following the brutal suppression of the student movement in 1989, to recover only in the late 1990s, paradoxically at the same time as the air went out of the wine craze in neighbouring Japan, Taiwan and Hong Kong following the so-called Asian financial crisis. China, which was much less affected by the upheaval, picked up the fallen mantle – and much unsold European wine in the region too. But China was not content with imported wine: within a few years, numerous new wineries were established, mostly with Chinese capital, but to a large degree working with imported machinery and expertise.

In the mid-1990s, China had about 250 wineries. This number has reportedly doubled by now, with wineries existing in about half of all provinces, regions and municipalities on the national level. However, most of these are local and far from all of them have their own vineyards. In 2002, 88 wineries produced more than 90 per cent of the national total, and the top six wineries – Changyu, Great Wall, Dynasty, Tong Hua, Fengshou and Grand Dragon – together produced more than half of the national total. Xinjiang is the country's largest wine district, but most wine is still produced in eastern China, especially in Shandong and Hebei. Dry and half-dry wine stands for more than half of the total production, and about 80 per cent of all wine produced is red, although this may be shifting in the future with more and more domestic online foodies arguing that white wine goes better with Chinese food. Branding has long been the main concern of the leading wineries, but this has recently been combined with efforts to promote *vin de terroir* within the frame of these brands. While wine is still very far from challenging the domestic dominance of distilled alcohol and beer, the industry has the highest profit margin in the drink sector, lobbies to get a national *Appellation Contrôlée* system approved by the state, and is in general predicted a profitable future.[10] Anticipating the normalization of this new drinking habit, wine advocates have already tried out exactly what wine goes with what Chinese dish and have started to spread their gospel. There are certainly problems: fake wine and sub-standard copy brands are often mentioned, and there is a lack of innovative research. But with prestigious and nationally leading distillers and breweries such as Moutai, Wuliangye and Tsingtao starting their own wine production, this is as good a sign as any of in which direction the wind is blowing.

On the 'international' side of the game, a number of foreign companies had already by the early 2000s established themselves as producers in China, among them Louis M. Martini, Louis Vuitton Moët Hennessy, Pernod Ricard, Rémy-Cointreau, Castel, Torres, and Scholle. Most of these established themselves in the form of joint ventures with big domestic companies, and perhaps not as much hoping for a quick return of interest as out of fear of missing the Chinese wine boat, once it was afloat. At the same time, smaller wine merchants dealing with expensive high-quality wine, especially French wine, seemed to be the ones with the best chance of striking it rich, although theirs often turned out to be a very rocky ride (Mustacich 2015). The lure of French wine has also made French vineyards a target for Chinese investments and takeovers, as a rule with the business idea of producing French wine exclusively for the Chinese market.

The official austerity policy, part and parcel of President Xi Jinping's anti-corruption campaign initiated in 2013, together with slower growth of the Chinese economy and turbulence on the Chinese stock market in 2015, led to dramatically diminished sales for high-end imported wine, and a rekindled focus on what was indeed always the main product, that is, domestically produced wine. Anderson and Nelgen (2011) estimated China's wine self-sufficiency already in 2009 to be 85 per cent. To be sure, this native product is one that comes complete with seemingly foreign traits, such as domestic châteaux tourism, vintage collections and 'nouveau' wine sales, as well as a high-end scene trying hard to combine what is seen as the best of both 'old' and 'new' wine to make up its own distinct brand.[11] But first and foremost, it is *Chinese* wine.[12]

Conclusion: A fluid modernity and its limits

For whom, then, is wine produced? Wine is a product that in China is strongly linked to the project of modernization. This project, as I have outlined, is carried out against the historical background of China's international humiliation in the late nineteenth century, and the introspective debate on the merits and perils of Chinese tradition that followed. But, while non-distilled rice wine, *huangjiu*, is trying its best to compete with grape wine by playing on feelings of continuity and tradition, grape wine strives to offer both tradition *and* modernity. By adopting foreign ideas and practices, turning them Chinese and branding the outcome international, the regime symbolically strives to put the period of a 'weak' China within brackets, equating the nation's glorious past with its glorious future, and identifying the national with the international, the latter representing what is basically a fantasy of the modern West, only no longer with Western world dominance. This is a modernity that in its apparent willingness to embrace the new and foreign supersedes the hitherto predominant Sino-Western dichotomy, while still adhering to century-old catchphrases such as 'make the old serve the present' and 'make the foreign serve the Chinese'.

The new culinary abundance of China signals the freedom from determination for the individual consumers who use their consumption to redefine what they are or strive to become. This freedom, however, is promised and negotiated by the market and distributed in direct proportion to wealth. Marx (1968 [1844]: 564–5) ironically wrote that what we are has little to do with personality and everything to do with purchasing power. Thus, rather than being what we eat, we are what we have the means to eat. A bottle of decent table wine today comes at what is for most citizens the prohibitive price of 60–80 Yuan (about 6–8 €) in the supermarket, much more than ordinary grain-based spirits of the same quality, and about twenty times the price of beer, testifying to the fact that this drunken modernity is not for everyone to enjoy. The common wine drinker in China is today, and will in the near future continue to be, a member of a socio-economic elite. These are likely to be young, urban, male professionals, aged twenty-five to forty, who can afford to enjoy wine, who can both benefit from and contribute to the positive social image of wine drinking, and who may even know enough about wine to tell if there is something seriously wrong with their drink.

However, one can also argue that wine is produced not only for those who actually drink it. As a sign of modernity, of the international, and of China joining ranks with the world through reclaiming its past glory, wine carries with it the promise of a brighter and healthier future also for the many who as yet cannot afford it, but upon whose efforts and continuing belief in the market the system relies. In the final analysis, the fulfilment of this liquid promise, a part of the 'Chinese Dream' that the present leadership has vouched to deliver no later than 2049, is one that the Chinese leaders may well have to realize, lest their own wine turn sour.

Notes

1. Estimates of Chinese wine production differ substantially, and official Chinese data have not been made public in a transparent way since 2009. As a rule, figures from international sources (WTO, OIV, FAO, Euromonitor, etc.) tend to be markedly higher than unofficial Chinese numbers attributed to domestic researchers. It should also be noted that roughly 90 per cent of the area under vine in China is producing table grapes, not wine.
2. Historically, there does not seem to exist any simple correlation between 'new food' and social class (e.g. Mintz 1985). In contemporary China, most of the new culinary diversity, be it Cantonese dim sum sold in Sichuan, McDonald's burgers in Beijing, French wine, or frozen dumplings, have been products catering first to the more affluent part of the local populations, although differentiations clearly exist also within this group. Given time, the process of normalization and the more widespread recognition of sociocultural distinctions will most probably land the poor with the low and the rich with the high. Signs of this are already to be seen in respect to, for example, McDonald's, although the price level even of these restaurants still makes them off limits to many (cf. Watson 1997).
3. See e.g. Mustacich (2015) for a partly sinophobic and decidedly Francocentric account of the relations between China and Bordeaux, and the documentary *Red Obsession*, written and directed by Roach and Ross (2013), also focusing on the relation between Bordeaux and a small but extremely wealthy Chinese elite. Compare also, for example, the 2013 Morgan Stanley report (Kierath and Wang 2013) warning of a global wine shortage (due to Chinese consumption), with a reoccurring concern for the global consequences of growing Chinese affluence and appetite (e.g. Brautigam 2015; Brown 1995).
4. A few Chinese sources divide the story of Chinese wine into four sections, with the addition of a special heading for the period between the founding of the PRC in 1949 and the advent of the reform policy of the 1980s. Even these sources with their adherence to official history-writing dividing lines do, however, treat the planned economy part of modern Chinese wine history with brevity.

5. Today, Left Mountain (Zuoshan) and Double Celebration (Shuangqing) are two indigenous 'mountain grapes' used to make sweet red wine in the northeastern province of Jilin, where *V. vinifera* cannot be used, unless grafted on the cold-resistant stocks of *V. amurensis* or *V. thunbergii*. Dragon Eye (Longyan) is another native grape, spread over the country and used to produce white wine (Zhu 1995). The last years have also seen minor plantations in South China using *V. davidii* and *V. heyneana*. Nonetheless, at least 80 per cent of today's Chinese wine is made with imported varieties.
6. Overton and Murray (2013) remind us that class formation when it comes to wine happens not only at the last stage, at the table with the symbolic consumption, but also very much at the production stage, through the relationships of investors, landowners and workers.
7. The health motive is most explicitly used by producers of so-called medical wine (yaojiu) and health wine (jiankangjiu). While it is beyond the scope of this chapter to go into the topic, it should be noted that the connection between food and health has a long and elaborate tradition in China.
8. Changyu's medal from 1915 is today seen as a symbol of early international recognition, but it has been observed that one rationale behind both the international fairs and national ranking systems that became popular in the late nineteenth and early twentieth century was to grant legitimacy to new kinds of food, establish new food hierarchies, and improve the public image of mass-produced products at a time when many of these were of sub-standard quality or even harmful. This rationale is very much alive in China, where an intricate system exists to label products in quality grades and to allow certain brands the right to special labels. As an example, in 2002, the Famous brand strategy committee of China granted Great Wall, Dynasty, Changyu, Tong Hua, Fengshou and Grand Dragon the title 'Famous national brands' in the wine category.
9. In the period 1892–1962, a total of 77 grape varieties were introduced to China from France, Germany, Austria, Switzerland, Bulgaria, Romania, the Soviet Union, the United States, Great Britain, Turkey, Iran, Hungary and Japan (Hong 2001).
10. The country's first such system has already been introduced in Ningxia, an up-and-coming wine region officially aiming at quality over quantity.
11. For a critique of this age-old distinction, perhaps soon to be without real meaning, see Banks and Overton (2010). In China, an example of the combination would be the trend of marketing wine with both wine district and grape variety; another would be experimentations with taste and flavour.
12. Or at least wine sold as such; mixing cheap imported wine with small quantities of Chinese wine (if at all) and labelling it 'Chinese' is supposedly still a common practice, despite a decade-long fight to curb this illegal practice. Indeed, this bottling is now reportedly taking place in international waters. Perhaps this can be seen as much as a sign of more active policing as of a market where domestic wine has a special allure.

References

Anderson, E.N. (1988), *The Food of China*, New Haven: Yale University Press.

Anderson, K., and Nelgen, S. (2011), *Global Wine Markets, 1961 to 2009: A Statistical Compendium*, Adelaide: University of Adelaide Press, www.adelaide.edu.au/press/titles/global-wine/Global-Wine-2009-EBOOK.pdf

Banks, G., and Overton, J. (2010), 'Old World, New World, Third World? Reconceptualising the Worlds of Wine', *Journal of Wine Research*, 21(1):57–75.

Barthes, R. (1957), 'Le vin et le lait' In: *Mythologies*, Paris: Editions du Seuil.

Becker, J. (1996), *Hungry Ghosts: Mao's Secret Famine*. New York: The Free Press.

Brautigam, D. (2015), *Will Africa Feed China?*, New York: Oxford University Press.

Brown, L.R. (1995), *Who Will Feed China?: Wake-up Call for a Small Planet*, London: Earthscan.

Chang, K.C. (ed.) (1977), *Food in Chinese Culture: Anthropological and Historical Perspectives*, New Haven: Yale University Press.

Constitution of the People's Republic of China (2004), *Zhonghua renmin gongheguo xianfa*. [The constitution of the People's Republic of China] (Promulgated for implementation in 1982, amended in 1988, 1993, 1999, 2004), Beijing: Falü chubanshe.

Fei, X. (2000), 'Chuangjian Zhongguoren ziji de shehuililun' [Create our own Chinese social theory] *Zhongguo shehui kexue jikan* (Chinese Social Sciences Quarterly), 31(IV).

Goldman, M., and MacFarquhar, R. (1999), 'Dynamic Economy, Declining Party-state', in Goldman, M. and MacFaquhar, R. (eds), *The Paradox of China's Post-Mao Reforms*, Cambridge: Harvard University Press, 3–29.

Hong, G. (2001), *Zhongguo niangjiu keji fazhanshi* [A history of wine production in China], Beijing: Zhongguo qinggongye chubanshe.

Huang, H.-T. (2000), *Joseph Needham, Science and Civilisation in China. Vol. 6, Biology and Biological Technology, Part V, Fermentations and Food Science*, Cambridge: Cambridge University Press.

Jiang, Z. (1996), 'Guanyu jiang zhengzhi' [About stressing politics] *Renmin Ribao* 01- 07- 1996[orig. in *Qiu shi* No. 13 1996].

Ke, S. (1920), *Xin Yuanshi* [New Yuan history], Tianjin: Tuigengtang.

Kjellgren, B. (2003), 'The Predicament of Indigenisation: Constructions and Methodological Consequences of Otherness in Chinese Ethnography', *Taiwan Journal of Anthropology/Taiwan Renleixuekan*, 1(1):147–78.

Li, H. (2002), *Zoujin putaojiu* [Approaching grape wine], Beijing: Nongcun duwu chubanshe.

Li, T. (ed.) (2003), *Zhongguo pengren cidian* [A Chinese culinary encyclopaedia], Taiyuan: Shanxi kexue jishu chubanshe.

Liu, Y. (2002), 'Suntime International Wine Company Striving for "Four Represents"', www.wineinchina.com (accessed 25 February 2002).

Marx, K. (1968 [1844]), 'Ökonomisch-philosophische Manuskripte aus dem Jahre 1844', In *Marx Engels Werke*, Ergänzungsband, Schriften bis 1844, erster Teil. Institut für Marxismus-Leninismus beim ZK der SED, Berlin: Dietz.

McGovern, P.E., et al (2004), 'Fermented Beverages of Pre- and Proto-historic China', *PNAS*, 101(51): 17593–98.

Mintz, S.W. (1985), *Sweetness and Power: The Place of Sugar in Modern History*, New York: Viking Penguin.

Mustacich, S. (2015), *Thirsty Dragon: China's Lust for Bordeaux and the Threat to the World's Best Wines*, New York: Henry Holt.

Nie, F. (1999), 'Wuchuijupeng yu shipeng shiqi' [The age of cooking without utensils or with stones], in Ren, B. (ed.), *Zhongguo shijing* [China's Book of Food], Shanghai: Shanghai wenhua chubanshe.

Overton, J., and Warwick, E.M. (2013), 'Class in a Glass: Capital, Neoliberalism and Social Space in the Global Wine Industry', *Antipode*, 45(3):702–18.

Polo, M. (1903), *The Travels of Marco Polo*, being the unabridged third edition of Henry Yule's annotated translation, as revised by Henri Cordier; together with Cordier's later volume of notes and addenda (1920), Project Gutenberg, www.gutenberg.org/cache/epub/12410 (accessed 26 February 2017).

Red Obsession (2013), [documentary film] dir. and writers: David Roach & Warwick Ross, Australia: Lion Rock Films.

Schafer, E.H. (1977), 'T'ang', in K.C. Chang (ed.), *Food in Chinese Culture: Anthropological and Historical Perspectives*, New Haven: Yale University Press, 85–140.

Sima, Q. (1965 [91BCE]), *Shiji* [The historian's records], Beijing: Zhonghua shuju.

Spence, J.D. (1999), *The Search for Modern China* (2nd edn), New York: Norton.

Kierath, T., and Wang, C. (2013), 'The Global Wine Industry: Slowly Moving from Balance to Shortage', Morgan Stanley Australia Ltd., 22 October 2013.

Tao, W. (1983), *Zhongguo pengren shilüe*. [A general history of the Chinese cuisine], np, Nanjing: Jiangsu kexue jishu chubanshe.

Wang, R. (1993), *Yinshi yu Zhongguo wenhua*. [Food and Chinese culture], Beijing: Renmin chubanshe.

Watson, J.L. (ed.) (1997), *Golden Arches East: McDonald's in East Asia*, Stanford: Stanford University Press.

Weber, M. (1914), 'Wirtschaft und Gesellschaft. Grundriss der verstehenden Soziologie', in *Grundriss der Sozialökonomik*, 3(2), Tübingen: Mohr.

Xiong, S., and Wen, T. (1998), *Zhongguo pengren gailun* [A general discussion of China's cuisine], Beijing: Zhongguo shangye chubanshe.

Xu Jieshu (1997), *Xueqiu: Han minzu de renleixue fenxi* [Snowball: The Anthropological Analysis of the Han Nationality], Shanghai: Shanghai renmin chubanshe.

Yan, Y. (2002), 'Managed Globalization: State Power and Cultural Transition in China', in P.L Berger and S.P. Huntingdon (eds), *Many Globalizations: Cultural Diversity in the Contemporary World*, London: Oxford University Press, 19–47.

Yantai Changyu Group Co. Ltd (October 2010), *Qianghua putaojiu zhiliang anquan tizhi jianshe cujin Zhangyu putaojiu chanye jiankang fazhan* [Strengthening the Construction of Wine Quality and Safety System to Promote the Healthy Development of Changyu Wine Industry], presentation material.

Zhu, B. (ed.) (1995), *Putaojiu gongye shouce* [Manual for the wine industry], Beijing: Zhongguo qinggongye chubanshe.

Zhu, G. (1999 [1117]), *Beishan jiujing* [North Mountain's wine classic], in Zhu, Y. (ed.), *Jiujing* [Wine classics], Beijing: Huaxia chubanshe.

8 The Globalization of the Wine Industry in Hong Kong: A Local and Global Perspective

HANG KEI HO

Introduction

In 2011, the global wine industry was stunned when the *Financial Times* reported that more than half of the global revenues of the fine and rare wine trade were generated through auctions that took place in Hong Kong, overtaking New York to become the most valuable wine auction hub (Lister 2011). By 2018, the Hong Kong wine world had further developed. An auction hosted by Christie's in Hong Kong witnessed 1,700 lots of rare vintages which were sold at $14.5 million (HK$ 113 million, £9.81 million),[1] $1.5 million more than the original estimate (Loos 2018). A particular lot of twelve-bottle 1982 Château Le Pin was auctioned for $206,000 (HK$ 1.6 million, £139,000).

One might think that wine has long been a popular drink in Hong Kong, but the wine culture there is relatively young. Until 2007, wine was only available in a limited range because it was expensive due to its high duty at 80 per cent. High taxation resulted in high retail prices, and coupled with the specific knowledge required for consumption, wine remained a drink for wealthy consumers. After years of lobbying by local businesses, the Hong Kong government reduced the wine duty to 40 per cent in February 2007, and since February 2008, wine duty has been completely withdrawn.

Meanwhile, during the global financial crisis in 2007, the sales of fine and rare wine for the North American and Western European markets dropped significantly. However, the global wine trade remained largely unaffected as the focus shifted to South East Asia instead. In 2008, $8.2 million (HK$ 63.8 million, £5.55 million) of the finest and rarest wines were sold at a single auction hosted by Acker Merrall & Condit in Hong Kong, in which more than five world auction records were broken (Pomfret 2008). Some of the lots included the 1990 Domaine de la Romanée-Conti, magnums of 1966, 1973 and 1976 Dom Perignon, as well as 1945 Mouton Rothschild. This auction has illustrated that the city is full of 'super-collectors' with unlimited financial resources to secure what is regarded as the best within the wine world. In essence, the withdrawal of the wine duty has not only revolutionized Hong Kong's drinking culture and alcohol industry; it has also had a huge knock-on effect in the wine trade in mainland China and the wine world at large.

Although trade figures present a clear case that Hong Kong has transformed into a significant wine-trading hub, academic discussion of the development of Hong Kong's wine trade has been limited. Moreover, there is very little qualitative data to explain the transformation of such a newly emerged industry. Therefore, this chapter uses Hong Kong as a strategic geographic location to study the globalization of wine for two major reasons. First, Hong Kong is a global financial centre, the freest economy in the world (Miller, Kim and Roberts 2018), and a well-established logistic hub, which allows the import of wine into the now postcolonial city-state. Second, not only is Hong Kong an interesting and important place to study because the city demonstrates the globalization of wine processes from the economic, social and cultural perspective within a part of East Asia, but more importantly, it is within this context that a large volume of wine is subsequently being re-exported to mainland China. Hence, Hong Kong is a crucial access point for the constant flow of global goods and culture.

Theoretical background

Academic literature has discussed research on alcohol consumption and, more specifically, the geographies of wine from anthropological, historical and technical perspectives. There is a large body of wine literature on production (e.g. Holly 1994; Orr 1995; Santon 1996; Simpson 2011), appellation (e.g. Gade 2004; Moran 1988, 1993, 2001) and *terroir* (e.g. Atkinson 2011; Dion 1959; Unwin 1991; Whalen 2010; van Leeuwen and Seguin 2006). Moreover, Dougherty's (2012) edited book on the *Geography of Wine* features a number of examples regarding wine in relation to the cultural, regional, physical, economic and technical context, and advances our current understanding of the Canadian wine tourism sector (Carmichael and Senese 2012), the physical and cultural characteristics of *terroir* in Burgundy and Bordeaux (Lemaire and Kasserman 2012), viticulture in California (Elliott-Fisk 2012), and how GIS (geographical information systems) and remote-sensing techniques can be deployed to manage vineyards (Green 2012; Johnson et al 2012), and so on.

Others have also written about the globalization of wine from a historical perspective. For example, Simpson (2011) explores the development of the wine industry in Europe between 1840 and 1914. Findings illustrate that phylloxera, a pest that damages the roots and leaves of grapevines, distorted the production and consumption of wine in France. Subsequently, the decline of the French wine industry created opportunities in Spain. By the late 1880s, a third of wine produced in Spain was exported to France (2011: 264). Regarding the wine trade, other works discuss the impact of networks and industrial districts in the English wine industry (Turner 2009), and industrial clustering in the Paso Robles wine region (Beebe et al 2013). In terms of wine consumption, other research also illustrates that wine concerns authenticity, taste and democratization (Smith Maguire 2018), as well as the projection of social identity, class and economic position (e.g. Ho 2015; Järvinen, Ellergaard and Larsen 2014; Rössel and Pape 2016).

However, despite the large amount of existing literature on wine, much of it is Anglo-European focused, with little attention paid to East Asia's winemarket in general, and Hong Kong's growing wine industry specifically. In order to fill this gap, this chapter aims to provide a general understanding of the globalization of Hong Kong's wine industry in three ways. First, it looks at existing theories and methods as to how research on alcohol and wine in Hong Kong and France has previously been carried out (e.g. Demossier 2005; Ho 2015; Ma 2001; Smart 2005). Then, through the analysis of wine trade figures and ethnography of wine fairs, as well as interviews with professionals who work for the industry, this chapter explores the Hong Kong wine industry from both local and global perspectives. Moreover, theories of indigenization (Appadurai 1996; Miller 1998), cultural capital (Bourdieu 1984) and conspicuous consumption (Veblen 2000 [1899]) are also applied to understand the localization (i.e. using a local form of culture to transform a foreign product into a more acceptable one) of wine in Hong Kong.

Research methods

This chapter draws on data collected between 2009 and 2015 during various visits to Hong Kong. Participants were contacted through personal and professional networks in which the non-random sampling of 'snow-balling technique' was applied to recruit a wider and larger sample size. Specifically, thirty semi-structured interviews were conducted between 2009 and 2010, with follow-up interviews carried out in the following years. Ten of those were categorized as strategic or elite interviews, as they were conducted with government agencies, high-end hotel restaurant employees, wine connoisseurs, wine traders and bar managers. The rest were conducted with local Hong Kong, as well as international, consumers from Australia, England, France, Germany, Scotland and so on. Participants included IT professionals, teachers, business owners, hedge fund managers, artists, exchange students and pensioners.

Four additional focus groups also took place, with a total of twenty-five participants who were asked to share their experience of wine-drinking practices and their understanding of the wine market. Interviews and focus groups were carried out in English as well as Cantonese. When permission was granted by the participants, recordings were made for transcription and analysis by the author. At times when participants declined to be recorded, interview notes were taken instead.

Furthermore, ethnographic research was carried out in wine bars, specialist wine shops and wine-tasting events. An ethnographic approach towards studying the wine trade has proven to be effective. For example, Demossier (2005) attended wine fairs in France and explored wine consumption, which provided an effective method for studying the interactions between suppliers, buyers and consumers. Similarly, I attended wine fairs and trade shows in Hong Kong and conducted participant observation, as well as conducting informal interviews with representatives and visitors from different parts of the world.

Names provided in this chapter are pseudonyms to ensure anonymity. The analysis of materials including marketing brochures, auction house catalogues and newspaper adverts in both Chinese and English was also included in the data gathering and analysis phase of the research. Local knowledge and language skills of the author were essential when accessing critical informants and analysing various marketing materials.

The chapter is structured as follows. First, it studies the operation of the wine trade in Hong Kong and mainland China through looking at how new companies have emerged to serve this emerging wine market. Second, it explores the popularization of wine consumption in Hong Kong in relation to changing consumption patterns. Third, it goes into the discussion of the changing levels of wine knowledge and education. Fourth, it demonstrates the local branding and tasting of wine through studying how a global product such as wine can be localized in the Hong Kong context. The chapter ends with a discussion of how globalization has not just changed the drinking culture in Hong Kong, but also how the global wine trade has evolved because of the globalization of cultural consumption.

The wine industry in Hong Kong and emerging wine businesses

In Hong Kong, the drop in the wine duty alone would not have transformed the city into one of the most important wine-trading hubs in the world. I argue that three government agencies – namely InvestHK, the official foreign direct investment (FDI) agency, the Hong Kong Trade and Development Council (HKTDC) and the Hong Kong Tourism Board – have been working together to come up with mechanisms, strategies and events that have enabled the promotion of the wine trade. For example, InvestHK has been working closely with a number of global wine businesses, educators and equipment providers to set up their presence in Hong Kong. Specifically, they give advice to investors on employment recruitment processes, labour legislation, the tax regime, office rental and warehousing. One of the most significant investment projects is by a Canadian investor who set up the winery Ap Lei Chau (an island in Hong Kong). Since Hong Kong's climate is not suitable for vine cultivation, grapes are being imported for winemaking. Although this is a small-scale production aimed at the hotel and catering industry, the concept of 'Made in Hong Kong' has made a positive contribution regarding how the world sees the local wine industry.

From the global wine trade perspective, the HKTDC and Hong Kong Tourism Board also organize international-scale events to provide platforms for business-to-business (B2B) and business-to-consumers (B2C) interaction. Two large-scale annual events have been taking place since 2008: the Hong Kong Wine and Dine Festival (formerly known as the Food and Wine Festival) and the Hong Kong International Wine & Spirits Fair have played important roles in promoting wine tourism, education and trade on the global scale. Exhibitors from wine-associated sectors, including wine ware, packaging, logistics, storage, wine education and catering have also been participating.

According to trade figures (Hong Kong Trade Development Council 2008), the Wine & Spirits Fair hosted 240 exhibitors from twenty-five regions and countries, and 8,758 buyers from fifty-five countries and regions in 2008. The last day of the event was open to the general public and 10,096 visitors attended. The exact figures are not available for the 2009 event, but in 2010 it was reported that nearly seven hundred exhibitors from thirty countries and regions took part in the fair. In addition, the fair was attended by more than 14,000 buyers, a 19 per cent increase from the previous year. The four biggest buyer increases in terms of buyers' countries of origin were Japan (39 per cent), the United States (23 per cent), Australia (22 per cent) and mainland China (16 per cent). The last day of the event was open to the general public and attracted over 14,000 visitors, a 15 per cent increase from the previous year. By 2014, the Wine & Spirits Fair was attended by approximately 20,000 buyers from seventy-five regions and countries (Hong Kong Trade Development Council 2015a). These figures illustrate that Hong Kong's wine trade continues to grow, and that consumers as well as the trade are now looking beyond France and beginning to purchase wine from other countries.

While HK$ 1.6 billion (£139 million, $206 million) worth of wine was imported in to Hong Kong in 2007, this figure increased more than fivefold to HK$ 8.4 billion (£730 million, $1.1 billion) by 2014 (Hong Kong Trade Development Council 2015b). Similarly, the volume of wine imports has increased by two and a half times to 52.4 million litres by 2014. The differing ratio between the increase in import value by the factor of five and volume by the factor of around 2.5, that is at two to one, suggests that Hong Kong is keen to purchase more expensive, fine and rare wines for which the global prices have increased significantly over the last few years. French wine is by far the most popular wine in Hong Kong, accounting for 52 per cent of the overall import value in 2014. More surprisingly, the UK was the second biggest exporter of wine to Hong Kong at almost 11 per cent. However, this was not necessarily because of its wine production, but was rather due to the fact that most fine and rare wines are sold through auction houses in London.

Despite Hong Kong being a valuable wine-trading hub that has seen a significant growth of local wine drinkers, both local and international wine merchants see Hong Kong as a strategic market, but not necessarily the final market destination. In the first nine months of 2015, around 90 per cent of the wine that was being imported to Hong Kong was re-exported to Macau and mainland China (Hong Kong Trade Development Council 2015b). The key reason is that the growing middle class in mainland China is increasingly interested in drinking wine. Regarding Macau, the casino industry is closely linked to the wine industry, because casinos need large quantities of wine for their customers. However, when the casino industry underperforms (e.g. in 2014), the sales of wine also decrease. Nonetheless, merchants still prefer to invest in the mainland through Hong Kong, and this is due to Hong Kong's robust financial, legal and logistical infrastructure. In order to get a better understanding of how to set up a wine business in Hong Kong, a case study is now presented, concerning how Georgia, a local Hong Kong woman, recently started a wine business with the intention of capitalizing on the wine boom.

Similar to other newly-established wine businesses in Hong Kong, Georgia exports a large volume of products to mainland China, but finds that supplying wine to mainland China is challenging. First, just like conducting other businesses in the mainland, it is difficult to gain access to networks without *guanxi*, a term in Mandarin which loosely translates into the notion of 'relationship'. Her company previously worked with a large-scale supermarket chain in Hong Kong, which already has a strong presence in the mainland. As a result, through existing business contacts, Georgia was able to use the already-established distribution channels and supply chains to transport goods across the border.

Second, as a result of corruption practices, Georgia's company also employs 'agents' to ensure trouble-free transactions. Exporting goods from Hong Kong to China is usually carried out by a third-party company, which may charge between 3 and 7 per cent of the value of the shipment. Georgia said that shipping three tonnes of goods may cost around HK$1,500 (£130, $193), but a further HK$750 (£65.2, $96.4) would be charged as a 'handling fee' by agents. The company sells wine in large volumes to mainland China, usually in containers capable of holding up to 1,000 bottles. The profit margin for this kind of low-cost French wine is around HK$5.00 to 10.00 (£0.43–0.87, $0.62–1.29) a bottle, and each bottle will then be retailed for between HK$30.0 and $40.0 (£2.61–3.48, $3.86–5.14). A number of mainland Chinese businesses have been known to purchase a container of wine as a one-off investment, in the hope it can be resold at a much higher value.

Georgia also explained that the number of bottles declared on export documents sometimes does not correspond to the actual number being shipped. Two 'books' are usually kept at the company warehouse, one to show to the customs officers and the other containing the actual figures, which are higher than the ones stated in the official export documents. It would be difficult to generate profits if the actual figures were declared.

In addition to supplying wine to mainland China, Georgia's company also trades with local Hong Kong businesses. She also works with bartenders in order to get her products marketed – the bar staff receive a percentage of the profit if the wine is sold. Hence there is an incentive for them to promote her products.

This newly established wine business tells us that breaking into the wine industry is not an easy task. Although Hong Kong has a robust legal and trading system, which eliminates the practice of corruption, doing business in mainland China remains challenging. In addition to the problems of corruption, China is notorious for producing and distributing counterfeit goods, and customers are aware of the existence of fake wines. Those wines can be made from chemicals, or in some cases cheap wine is bottled in used expensive bottles to trick customers. A Hong Kong-based informant said there is now an underground market in both Hong Kong and mainland China in which empty bottles of fine and rare wines can be traded for a considerable amount of money for refilling purposes.

As the wine trade begins to mature in Hong Kong, local wine businesses have to adapt. Another informant who runs a wine business said that when the wine industry took off in 2008, a large quantity of low-quality wine was being imported to Hong Kong, and these French wines being sold by new businesses were often considered unsaleable in France. These wines would have been destroyed or distilled into alcohol for other uses. Yet the same wines proved popular and profitable in Hong Kong and the mainland. But as local consumers are becoming more knowledgeable, they have begun to demand higher-quality wine, a trend which is also being reflected in the value-to-volume ratio already mentioned above.

The popularization of wine consumption in Hong Kong

Exploring marketing materials of wine exhibitions and trade fairs can tell us about the image of wine that the industry aims to project. For example, from the official promotional leaflet of the Hong Kong International Wine and Spirits Fair in 2011, it can be seen that the focus of the map is on the Asia Pacific region. The front cover of a similar event brochure presents two trendily dressed couples, one of Chinese origin and the other one of European origin. All appear to be cheerful, holding a glass of red wine, toasting each other. This implies that wine is not just trendy and stylish, but also represents cosmopolitanism. The background is presented with the skyline of Hong Kong Island in which the International Financial Centre building particularly stands out. In this version of the brochure, the content is written in both Japanese and Chinese, which corresponds to the importance of both markets. An English version of this brochure was also available. This brochure gives the impression that Hong Kong is a rich, stylish and cosmopolitan city where the West meets the East.

Another leaflet which was also being handed out to visitors places the emphasis on the promotion of Hong Kong's wine trade. This leaflet illustrates three important messages. First, the label shows Hong Kong's skyline, and the description reads 'Hong Kong Asia's wine capital', which gives the impressions that Hong Kong is now a key wine-trading hub. Second, '0.00' is printed on the 'price tag', which represents Hong Kong's zero per cent wine duty rate. Third, 'Magnum Force' refers to a 1.5L magnum bottle, illustrating that the wine trade in Hong Kong is large and growing. Importantly, it is also a pun that refers to Clint Eastwood's film *Magnum Force* where Eastwood plays the violent policeman called Dirty Harry. It could be interpreted that the joke aims to connect wine to the glamour of Hollywood productions.

Along with the changing marketing image of wine in Hong Kong, local alcohol consumption patterns have also been transformed. For many decades Chinese rice wine was a popular drink in Hong Kong. Although it was often consumed as an alcoholic drink by male manual labour workers as well as other members of the working-class population, it was also used in the making of traditional Chinese medicine, domestic cooking and ancestral worshipping rituals (Ho 2015).

Post–Second World War Hong Kong was poor, but with the growing manufacturing, real estate and electronics industries in the 1960s and 1970s, Hong Kong became wealthy. Some forms of Western cultural consumption and culinary practice have been adopted, since there have long been Europeans working in Hong Kong. For example, cognac is expensive, of French origin, and often perceived as the symbol of wealth and status in Hong Kong (Smart 2005) as well as in other parts of the world. For almost five decades, cognac was the choice of drink in birthday celebrations, wedding banquets and business meetings. At the same time, since Hong Kong is a former British colony, some forms of Western drinking culture were also introduced by the British in workplaces. For example, one retired Hong Kong policeman said that drinking was used as a way to bridge the hierarchy between the Hong Kong locals and British policemen within the Royal Hong Kong Police Force. Disagreements among colleagues often occurred during work, but after-work social events which involved alcohol consumption gave opportunities to junior and senior colleagues to discuss openly work-related as well as personal issues. Through research on the longshoremen working community in Newfoundland, Canada, Mars (1987) argues that drinking acts as a feature of social hierarchy, inclusion, exclusion and social identity. Similarly, in the Hong Kong police context, drinking became a way for colleagues of different ranks to establish social bonds. Drunkenness also allowed the temporary removal of work hierarchies.

Other types of alcohol such as imported European beers (Ma 2001) and whisky were popular, but wine remained expensive and was only offered in high-end restaurants and specialist shops. With the popularization of North American and Western European popular culture in the 1980s, wine was perceived as a drink associated with class, sophistication, and high culture. In Bourdieu's (1984) terms, it was a form of cultural capital which was socially legitimate.

Perhaps it is also important to acknowledge the existing drinking culture today. For example, younger consumers tend to be less superstitious and do not place much emphasis on traditional customs. But older drinkers may avoid white wine at weddings and birthday gatherings, as white is traditionally associated with the dead. In contrast, red wine is more widely accepted, not only as a fashionable drink, but also because red represents good luck.

In one focus group made up of eight local consumers (men and women aged between their forties and sixties), all of the participants agreed that beer is slowly being replaced by red wine when people dine out in local Chinese restaurants. This is driven by the cost of wine having become significantly lower. Moreover, they believed that drinking wine has become more commonplace in Hong Kong, while rice wine is going out of fashion because 'it tastes awful'. In other words, social factors have contributed to how taste is being perceived: some consumers *think* that rice wine tastes awful, rather than rice wine becoming awful-tasting recently. This is due to a shift in the taste culture, as well as changes in habitus and the perception of cultural capital (Bourdieu 1984).

According to interviews with two experienced employees of a five-star hotel in Hong Kong, a connoisseur and a French restaurant manager, there is a group of wealthy local elite people who have been collecting wine for decades. Traditionally they bought wine through overseas auction houses, and stored their collections, mostly of French origin, in the UK. The purchase would then be shipped between 10 and 15 cases at a time from overseas warehouses to Hong Kong, for consumption or personal collection. The wine would be taxed accordingly at 80 per cent. They also explained that wine has been served in luxury hotels for many years. When wine tax was at 80 per cent, a bottle of wine that cost HK$100 (£8.70, $12.90) from an overseas supplier would be HK$180 (£15.70, $23.10) when import tax was added. With markup and overheads, that bottle would be listed on the menu at HK$800 (£69.60, $103), about eight times the import price. This has now changed with the popularization of wine and the withdrawal of wine duty, and wine is now available in most restaurants. Regular customers sometimes prefer to have their wine collections directly shipped to the restaurant, but those tend to be fine and rare wines which the hotel may not supply. In such cases, a corkage fee is imposed, as is usual.

For many Hong Kong consumers, France was traditionally perceived as the most prestigious wine-producing country, and during my visit to wine fairs and trade shows in Hong Kong, many exhibitors came from France. Based on discussions with a number of exhibitors, the general feedback was that visitors were overly enthusiastic about tasting French wines and most of the visitors flocked to these stands, resulting in several 'scuffles' and altercations. A representative from the Rhône-Alpes Regional Council (Entreprise Rhône-Alpes International), who was in attendance to promote wines from that region, said that his stand was popular. Visitors were keen to try the wine due to the Rhône's association with France. The council has also established a regional office in Shanghai, and acknowledges that mainland China is one of their key targeted markets. There were also Hong Kong suppliers specializing in French wine, including one which specialized in selling wines from Saint-Émilion.

In addition, there were a number of wine suppliers attending these events from countries less renowned in Hong Kong for wine production, such as Argentina, Australia, Austria, China, Germany, Italy, Portugal, Spain, New Zealand and the United States. Although these wines were often of good quality, the stands were less popular with consumers because they were unfamiliar to them. The marketing manager of the Austrian Wine Marketing Board (Österreich Wein Marketing GmbH) said that they supplied wines to a number of local hotels, but consumers' lack of knowledge about these wines made it difficult to sell their products.

Gender plays an important role when choosing wine. Alcoholic drinks were often perceived as a male preserve in traditional Chinese society. Many trusting friendships were established through drinking. At the same time, alcohol would also be drunk before battles against enemies and after victories. Thus alcohol has played an important role in Chinese history. In comparison, women who drank alcohol in the public sphere were most likely to be seen in brothels and often were regarded in a negative way. However, these views have been changed with the globalization of consumer culture.

Mary, a participant in her mid-twenties who grew up in different parts of the world, believed that women now drink more wine than men in Hong Kong. She had many single female friends in their late-twenties who would like to meet men. This group of women believed that they would look and feel more 'attractive and sophisticated' if they held a glass of wine in a bar, rather than drinking a large glass of beer. Moreover, her friends were health conscious, as is Mary herself (she is a personal trainer). Generally speaking, a glass of wine contains fewer calories than a glass of beer. Furthermore, it is more difficult to share a beer or cocktail, and therefore drinking wine seems to act as a social practice, as a bottle can be shared among a group of friends. It is of course possible to share a round of drinks with friends, but this could lead to overconsumption of alcohol if there is a large group involved and everyone feels obliged to buy a round of drinks. In addition, some may feel obliged to spend money on a round of drinks, while what they actually want is to have one drink. Mary also believed that Chinese women 'can catch up quicker than men on wine drinking, because a lot of Chinese girls who come back from overseas tend to date Western men'. Therefore they are more likely to go out for Western-style meals and social events. As a result, these women have a higher exposure to wine consumption. Chinese women also tend to feel more comfortable and act more at ease when drinking wine than other alcoholic drinks. In contrast, Mary had not come across many Chinese men dating Western girls. To these men, as she described it, 'it is probably harder to learn about wine'. Perhaps her views are slightly biased, as there are local men who are also knowledgeable about wine and who have been attending wine courses and wine-tasting events. Nonetheless, wine is deemed as a popular drink with local women. Informants from another focus group also claimed that while men prefer dry wines, women tend to go for sweeter wines. White wine seems popular with women according to some, but this claim contradicts other participants' views that red wine is popular among women. Some customers may not be familiar with ordering wine, but nevertheless it remains a popular choice when dining in local Chinese restaurants and drinking at bars.

Changing levels of wine knowledge and education

We have so far discussed the popularization of wine in Hong Kong and illustrated the changing alcohol consumption patterns. The key finding so far demonstrates that local consumers' affection for French wine is apparent, and because of this, they are reluctant, or lack the knowledge, to explore other wines. But as consumers are becoming more educated, they begin to take courses in wine-tasting and explore wines of other countries. This section further discusses Hong Kong's emerging wine education and wine culture.

Anthropologists view alcohol consumption as a way of constructing meanings, and Douglas (1987) in particular describes this through the notion of 'constructive drinking'. Similarly, there are two reasons as to why consumers in Hong Kong may want to pursue wine drinking to construct social meanings: to acquire cultural capital

(Bourdieu 1984), and to carry out conspicuous consumption (Veblen 2000 [1899]). Both ideas are related to the display of identity and knowledge, and of having the financial ability to consume a product.

Bourdieu (1984) defines three forms of capital with regard to social class, which are economic, social and cultural capital. He further defines three forms of cultural capital: embodied, objectified and institutionalized (Bourdieu 1984: 47). The key argument is that cultural capital is not a form of knowledge that can be acquired in a short period of time. Developing such forms of capital requires time and resources. Furthermore, skills and knowledge can be defined as cultural capital, which are institutionalized because one's knowledge can be accredited through attending an educational establishment.

Bourdieu's notion of cultural capital allows us to understand why consumers may want to learn about traditional wine-drinking practices, but we can also use Veblen's (2000 [1899]) theory of conspicuous consumption to explore the ways in which drinkers purchase expensive wine in Hong Kong. Conspicuous consumption has become one of the most discussed topics within the consumption framework. Through observations in nineteenth- and early twentieth-century North America, Veblen describes the way in which upper classes carried out luxury shopping to flaunt their wealth. As such, these 'are methods of demonstrating the possession of wealth' (Veblen 2000 [1899]: 40). Conspicuous consumption is a waste of time and effort, as well as a waste of goods. In addition, objects are used to communicate meanings and to portray one's wealth and social status (1899: 31–7). This was particularly important to the entrepreneurs who became wealthy quickly during the industrial boom periods. This class acquired tremendous wealth in a short amount of time and, as a result, also resorted to conspicuous consumption. They often mimicked the way that the upper class consumed, a practice Veblen referred to as emulation. Along these lines, some consumers in Hong Kong may choose to consume expensive alcohol in order to flaunt their wealth in bars and restaurant. However, wine consumption requires cultural capital, which some consumers may lack, and taking part in a wine-tasting course will compensate for that.

The increased availability of wine in Hong Kong has led to consumers wanting to learn about wine drinking, and new wine businesses are being established to cater for these new consumers who emerged when the wine trade took off. In 2008 there was a lack of recognized wine experts in Hong Kong. It is important for the professionals who work in the industry to have a strong understanding of the products that they offer to their customers. One informant describes such issues when dining at a local restaurant: 'If you ask the waiter about what dishes go with what kind of wine, he probably wouldn't be able to tell you.' This tends to be true because waiting staff do not usually have adequate training or knowledge to make suggestions to customers. According to field observations, a number of local restaurants had only begun selling low-quality red and white wine. On various occasions, wine options were limited, and some restaurants in particular only offered two choices: house red and house white. But this is changing as restaurant staff become better trained and informed about wine. At the same time, many local and global wine connoisseurs have recently emerged. Wine-tasting courses are now widely available. Most notably, the Open University of Hong Kong and the University of Hong Kong School of Professional and Continuing Education (HKU SPACE) have introduced professional diploma and certificate programmes for those who work in the wine and related industries, and for those who want to learn more about wine in general. Many restaurants now also run food and wine matching events for enthusiasts.

Running wine fairs is also a good way to promote wine education and knowledge. I collected marketing materials on wine education during wine fairs and events. For example, one brochure advertises a workshop on 'wine tasting technique' run by the Hong Kong Management Association. The front page reads, 'Learn how to taste and how to talk about it', and this idea perfectly fits into Bourdieu's notion of acquiring cultural capital. More importantly, it relates to the overarching theme of the wine field as highlighted in this book (see Chapter 1). The two two-and-a-half-hour evening workshops cost HK$2,000 (£174, $257) for members and HK$2,200 (£191, $283) for non-members. The course is taught in Cantonese, even though the advert is in English. Another brochure advertises a diploma course in 'Wine Business'. This diploma is made up of seven modules, and each module costs HK$2,850 (£248, $366) for members and HK$2980 (£259, $383) for non-members. Wine-tasting courses on wine from specific countries and regions such as California and Bordeaux are also available. These brochures promote the idea of wine education, and the courses are mostly designed for those who have no prior knowledge of wine but would like to learn. We can clearly identify from the printed materials that wine consumption is portrayed as a Western practice – very little Chinese is being used on such materials.

When wine was becoming popular in Hong Kong in 2008, only Bordeaux was perceived as the preferred choice. As consumers have become educated and adventurous, they have moved beyond drinking wines of the Old World such as France, Germany and Italy, to the New World, including Argentina, Australia, Chile and New Zealand and the United States. Now wine can easily be bought from supermarkets and convenience stores, which would have been previously impossible. As wine has become increasingly popular, consumers are not only interested in purchasing expensive cognac or fine and rare wine to display their wealth, which in Veblen's terms is conspicuous consumption. They are also aspiring to accumulate cultural capital through developing wine knowledge, and subsequently developing cultural capital in wine for its own sake.

Local branding and tasting of wine

Globalization has also allowed the constant exchange of goods and cultures between the local and global context. In particular, one product that stood out at the Hong Kong Food and Wine Festival was the 'Hello Kitty' wine, which captures the importance of local branding and marketing in order to appeal to local cultural tastes. The promotional banner at the stand reads 'Hello Kitty Wine'. Underneath, it has a pink Hello Kitty figure, and below that, it reads 'Made in Italy'. 'Imported from Italy' is also printed in traditional Chinese for those who may not read English. Both male and female customers showed interest in this product. This kind of product has a certain appeal in South East Asia because of a perceived 'cuteness'.

A point that has been overlooked in previous studies involves cultural differences in consumption, or, in this case, subcultural differences. Products with Japanese cartoon characters such as Mario, Astro Boy and Doraemon, as well as characters by Western artists including Miffy, Snoopy and Forever Friends, are popular in Hong Kong, Japan and South Korea. Not only are there a number of shops which specifically sell cartoon-themed merchandise including T-shirts, bags, wallets, dolls, photo albums, notepads, pens and so on, but they also attract a wide range of customers from different age groups. Miller (1998) uses the example of consumption of Coca-Cola in Trinidad to demonstrate how a product can be indigenized such that the end-product is no longer global (American) but rather local (Trinidadian). Using a similar understanding, we can say that Italian wine is also being transformed. It is localized, and stops being only a product of Italy, through the use of the packaging of the Japanese cartoon character, and subsequently being marketed in Hong Kong. Appadurai (1996) has theorized the notion of globalization as indigenization. He argues that under the influence of globalization, things appear to be homogeneous, but it is the localization of global trends which allows these things to become more acceptable to a particular local society. Therefore, wine drinking, which is often perceived as a form of high culture, is being popularized through a Japanese cartoon cat that has made the product from the West more acceptable to Hong Kong consumers.

It is common to see both adults and children wearing items with distinct designs such as Hello Kitty and Paul Frank in Hong Kong. Such practices for adults might be alien to Westerners and perceived as childish, but for the locals this is an expression of identity and 'cuteness'. Conversely, one frequently comes across female teenagers in the UK wearing clothing items which often convey a sense of mature femininity. These could be perceived by a different culture as vulgar. Therefore, consumers' practices within particular cultures should be commented on with caution. In addition, emotions (Colls 2004) can be communicated through objects, and I argue that a bottle of wine with Hello Kitty labelling is likely to be bought as a gift and given to younger women. Once again, this kind of product seems to be popular in the South East Asian regions, but may struggle to sell in other parts of the world.

To elaborate on the concept of indigenization, the Hello Kitty branding of wine communicates three key messages simultaneously. First, it can be understood as a local product, as it is aimed at certain types of Hong Kong consumers, presumably younger women. Second, it is also perceived as a regional product, because cartoon-branded items are well regarded in South East Asia. Third, the imagery of Hello Kitty has also been promoted around the world. Essentially, a bottle of Italian wine with Hello Kitty branding demonstrates a process of globalization that cuts across national cultural boundaries. From the above observations, although we can see that Hong

Kong is largely a globalized city within which Western forms of consumption are widely accepted, more local cultures and customs are also important when a new product or idea is being introduced.

Conclusion

From wine being only a product for very wealthy Hong Kong consumers, to now being a drink served in most restaurants, the local wine culture has been transformed in less than a decade. It is undeniable that Hong Kong's continuous growing demand for wine has pushed up the prices of rare vintages, and this trend is being reflected in record-breaking wine auctions taking place in Hong Kong. The domination of imported beer, cognac and whisky is now being replaced by mostly red wine, but white wine has also become more popular. This was made possible when the wine duty was completely removed in 2008. However, I argue that the transformation could not have been achieved without the support offered by three Hong Kong government agencies, namely InvestHK, the Hong Kong Trade and Development Council and the Hong Kong Tourism Board. Together they have been hosting events to create platforms for wine businesses and consumers to interact within. When combined with the change in the tax regime, this kind of government-backed trade promotion has proven to be effective when creating a new industry, that of wine. Perhaps other industries can also be created using a similar model. Trade figures illustrate that the wine trade is growing, specifically with more high-quality wine being imported to Hong Kong. In addition, with Hong Kong being the gateway for the mainland's wine trade, a large quantity of wine is being re-exported for the growing Chinese middle class. Although the mainland market accounts for most exports in Hong Kong, questionable business practices such as corruption may yet discourage foreign investors investing in it directly.

The popularization of wine has also illustrated changing trends in alcohol consumption patterns in Hong Kong. More specifically, we see a shift from cognac consumption to wine consumption, from elite consumers to middle-class consumers, from wine being difficult to purchase to a wider range of wines being available in more outlets, from older to younger consumers, from male to female consumers, from red wine to white wine consumption, from France to other countries, and so on. Wine has become a mass phenomenon, and at the same time the market itself has become more diversified, with new types of consumers constantly emerging.

With wine being more widely available, local consumers have developed a desire to take courses in wine appreciation. They want to be seen as wealthy by flaunting the financial ability to purchase expensive wine through conspicuous consumption (Veblen 2000 [1899]). But more than this, sophisticated consumers want to show their knowledge of food and wine pairings in social settings, and this behaviour can be understood as the display of cultural capital (Bourdieu 1984). Therefore, wine education providers have emerged in Hong Kong, teaching drinkers how to taste wine.

With consumers being more educated, they have gone beyond drinking wine from France, which was traditionally associated with prestige and authority. This trend is reflected by trade figures illustrating that the sales of wines from the New World are growing.

Another way of thinking about the globalization of cultural consumption is through the notion of indigenization (Appadurai 1996; Miller 1998). The example of Hello Kitty wine captures the glocalization of culture, in which the meaning of a product can be transformed from its place(s) of origin to a new location. Marketers should pay attention to such factors when they introduce a product to a new region.

In short, Hong Kong is a strategic geographic location which helps us understand the globalization of wine, both within Hong Kong itself and through its acting as a connection point between mainland China and the West. Wine has become a popular drink in Hong Kong because it captures the notions of high culture, flaunting wealth and being Westernized. This chapter has shown how wine consumption practices have changed over the years, and how the global wine trade has adapted itself to serve the newly-emerged Hong Kong and mainland Chinese markets.

Acknowledgements

Earlier versions of this research were presented at the Foodscapes: Access to Food – Excess of Food conference organized by the University of Graz, Austria, at the Castle of Seggau in September 2013, and The Worlds in a Wine Glass conference organized by the University of Newcastle, Australia, at King's College London, UK, in May 2016. The author would like to thank the University College London Graduate School, University College London Department of Geography, and Swedish Research Council (Vetenskapsrådet) for their funding of the project this chapter is based upon. The author would also like to thank the editors whose comments and suggestions helped improve this chapter. Additionally, the author would like to thank all the participants who took part in this research.

Note

1. Exchange rate at £1 to HK$11.5 and $1 to HK$7.78 is used throughout this chapter.

References

Appadurai, A. (1996), *Modernity at Large: Cultural Dimensions of Globalization*, Minneapolis: University of Minnesota Press.

Atkinson, J.M.W. (2011), '*Terroir* and the Côte de Nuits', *Journal of Wine Research*, 22(1):35–41.

Beebe, C., Haque, F., Jarvis, C., Kenney, M., and Patton, D. (2013), 'Identity Creation and Cluster Construction: The Case of the Paso Robles Wine Region', *Journal of Economic Geography*, 13:711–40.

Bourdieu, P. (1984), *Distinction: A Social Critique of the Judgement of Taste*, London: Routledge.

Carmichael, B.A., and Senese, D.M. (2012), 'Competitiveness and Sustainability in Wine Tourism Regions: The Application of a Stage Model of Destination Development to Two Canadian Wine Regions', in Dougherty, P.H. (ed.), *The Geography of Wine: Regions, Terroir and Techniques*, Dordrecht: Springer, 159–78.

Colls, R. (2004), '"Looking Alright, Feeling Alright": Emotions, Sizing and the Geographies of Women's Experiences of Clothing Consumption', *Social and Cultural Geography*, 5(4):583–96.

Demossier, M. (2005), 'Consuming Wine in France: The "Wandering" Drinker and the Vin-anomic', in Wilson, T.M. (ed.), *Drinking Cultures: Alcohol and Identity*, Oxford: Berg, 107–28.

Dion, R. (1959), *Histoire de la vigne et du vin en France: des origines au XIXe siècle*, Paris: Les Belles Lettres.

Douglas, M. (1987), *Constructive Drinking: Perspectives on Drink from Anthropology*, Cambridge: Cambridge University Press.

Elliott-Fisk, D.L. (2012), 'Geography and the American Viticultural Areas Process, Including a Case Study of Lodi, California', in Dougherty, P.H. (ed.), *The Geography of Wine: Regions, Terroir and Techniques*, Dordrecht: Springer, 49–57.

Gade, D.W. (2004), 'Tradition, Territory, and *Terroir* in French Viniculture: Cassis, France, and Appellation Contrôlée', *Annals of the Association of American Geographers*, 94(4):848–67.

Green, D.R. (2012), 'Geospatial Tools and Techniques for Vineyard Management in the Twenty-first Century', in Dougherty, P.H. (ed.), *The Geography of Wine: Regions, Terroir and Techniques*, Dordrecht: Springer, 227–45.

Ho, H.K. (2015), 'Hong Kong', in Martin, S.C. (ed.), *The SAGE Encyclopedia of Alcohol: Social, Cultural, and Historical Perspectives*, Thousand Oaks, CA: Sage, 701–03.

Holly, P. (1994), 'Organisational Structure of Wine Production in the US', *Journal of Wine Research*, 5(2):91–101.

Hong Kong Trade Development Council (2008), *A World of Fine Wine*, http://hkwinefair.hktdc.com/dm/200812/issue01.htm (accessed 26 November 2018).

Hong Kong Trade Development Council (2015a), *Asia's Premier Wine Event Draws to Successful Close: Global Wine Merchants Set Sights on Asia Expansion*, http://www.hktdc.com/fair/hkwinefair-en/s/8843-For_Press/HKTDC-Hong-Kong-International-Wine-and-Spirits-Fair/PressRelease8Nov2015.html (accessed 26 November 2018).

Hong Kong Trade Development Council (2015b), *Wine Industry in Hong Kong*, http://hong-kong-economy-research.hktdc.com/business-news/article/Hong-Kong-Industry-Profiles/Wine-Industry-in-Hong-Kong/hkip/en/1/1X000000/1X07WNW7.htm (accessed 26 November 2018).

Järvinen, M., Ellergaard, C.H., and Larsen, A.G. (2014), 'Drinking Successfully: Alcohol Consumption, Taste and Social Status', *Journal of Consumer Culture*, 14(3):384–405.

Johnson, L.F., Nemani, R., Hornbuckle, J., Bastiaanssen, W., Thoreson, B., Tisseyre, B., and Pierce, L. (2012), 'Remote Sensing for Viticultural Research and Production', in Dougherty, P.H. (ed.), *The Geography of Wine: Regions, Terroir and Techniques*, Dordrecht: Springer, 209–26.

Lemaire, D., and Kasserman, D. (2012), 'Bordeaux and Burgundy: A Comparison of Two French Wine Regions in Transition', in Dougherty, P.H. (ed.), *The Geography of Wine: Regions, Terroir and Techniques*, Dordrecht: Springer, 61–80.

Lister, E. (2011), 'Fine Wine Auctions: Hong Kong Confirms Its Place at Top of the Podium', *Financial Times*, 17 June, www.ft.com/intl/cms/s/0/bc0e571c-989c-11e0-94d7-00144feab49a.html (accessed 16 February 2016).

Loos, T. (2018), 'For Wine Auctions, It's Been Another Very Good Year', *The New York Times*, 2 October, https://www.nytimes.com/2018/10/02/arts/wine-auctions-spirits.html (accessed 26 November 2018).

Ma, E.K.W. (2001), 'The Hierarchy of Drinks: Alcohol and Social Class in Hong Kong', in Mathews, G., and Lui, T.L. (eds), *Consuming Hong Kong*, Hong Kong: Hong Kong University Press, 117–39.

Mars, G. (1987), 'Longshore Drinking, Economic Security and Union Politics in Newfoundland', in Douglas, M. (ed.), *Constructive Drinking: Perspectives on Drink from Anthropology*, Cambridge: Cambridge University Press, 91–101.

Miller, D. (1998), 'Coca-Cola: A Black Sweet Drink from Trinidad', in Miller, D. (ed.), *Material Cultures: Why Some Things Matter*, Chicago: University of Chicago Press, 169–87.

Miller, T., Kim, A.B., and Roberts, J.M. (2018). 2018 Index of economic freedom. Washington, DC: The Heritage Foundation. Retrieved from https://www.heritage.org/index/pdf/2018/book/index_2018.pdf (accessed 16 May 2019).

Moran, W. (1988), 'The Wine Appellation: Environmental Description or Economic Device?' in Smart, R.E., Thornton, R.J., Rodriguez, S.B., and Young, J.E. (eds), *Proceedings of the Second International Symposium for Cool Climate Viticulture and Oenology: Auckland, New Zealand*, New Zealand Society for Viticulture and Oenology, 356–60.

Moran, W. (1993), 'The Wine Appellation as Territory in France and California', *Annals, Association of American Geographers*, 83:694–717.

Moran, W. (2001), '*Terroir* – The Human Factor', *Australian and New Zealand Wine Industry Journal*, 16(2):32–51.

Orr, S.C. (1995), 'Production Practices in the Australian Wine Industry', *Journal of Wine Research*, 6(3):179–93.

Pomfret, J. (2008), 'Asian Wine Auction Uncorks $8.2 mln in Sales', *Reuters*, 31 May, https://www.reuters.com/article/arts-hongkong-wine-dc/asian-wine-auction-uncorks-8-2-mln-in-sales-idUSL3136032920080531 (accessed 26 November 2018).

Rössel, J., and Pape, S. (2016), 'Who Has a Wine-Identity? Consumption Practices between Distinction and Democratization', *Journal of Consumer Culture* 16(2):614–32.

Santon, T.J. (1996), 'Columella's Attitude towards Wine Production', *Journal of Wine Research*, 7(1):55–9.

Simpson, J. (2011), *Creating Wine: The Emergence of a World Industry, 1840–1914*, Princeton: Princeton University Press.

Smart, J. (2005), 'Cognac, Beer, Red Wine or Soft Drinks?' in Wilson, T.M. (ed.), *Drinking Cultures: Alcohol and Identity*, Oxford: Berg, 107–28.

Smith Maguire, J. (2018), 'The Taste for the Particular: A Logic of Discernment in an Age of Omnivorousness', *Journal of Consumer Culture*, 18(1):3–20, DOI: 10.1177/1469540516634416.

Turner, S. (2009), 'Networks of Learning within the English Wine', *Journal of Economic Geography*, 10:685–715.

Unwin, T. (1991), *Wine and the Vine: An Historical Geography of Viticulture and the Wine Trade*, London: Routledge.

van Leeuwen, C., and Seguin, G. (2006), 'The Concept of *Terroir* in Viticulture', *Journal of Wine Research*, 17:1–10.

Veblen, T. (2000 [1899]), 'Conspicuous Consumption', in Lee, M.J. (ed.), *The Consumer Society Reader*, London: Blackwell, 31–47.

Whalen, P. (2010), 'Whither *Terroir* in the Twenty-first Century: Burgundy's Climats?', *Journal of Wine Research*, 21(2–3):117–21.

9 Enduring Wine and the Global Middle Class

PETER J. HOWLAND

Introduction

The globalizations of grape wine – historic and contemporary, field-based and cultural – have been underpinned by a nexus of enduring, capital-based modalities. Noted here in both an unfolding order of consequence and a descending order of fixity – natural: material: commercial – these capital-based modalities have influenced the histories of transplantation, adaptation and change since grape wine's invention in circa 6000 BCE (Johnson 2004 [1989]; Unwin 1991). The nature capital (Taylor 2018) of grapes – their genetic, biological, chemical and other inherent characteristics – provides a foundation for human recognition and valuing of varied wine tastes, together with the construction of associated quality assertions and social hierarchies of possession and appreciation that are, of course, expressly sensitive to the wine-enabling and wine-restrictive interventions of human agents at specific moments in history and within different societies. Furthermore, the nature capital of grapes and the material capital (Miller 1987)[1] of wine have combined unfailingly to underscore the scale and technical exactitudes of grape wine production. This is particularly notable in the production of 'beyond sustenance' or 'surplus' wines. This is essentially any grape cultivation and wine production above the consumption needs of an 'ordinary' household (however historically and socially constructed) – and particularly production for elite institutions such as pharaohs, kings, cardinals and other bigwigs who regularly host large numbers of guests, or who indulge in frequent, ritual and ceremonial consumption, and/or those who are entrepreneurially committed to producing wines for market trade. In such cases significant scaling-up in terms of production acreages, equipment, labour and storage is necessary. Surplus wine producers are also likely to deploy whatever is considered the most judicious and comparatively 'cost-sensitive' techniques (quantity- or quality-orientated), specific to, and yet variable within, their historical locations. These economies of scale – of planted acreage, labour capacities, production and storage facilities – have always meant that wines, particularly commodified and quality wines (however historically framed), have routinely been the reserve of the privileged (Howland 2013; Johnson 2004 [1989]). Accordingly, a focus on the enduring in wine provides a complimentary, yet differently hued, optic to studies currently acutely attentive to the shifting homogenic and heterogenic dynamics of the global-glocal-local, and importantly directs our attention to the significance of the durable, commonplace and banal in wine worlds, fields and cultures across the globe.

In this chapter I assume the modest, yet wilfully polemic, register of a knowingly misrecognizing wine tourist/sociologist/anthropologist, and as such seek to foreground the enduring or durable evident in both my New Zealand and Peruvian wine tourism experiences. My aim is to contribute to studies of everyday globalization (Ray 2007; Shortell 2016) and to analyses attentive to the globalizing possibilities (Leichty 2012) of standardization and differentiation. Well-founded concerns about homogeneity and universalization credited to varied globalizing phenomena can unwittingly direct attention away from the 'striking resonances' (Heiman et al 2012: 7) across diverse societies and cultures. Such resonances are as evident in the fact that wine is customarily made from grapes, and in the systematic, commonplace routinization of market-commodity wine production, as they are in the widespread, contemporary 'longing for middle-class lifestyles, spaces, and modes of consumption' (Heiman et al 2012: 7).

My aim is not to find fault with studies that bear witness to the pluralities, hybridizations and resistances that distinguish people striving to exist morally at concurrent reflexive, domestic, local, national and global scales of being. These studies are vital correctives to accounts (especially economic) of globalization that appear totalizing, and they function as important bulwarks against the universalizing aspirations of global ideologues everywhere. They also remind us to celebrate divergent modes of being and provide much-needed platforms for emancipation (e.g. Holton 2005; Inglis and Gimlin 2009; Turner 2010). However, overemphasis on glocal and local differences, pluralities and the resistant – so often a feature of anthropological studies of globalization (e.g. Inda 2001) – runs the risk of backgrounding the most commonplace and enduring of phenomena in contemporary globalization. Similarly, globalization studies that foreground the homogenic, standardizing and universalizing – a tendency among sociologists enamoured by Western-centric theories generated in the nineteenth century and beyond (e.g. Ritzer 2004) – can underemphasize the very long histories, and the consistently marked migratory and globalizing temperaments, of market-orientated production and economics.

The history of wine coincides with many pivotal moments of the archaic, early modern and modern epochs of globalization. Convergences are evident in the 6000–4500 BCE origin and spread of peoples, cultures and wine from Georgia to Iran to Greece; in the extensive wine production and trade networks of the Roman Empire marked by the first treatise devoted, in part, to optimizing wine grape agriculture – Cato the Elder's *De Agri Cultura* (circa 160 BCE), the oldest surviving complete Latin prose; in the Bordeaux invention of single-vineyard, vintage-specific, fine wines in 1660 and the consequent 1666 opening of a luxurious tavern in London dedicated to their sale, innovations that amplified both the emergence of distinction-attuned middle classes and public theatres of conspicuous consumption; in the King of

Spain's seventeenth-century ban on imported South American wines to protect the Iberian industry, which in 1766 prompted winemakers in Peru to make Pisco (a distilled grape alcohol) to usurp the prohibitions; and in the great wine merchants of Bordeaux, who since the middle ages have been aligned (albeit variably) with the English crown – indeed, in eighteenth century Bordeaux many wine brokers and négociants were of Irish descent, both Catholic and Protestant (Charters 2006; Johnson 2004 [1989]; Ludington 2013; Unwin 1991). Moreover, French and other European quality wines repeatedly feature in eighteenth- and nineteenth-century colonial records of the New World as vanguard artefacts in the form of imported wines and vine cuttings transplanted to nascent vineyards. Disseminated by the colonial elite, wine fulfilled the role of a translocated, yet durable, practice of Eurocentric commercial, religious and secular civilization (Hannickel 2013). Similarly, since the widespread neo-liberal reforms of the 1980s onwards, the aesthetic consumption of quality wine has emerged as a key component of a globalized wine culture, and as a ubiquitous marker of cosmopolitan refinement for the affluent, educated 'global middle-class' (Koo 2016: 3).

The commodity-based production and market trade of grape wine has long been a significant, and nowadays increasing, social, cultural and globalizing force – even if you only assume consistencies from the nineteenth-century rise of industrial capitalism onwards (Harvey 2014). Furthermore, in the twenty-first century, the enduring, now commonplace and banal, commodity-based, ideally profitable, creation and appropriation of surplus goods and value; the routine exploitation of physical labour, knowledge, nature and everything else; the relentless, competitive pursuit of increasing profits and market control; and the obstinate regimes of proprietorship, territoriality and stratification should all warrant our primary analytical considerations, even in these times of global postmodernity: 'The attention that post-Marxist analysis places on the fluidity and provisionality of social patterns of identification – over and above the systematicity and stability of the exploitative processes of those patterns – tacitly reproduces the logics of capital' (Tie 2015: 74–5).

As a knowingly misrecognizing wine tourist/sociologist/anthropologist, I visited the front-stage, cellar door[2] of Tacama in Peru, and compared this with my experience of cellar doors in New Zealand. I was sensitive to differences, yet within the oasis where Tacama is situated, I was inundated with familiarity and remained well insulated within my middle-class/tourist/consumer bubble (Jacobsen 2003), which was foundationally generated in my everyday New Zealand-located, yet clearly globalized and globalizing, habitus. Similar thin ethnographic experiences are replicated by wine tourists around the globe, and on this basis alone are a worthwhile measure of the globalized scope, scale and hegemonic efficacy of quality wine tropes and practices. Such experiences also highlight the enduring ordinariness of the commodification of wine and of accordant wine aesthetics, along with increasingly globalized reflexive modes of consumption, middle-class lifestyle distinctions, and the generation of benign, commensal cosmopolitanism and apolitical citizen-consumers (Srivastava 2012).

Grape wine – Nature and material capitals

The most prized wines have overwhelmingly been – and still are – those made from grapes,[3] and in particular those of the *Vitis vinifera* species. And as wine can be made from most fruit or vegetable matter – I personally have enjoyed plum, parsnip, apple, rice and feijoa wines (not to mention a hallucinogenic beetroot wine!) – it begs the question of why and how *grape* wine? In answering this question we must first note that wine grapes have nature capital that necessarily predates and ultimately transcends (given the probabilistic limits of science) the ecological, economic, cultural and all other mediations of humanity. Key nature capitals include grape vines' adaptability, sweet fruits, naturally occurring yeasts on grape skins that spontaneously provoke fermentation of embodied sugars into alcohol, and a highly complex amalgamation of sugars, acids, tannins, esters, lactates, etc., that produce juices with an unrivalled sensitivity to variations in weather, climate, topography, soil conditions (particularly water availability) and to viticultural and vinicultural interventions. Grape vines are hardy, woody perennials, which before the invention of wine grew naturally in the Mediterranean (*Vitis vinifera*), Central Asia (*Vitis amurensis*) and North America (*Vitis labrusca*). Grape vines typically grow in regions where temperatures range from 13–21°C (55–70°F) during the growing season, display a variety of tolerances to drought and rainfall, and grow in fertile to very poor soils (Jones 2006). This latter capacity makes grapes particularly suitable for cultivation as non-staple, gastronomically valued, agricultural plants (Farrington and Urry 1985). The combination of adaptation to poor soils (and non-competition with staple crops requiring arable land), and the production of a storable, intoxicating, ideally sterile, and transportable beverage that naturally provisions a constantly evolving imbrication of complex, nuanced flavours, has been valued at least since the wine appellations of ancient Egypt in 2740 BCE (Johnson 2004 [1989]; Unwin 1991), and reaches an escalating zenith from the nineteenth century onwards, with the increasing dominance of fine and singular wines (i.e. vintage, vineyard and varietal specific) and consequent modes of wine connoisseurship (Howland 2013). The noted wine historian and commentator Hugh Johnson argues that *Vitis vinifera* is the most adaptable plant and produces the sweetest fruit of any that humans have cultivated. Moreover, grape wine has long been revered for its 'brisk and refreshing' flavours that live 'so happily with food', and is 'the most repeatable of mild narcotics without ill effects – at least in the short and medium term' (2004 [1989]: 11).

Similarly, the production of grape wine has a material capital. Grape wine production as a primarily, but not a necessary, human endeavour is significantly more open to the specific cultivations of different peoples, times and places. Yet it also has enduring threshold limits and restrictions. Fail to achieve the minimal (i.e. ripened grapes, fermentation and, for practical purposes, a containing vessel) and you have a puddle of unpalatable juice. Exceed the maximum and you have vinegar. However, if enacted successfully to produce a palatable beverage (notions of which vary according to historic, social and subjective constructions of taste – Simpson 2011), the winemaker will possess a product prized since 6000 BCE for a variety of intoxicating, sanitary, medicinal, religious, hedonic and/or status-based reasons (Charters 2006; Johnson 2004 [1989]; Unwin 1991). Grape wine organically provokes a highly complex, constantly evolving, entangled bio-neural-cultural assemblage of sights, sounds, smells, tastes, ingestion, language, emotion, memories, socio-subjective rewards, and the metabolics of digestion and intoxication that the 'neuroenologist' Gordon Shepherd argues 'engage more of the brain than any other human behaviour' (2015: 1). As such, wine is an exemplary product upon which to generate the hierarchies of social distinction, which have been enduringly assigned to the possession of quality wine (however rendered) and its knowledgeable, appreciative and/or hedonic consumption.

Furthermore, in the right conditions grape wine can be stored without spoilage for decades (ideally with palatable evolutions in flavour), and is amenable to the addition of sugar, resin and fortifying alcohols such as brandy, all of which may enhance its palatability and storability. Last, but not least, grape wine, its production techniques, and desire for wine are all readily transported, transplanted and adapted along a shifting medley of migration, trade and communication routes.

In new lands, amidst different people, wine has clearly been subjected to myriad deterritorializations and adaptations. These include adulterations such as the addition of sugar, water, colouring agents, spices, fortifying alcohols and fake labels, which have been variously regarded as acceptable or fraudulent. And viticultural and vinicultural innovations encompass things like hybrid and grafted vines, innovative trellising techniques, barrels made from acacia, cypress and other woods, manual and automated presses, and transplanted vines, wine producers and consumers. These variations raise questions similar to those that invigorate critical analyses of contemporary globalization: the focusing of attention on origins; the political-economic hegemonies of, and oppositions to, various Euro-American-centricities and other standardizing flows; and pluralistic, glocal modes of being.

Yet unlike the kaleidoscopic vagaries of globalization, constitutive definitions of wine have remained comparatively fixed. As noted, it is widely agreed that wine is best made from fermented grape juice and, since Dom Pierre Pérignon's 1718 'golden rules' of winemaking, ideally from forty or so *Vitis vinifera* vines. Since the late seventeenth century, wine has also been increasingly (though not solely) transported and marketed in singular glass bottles. Moreover, the enduring valorization and increasing codification of wine tastes and quality is as wholly evident in the 'miraculous "Opimian" vintage of 121 BC[E]' (Johnson 2004 [1989]: 61), which prompted the first mention of a Roman 'first growth', as it is in Robert Parker's contemporary 100-point rating system (a globalizing phenomenon in its own right). Perceived variations in wine tastes and quality have also long been associated with the variable influences of place and *terroir*, time (seasonality, vintage, cellaring) and people (particularly grape growers, winemakers and appreciative consumers). This foundation has been utilized to ascribe elite status to those in possession of quality wines and/or with apposite wine appreciation. I suggest such enduring phenomena, no matter how commonplace or banal, are *fidelities* to perceived *truths* (Badiou 2007), and although pervasive, yet variable, across time and space, I am confident that historically distinct consumers such as Benjamin Franklin (1706–90) and myself could find enough mutual comprehension across several hundred years to share meaningfully in our respective recognitional and aesthetic responses to a 1660 Haut-Brion (modernity's first named, single-vineyard, vintage-specific wine) as we would to Haut-Brion's 2018 vintage.

So while wholly open to human recognition and adaptation – most notably through the judicious cultivation of desired cultivars, clones and hybrids, the deterritorializations and re-territorializations of varied planting sites and consumption cultures, and via the deployment of evolving viticultural and vinicultural techniques designed to enhance quality and/or quantity – the nature capital of wine grapes and the material capital of grape wine production nevertheless habitually combine to underscore the economic production, the aesthetics of taste and the politics of quality assertion, the assignment of accordant social distinctions and hierarchies, and the transmigratory potentialities of wine across all globalized wine worlds, fields and cultures (Inglis and Almila in this volume). And while these natural and material capitals will appear achingly obvious, even trite, to wine scholars and oenophiles alike, they nevertheless draw our attention – not in deterministic, essentializing or reductionist ways, but more with a lens of first principles – to the enduring, durable and fundamental aspects of grape wine at different moments of history and across different sites of production, exchange and consumption.

Elite and vanguard wines

In this section I outline a speckled history of the wine/globalization dyad, focusing on aspects that informed my wine tourist experiences. I discuss a) the incessant differentiation of wine tastes and quality ascribed to place and vintage specificities; b) wine as a vanguard artefact in European religious and secular colonization; c) wine's persistent elite associations; and d) its contemporary promotion as a consummate middle-class commodity that exemplifies novelty, progressive ephemerality and socio-reflexive distinctions.

The production of wine is rooted in the biocultural, glocalizing dialectics of local place/other place, and the accordant mutual constitutions and specificities of space, people, products, etc. Accordingly, wine never has been, and likely never will be, regarded as a 'homogenous product' (Simpson 2011: 30). Constructed recognition and idealization of difference form an enduring core of wine's ever-changing assemblages, with taste and quality variations often variously ascribed to perceived specificities of place (*terroir*) and time (seasonality and cellaring), the production techniques and the aspirations of grape growers, winemakers and vintners, grape varietals, the singularity or blending of juices, and evolutions in consumer tastes.

Such assemblages are evident across many historical moments. These include the six wine appellations of ancient Egypt (2740 BCE); the New Kingdom's (1550

BCE) labelling that specified year of production, vineyard, vineyard owner and head vintner; and the Cistercian monks' twelfth-century CE notion of the *clos,* which foreshadowed the twentieth-century Burgundian provocation of *climat* – a 'homogeneous section of vineyard whose wines year after year proved to have a discernible identity of quality and flavour' (Johnson 2004 [1989]: 131).

The ideals of progressive ephemerality in wine taste and quality were also evident in the New Kingdom (1550 BCE), where experts could 'discriminate between qualities of wine as confidently and professionally as a sherry shipper or Bordeaux broker of the twentieth century' (Johnson 2004 [1989]: 24). Contemporary notions of quality wine – valued for aesthetic taste characteristics, singularity (vintage, vineyard and commodity form), and as a marker of individual choice and social distinction – can be directly traced to the seventeenth-century initiatives of Lord Arnaud de Pontac. In 1660 de Pontac established the modern custom of naming individual vineyards and making vineyard-specific wines when he sold his Bordeaux wine, *Haut-Brion*, under the name of the estate where it was produced, and so established the 'prototype of every chateau wine from that day to this' (Johnson 2004 [1989]: 201).

De Pontac was a perfectionist and limited yields to increase wine flavour and strength, rejected mouldy grapes and unsuccessful barrels, used new barrels and ensured they were topped to the bung to limit oxidation. He made *Haut-Brion* his first-growth wine, lent his family name to his *Médoc* wine, and in 1666 opened a luxurious tavern called Pontac's Head, situated behind the Old Bailey in London. There *Haut-Brion* sold for seven shillings a bottle, when two was normal for a quality wine, and the tavern attracted London's aristocracy and fashionable men of letters. De Pontac's wines were also sold retail or 'off-licence' (Charters 2006; Johnson 2004 [1989]).

De Pontac's initiatives combined with the mass manufacture of thicker, stronger and darker bottles, with oxidation-resistant cork stoppers and the corkscrew from the 1630s onwards, and the realization that laying wine bottles on their side reduced oxidization and promoted cellaring to enhance taste characteristics. These innovations also enabled wine to be more effectively transported, and wine was increasingly sold and consumed in singular, performative forms (i.e. in labelled bottles, as opposed to barrels and non-descriptive goblets).

These initiatives also laid the foundation for the ascription of quality wine from the eighteenth century onwards as a hyper-differentiated commodity valued for its distinctive, evolving varietal, vineyard, vintage and ephemeral cellaring characteristics. Wine's capacity to be singularly acquired (in bottles) meant that it was increasingly conspicuously consumed as a mark of distinction in public (and domestic) theatres of consumption by the emerging middle classes. This also heralded a rise in wine connoisseurship, and was marked by the 'golden age' of wine books, including the 1816 publication of the 'most remarkable book on wine ever published' (Fielden 1999: 409) – *Topographie de tous les vignobles connus* – written by André Jullien, a Parisian wine merchant. Jullien rated all the known wines of France, California, South America, South Africa's Cape and 'Chinese Tartary'. He forecast the 1855 Bordeaux classifications by rating as first-class the wines of Lafitte [sic],

Latour, Ch-Margaux and Haut-Brion. Wine differentiation involves complex practices and discourses that still underpin contemporary appreciation, where wine is valued as an intensely aesthetic, evolving product, notable for its nuanced characteristics (including aroma, colour, clarity, flavour, texture or mouth-feel, etc.) and quality variances.

Terroir and other place-based assertions (e.g. appellation classifications, geographical indications, etc.) are increasingly prevalent within globalized wine fields. These assertions function as truth claims that seek to embed grape-growing and wine production – in terms of consequent taste and quality – within the perceived 'natural facts' of specific places (especially soil 'minerality') and vintages (seasonal differences) and/or the 'historical facts' of local wine cultures and winemakers. This is wilfully done to produce non-replicable, authentic and seemingly truthful (and highly marketable) notions of local places of origin and inalienable product associations. Wine is distinctive in this regard due to the 'widespread acceptance that different places, because of both their environmental characteristics and winemaking traditions, make different wine. Place is a marker of wine quality and thus a key element in product [and price] differentiation' (Overton et al 2012: 276). More generally, contemporary wine narratives relentlessly assert non-replicable uniqueness of place, vintage, varietals, winemaking techniques and winemakers, as valued criteria for assessing wines: 'Particularization: the minutiae of provenance (where, how, by whom, when an object was produced) has become a device for distinguishing what counts as good taste' (Smith Maguire 2018: 2).

Terroir is, however, a highly malleable concept and form of morality, primarily because its parameters – sociocultural and historical, but also geographic, cartographic and climatic – cannot necessarily be fixed nor agreed upon empirically or politically (Demossier 2011). Accordingly, *terroir*-based assertions of unique taste and quality characteristics are found both in the romanticized discourses of small-scale, place-specific and artisan-inspired winemakers, and in the glossy, global advertising campaigns of large-scale, poly-geographic corporations (i.e. grapes sourced from different vineyards, regions or countries). *Vitis vinifera* cultivars have been transplanted globally and subjected to widely different environmental conditions, innovative production technologies and divergent consumer cultures. This has repeatedly resulted in local, glocal and trending wine taste and quality ascriptions, such as the 1980s emergence of New Zealand (particularly Marlborough) Sauvignon Blanc and its fruit-forward, tropical fruit overtones, compared with drier, more astringent, French versions of the same varietal.

Wine has long been assigned and valued for its perceived glocal tensions and creativities. The caprices of seasonal production and vine growth alone effectively stymie the *Mondovino*-like[4] efforts of large-scale, corporate producers to standardize wine. However, the valuing of wine variance underpins another enduring fidelity – the ascription of social distinction assigned to differences in the knowledgeable appreciation and/or possession of quality wine. In other words, the 'best wines' (and vineyards, production technologies, and consumption contexts) have long been the preserve of the 'best people'. For example, wine repeatedly appears in sixteenth- to nineteenth-century colonial records as a vanguard artefact, favoured by many colonializing elites as a progenitor of Euro-religious and secular civilization for indigenous and settler populations. Tacama, Peru – which I visited in early 2016 – was reputedly founded in 1540 by Francisco de Carabantes, a Spanish priest, who is also credited with establishing vineyards in Chile in 1548 (del Pozo 2004). Established primarily to provide sacramental wine, similar vineyards were also founded by seventeenth- and eighteenth-century Jesuit and Franciscan missionaries throughout California (Fuller 1996). The first recorded grapevines in New Zealand were planted by the Anglican missionary Samuel Marsden in 1819. Marsden believed indigenous Māori would be civilized through acceptance of Christian scripture and by adopting the rational, systematic practice of European agriculture (Stewart 2010).

Marsden's outlook was shared by James Busby, a British colonial bureaucrat in New Zealand and Australia, and credited as the 'father' of Australian viticulture. Busby strongly believed in the humanist, civilizing efficacy of viticulture: 'Wine to him was not just an item of trade or produce from his budding farm, it was also the beverage of utopia' (Stewart 2010: 32). Before emigrating in 1832, Busby visited vineyards in Jerez, the Rhone valley and Burgundy, collecting vine stock, of which 362 were shipped to Sydney. Committed to 'the supremacy of the British Empire and its Tory inclinations, yet a supporter of the Mediterranean culture of the vine', Busby wrote that the colonists would be advanced 'if their habits were assimilated ... to those of the inhabitants of wine countries' (Stewart 2010: 29, 30). The appreciative consumption of quality wine – imported from Europe at considerable expense – was regarded as a particularly civilized endeavour, conducive to collegial ruminations on matters of politics and theology, while comparing tasting notes was a frequent pastime among the elite (predominantly male) colonists.

A similar wine/elite status dynamic is evident today. Since the globalization of the 1980s neo-liberal reforms, there has been a correlated increase in the global flows of wine investment capital, technical knowledge and winemaking personnel. This has resulted in the development of industries in places where grape wine historically had little presence (e.g. India and China) in the expanding influence of transnational alcohol corporations (e.g. *Constellation*), and in increasing wine exports (Anderson and Neglen 2011). Furthermore, the emergence of a conspicuously wealthy, transnationally-investing elite in China has seen intense speculation in the premium French wine market, the acquisition of quality French and European vineyards, and the construction of emulative domestic vineyards and chateaux (Smith Maguire and Lim 2015).

The globalized compression of time and space, together with increases in social and cultural connectivity and the exchange of commodities, ideas and people, has resulted in the emergence of a global middle class (Heiman et al 2012; Koo 2016; Lopez and Weinstein 2012) who are affluent, educated, mobile (as white-collar, professionalized labour and tourists) and transnationally alert. A loose cohort, the global middle class are as delineated as they are differentiated. For example, they typically value tertiary education for its capacity to enhance individual well-being (in economic, social, and knowledge terms). However, specific disciplines and qualifications (e.g. IT, economics, social sciences) often provide divergent, post-education, occupational and financial pathways, and can result in variable political inclinations. Local variance in ethnicity, religion and culture also routinely differentiates this cohort. Nevertheless, the global middle class increasingly share consumer and lifestyle aspirations that are reflexive (Howland 2014), omnivorous (Peterson 2005), and aesthetically attuned, distinction-affirming and hedonistic (Bourdieu 2010 [1984]).

Quality wine is arguably a consummate global middle-class commodity (Overton and Murray 2012) – notwithstanding ethnic, cultural or religious restrictions on alcohol – and is widely perceived to possess, as core and natural attributes, originality, uniqueness, nuance, progressive ephemerality and variegated, shifting taste and quality profiles. These attributes underpin the status differentiations and fashionable consumption favoured by the middle classes (Bourdieu 2010 [1984]). Popular ideas of quality wine are often reverentially aligned with mythical notions of French wine connoisseurship (Demossier 2010), and are part of an assemblage of refined 'Euro-chic' (Howland 2012: 113) commodities that include expensive watches, stylish clothing and gourmet foods.

Quality wine narratives are also espoused by a celebrated global/glocal coterie of artisan winemakers, wine critics, sommeliers and other cultural intermediaries (Smith Maguire 2018), who find limitless cause to express subjective, yet informed, perspectives on historical and emerging wine styles, quality assessments and other trends. This cohort voice their 'wine opinions' in national and transnational wine, food and lifestyle magazines (e.g. *Decanter, Vogue Entertaining*), through an assortment of wine and vineyard websites, blogs, shows and awards, and via publicly accessible wine clubs, vineyard cellar doors, and wine and food events. These promotional nodes effectively collude to mediatize (i.e. generate hegemony through media saturation) widely accepted quality wine tropes and thereby reinforce the association of elite status with appreciative wine consumption.

The influence of these wine culture brokers should not be underestimated. Many in the industry operate on the perception that '90 per cent or more of wine drinkers know very little about wine' (personal communication, anonymous Wellington sommelier). Many consumers make their wine choices 'by proxy' (Howland 2013: 325) and through referencing the readily accessible assessments of experts, tasting notes, wine awards and varietal bottle labelling. Unsurprisingly, aesthetic, explorative and trending knowledges of wine variance are global markers of middle-class distinction, and those with particularly knowledgeable palates are accorded significant status.

Research has shown that wine tourists – irrespective of their originating residential locales (regional or overseas) – not only coalesce around the middle-class attributes of tertiary education, white-collar employment and above average incomes, but also visit vineyards for the same reasons: to sample wines, to purchase wines they find personally agreeable (by taste and price) and to enjoy the countryside. International tourists tend to purchase less wine, possibly due to concerns about bottle weight and other travel restrictions (Mitchell 2004; Sigala and Bruwer 2016). In the following section I explore the global/glocalized ordinariness of my own wine tourist experience at Tacama, Peru, and compare this with my New Zealand vineyard experiences.

Globalized quality wines

In early 2016 I visited Tacama vineyard, situated in the oasis of Ica and surrounded by arid coastal plains. Tacama is 300 kms from Lima, and was established in 1540 to provide sacramental wine to the conquering Spanish. The vineyard has an alternating history of private and missionary ownership, and was the Saint Agustin Convent in 1821, before being purchased by the current owners – the Olaechea family – in 1889. The vineyard covers 220 hectares, and produces twenty single-varietal or blended red and white wines. These are classified as 'fine', 'classical', 'varietal', 'traditional sweet wines', 'sparkling' and 'semi-sparkling', and are made from a variety of *Vitis vinifera* grapes (including Petit Verdot, Tannat, Malbec, Sauvignon Blanc, Chenin, Chardonnay). All are promoted as good quality yet variant in fineness and price. Tacama also produces Pisco (distilled grape alcohol), a mainstay product from when the Spanish prohibited the export of South American wines in 1776.[5]

Before visiting the vineyard, I consulted Tacama's website (www.tacama.com). The site was very similar to those promoting New Zealand vineyards, although it had both Spanish and English versions. It had notes on the vineyard's history, land, products, people (owners, winemakers, etc.), wine reviews, awards and tasting notes, which most wine consumers in the Global North will find familiar. Space precludes a detailed analysis of this important communication node, other than to note that like most contemporary forms of advertising, and especially of hedonic, lifestyle and leisure commodities (Williamson 1978), its narratives are selective, naturalizing, triumphal, progressive and fetishizing. The narratives repeatedly directed attention towards wine aesthetics, and functioned as invitations to consumers to share in the winemakers' prosuming[6] passion for, and commitment to, high-quality wines, with Tacama wines advertised under the flagship banner *Vino con pasión*.

Potentially problematic issues like historical land ownership were presented as a form of progressive transfer, even when acknowledging conquest. While I have yet to encounter a New Zealand vineyard that directly addresses Māori land appropriation, the Tacama website notes its land:

> was conquered by the quechua [sic] from Cusco ... The referred area was set aside by the Inca ruler for his sacred crop: the coca leaf. With the arrival of the Spaniards, the lands of Tacama were transferred from one monarch to another ... It must be noted that despite the change of owners, its crops, the coca leaf and subsequently the grape, continued to serve those whose men [sic] considered as their only god.[7]

Unsurprisingly, the website omitted to mention the political economies of wine, aside from noting the eighteenth-century Spanish prohibition on Peruvian wine exports that parenthetically 'promoted' the invention of Pisco. The Tacama website did not list the prices of its wines, possibly because it did not have any provision for online purchasing. The website, however, repeatedly asserted the *terroir*-cum-geological distinctiveness and resultant quality of its wines, together with the progressive technical adroitness and passion of its owners:

> It is situated on alluvial land, formed during the large prehistoric ice ages, when giant landslides slid down the Andes into the Pacific Ocean and formed the valleys of today. As a result, the subsoil of the valley of Ica is sandy and rocky – similar to some of the best vineyards of France – which exercises an influence on the properties of the vines and on the quality of their fruit.[8]

One notable difference with New Zealand was the repeated mention of the employment of French oenologists who confirmed the suitability of Tacama's *terroir* for producing good-quality wines, and who sanctioned various technical developments (including 'modern' techniques, such as temperature-controlled, stainless-steel vats). Similar narratives are evident in other wine industries (e.g. Lebanon – see Saleh 2013) seeking to establish footholds in global wine worlds, cultures and fields. This compares with the more discreet, yet still reverential, ethos of many New Zealand vineyards, where promotional discourses characteristically proclaim that they have appropriated the best of French winemaking traditions, and improved these with New World innovations such as refrigerated, temperature-controlled fermentation (Howland 2012).

Such promotional nodes also act as invitations – explicit in advertising cellar door accessibility and opening times, and latent in directing the consumer's gaze towards the aesthetic, hedonic, idyllic and distinction-conferring aspects of quality wine. In this, the '"objective" truth[s] of "economic" practices' (Bourdieu 2010 [1990]: 118) – for example, the profit realization, labour exploitation, debt servicing, etc., of wine production, sale, purchasing and consumption – are rendered unrecognizable and wine drinkers are cast as misrecognizing consumers. Yet many wine consumers I have researched are either embryonically or plainly aware of the myriad economic demands generated and responded to by capitalist enterprises. Many accept (and celebrate) these as normative aspects of 'doing business' and praise the financially successful. However, many also do not define success solely, or even predominantly, in economic terms, especially in regard to innovative, creative or artisanal enterprises, where success is more likely measured in the production of superior commodities. For example, winemakers in New Zealand are routinely adulated for their urbane, balanced (work-leisure-family), creative, self-actualizing and idyllic lifestyles, while their economic success is perceived as a fitting affirmation of their winemaking abilities. Boutique winemakers are particularly adept at generating this form of enchanted forgetting. Accordingly, holidaying in the countryside to visit a vineyard and to leisurely sample a resident winemaker's creative efforts, is for many urbanites welcome time out from the cynicism of their everyday lives, although it simultaneously affirms their metropolitan-derived productionist, consumerist, lifestyle and sociality ideals (Howland 2014).

Consumers are prompted willingly to suspend or forget their knowing and instead adopt enchanted (aesthetic, hedonic, reflexive and status-conferring), fetishizing perspectives on quality wine production and consumption. The wilfully misrecognizing wine consumer effectively engages a Goldilocks sensibility (i.e. not too much, not too little, just enough) to the economic demands of commodity winemaking, and in doing so foregrounds the winemaker's creativity, passion and artisanship.

As an anthro-sociologist, who has analysed and participated in wine consumption and tourism for more years than I care to recall, I cannot in good conscience lay claim to being either a misrecognizing or enchantedly forgetting wine tourist. I can, however, adopt the guise of a consumer who is critically attuned to the differences and similarities, absences and presences that I experienced in my thin ethnographic engagement with Tacama vineyard compared with vineyards in New Zealand. Primed by the website, I was excited by the prospect of visiting Tacama, particularly as any 'exotic' wine experiences would add to my cachet as a globalized wine consumer. I was also keen to assess how Tacama's wines and cellar door compared with my experiences of wines and vineyards in New Zealand.

Beyond the internet presence differences noted above, the first major difference I noted was in the supporting infrastructure. Road signs directing travellers to the vineyard were absent or easily missed, while the roads from the central township of Ica became increasingly potholed, eventually disintegrating into a deeply rutted, one lane, dirt road for several kilometres before arrival at the vineyard's impressive archway entrance. Fortuitously the taxi driver, who transported myself and my Spanish-speaking daughter, knew the route well and negotiated the road with the sensibility of a cautious rally driver.

Mud and corrugated iron 'hovels' situated close to the dirt road, and presumably housing vineyard workers (similar abodes are evident near agricultural plantations dotted along the coast between Lima and Ica), signalled that we were soon to arrive at the vineyard. Visible and tangible manifestations of poverty are evident throughout Peru, and can give ready cause for reflection on the pronounced economic and political stratifications that exist there and throughout the Global South. However, I was also prompted to reflect on how similar stratifications exist in New Zealand, although they are not as visible or necessarily as acute. Yet seasonal vineyard workers (both domestic and those recruited from Melanesia, the Pacific Islands and other countries) in New Zealand typically earn the minimum wage without necessarily having security or continuity of employment. For many, several hours, if not whole days, of employment are required to earn enough to purchase a single bottle of the wine they are helping to produce, and that is without the demands that necessities, such as food and shelter, make on their incomes.

On arriving at the vineyard entrance, we were greeted by two uniformed security guards, one with a machine gun slung across his shoulder. These guardians of private property were welcoming and requested our passports, of which they took copies. The recording of identification details is fairly routine in Peru (regional bus operators require the same). Moreover, a search of Tripadvisor.com reviews posted by other Tacama visitors had alerted us to this possibility. Accordingly our passports were at the ready. Just as importantly, however, the view behind the guards revealed hundreds of rows of systematically spaced and trellised grape vines that also immediately engendered a welcoming familiarity of place, particularly of the commercial vineyards of New Zealand and elsewhere. A quick drive up a winding dirt driveway – mercifully flat and lined with tree and vineyard vistas – revealed another machine-gun-armed security guard standing disinterestedly in front of the entrance to the impressive Spanish-colonial, missionary architecture of the cellar door, restaurant and winery. Although the sight of another armed guard was unsettling, the vista of neatly shelved and displayed wine bottles, Visa and Mastercard welcome signs, and a smiling cellar door host, quickly reasserted that we were still in a familiar and comfortable setting. We spent a very enjoyable few hours touring the winery, lunching at the restaurant, purveying the wine and assorted sundries on offer at the retail store, and generally appreciating the idyllic locale. Moreover, I had pre-emptively ensured my credit cards were 'at the ready'.

The bilingualism of the Tacama website was replicated in the video that explained the history and production of Tacama wines and pisco, in the restaurant menu (that offered a variegated Anglo-Peruvian cuisine), and by the tour guide, waiter and shop assistant who were all competent in 'tourist English'. Besides, like many middle-class individuals in the Global North, I had the foresight and resources to ensure specialist services (my Spanish-speaking daughter) were recruited to ensure the ease of my venture. The winery tour and video focused on the production techniques (historical and contemporary) employed at Tacama. It was shown how these techniques were hygienic, were being progressively modernized, were endorsed by French oenologists, and were being adroitly deployed to enhance the natural *terroir* conferments of taste and quality. This differs from New Zealand cellar doors, where the aesthetics and experience of consumption are typically foregrounded, and where production details are framed as supporting narratives. I had, however, been alerted to this possibility by colleagues and friends who had visited vineyards in Chile and Argentina, and besides our tour of the Tacama winery ended with a familiar wine-tasting designed to affirm the quality, *terroir* distinctiveness and subsequent purchase of Tacama wines.

Long before I had sampled several wines and had assessed they were mostly of 'quaffing', or mid-range, quality compared to quality New Zealand wines, I was thoroughly charmed by my visit. The vineyard was an environment I knew well, and as such was a temporary and spatial break from the heat, aridity and sociocultural intensity I had experienced since arriving in Peru, which itself was both differentiating and concentratedly familiar. (Indeed, the last time *Coca Cola* had occupied such a salient position in my life was when I was ten years old). Tacama was not only a geographic oasis but also a dispositional one. The exotic, idyllic and urbane surroundings, the enchanted discourses of wine and food, fellow middle-class clientele from America and Peru (readily identifiable by their casual, yet chic dress, deportment and dining mannerisms), and my institutionally acknowledged status as a 'welcome' consumer-guest (of which I remained confident even when confronted by machine-gun-wielding security guards), all combined to reaffirm and invigorate my middle-class consumer subjectivity.

My Tacama experience contained other highly familiar, emphatically mundane aspects, which are firmly situated in the territorializations of globalizing capitalism and the market commodification of wine. These included the monetized sale and purchase of wines and food – facilitated by internationally accepted credit cards and well-rehearsed, consumer-retailer conventions, and the singular bottling and labelling of wines, from which (with my appalling Spanish, and only marginally better 'wine French') I was able to decipher grape varietals, taste characteristics and award ratings. Along with commonplace eating and drinking conventions, such as sitting in chairs around tables and drinking from singular bottles and glasses, I was securely cocooned by the idyllic, consumerist and lifestyle ordinariness of the experience. This was despite the prevalence of Spanish-speaking individuals, machine guns and the somewhat disconcerting, yet also thrilling, sight of the vineyard owner riding a majestic white stallion amidst the vines, as his peasant workers rode on the back of tractor-hauled trailers.

The differences I encountered at Tacama were enacted as re-territorializing, auxiliary support of a globalized culture of quality wine. Troubling historical, economic and political concerns were absenced, veiled or framed in progressive, triumphal terms. Safely corralled within the dominant, globalized logics of quality wine and associated social distinctions, Tacama was rendered both as a desirable exotic experience for the wandering wine consumer, and also as a form of benign, commensal cosmopolitanism. The omnivoristic consumption of 'foreign' foods, clothing and other lifestyle commodities is a form of benign or weak cosmopolitanism (Woodward and Skrbis 2013). This frequently consists of appropriated, abridged and exoticized narratives and materialities of ethnicity, which are purposefully skewed to provide moral, triumphal support for late-modern Western capitalism and consumerism. The globalized practices of quality wine promote commensal cosmopolitanism in regard to the cordial fellowship and civilizing discourse – the 'social jollification' (Fuller 1996: 22) – that its aesthetic, contemplative consumption supposedly engenders.

Commensal cosmopolitanism is effectively limited to those who ascribe to the globalized moralities and apoliticity evident in the commodity economics of middle-class urbaneness in New Zealand and Peru. My Tacama experience was thus cast as a shift from the compulsions of everyday necessity to the subjective electivity of recreational commerce, and, just as importantly, from the ordinary to the extraordinary or the idyllic/exotic. The idyllic vineyards of Tacama, New Zealand, and elsewhere are arguably enclaved moments of middle-class utopian being and dreaming (Howland 2019). In these settings, quality wine production and consumption represent the reproduction, and a reward for the acquisition, of valued middle-class capitals (economic, cultural, social and symbolic). Enacted within the idyllic, urbane and untroubling, the wine drinkers' middle classness is rendered exemplary and emancipatory, and wine tourists are thrice cast as apolitical citizen-consumers (Srivastava 2012).

Conclusion

The natural capital of grapes provides the necessary foundations and fundamental thresholds by which interventions of material capital may be wilfully deployed to produce palatable and intoxicating grape wines fit for human consumption and trade. Grape wine is effectively an arrested by-product of ripening grapes as they ferment into vinegar and compost. As micro-wineries, grapes possess the nature capital needed for wine – the pulp consists of water, sugar and fruit acids, while the skin contains colour pigments, flavours, tannins and the wild yeasts that turn grape pulp into wine.

Along with the land in which vines grow, grape wine thus seemingly has a natural-material solidity (Ritzer 2004) that can function as fact or truth, and which demands fidelity (Badiou 2007). Yet like all organic matter, grapes and grape wines are also persistently subject to natural evolutions, especially seasonal new growth on lateral shoots that potentially 'release mutant genes to express themselves by somatic segregation' (Olmo 2005: 39), the phenotypics of vine-aging, and the bio-physical responses to changes in climate and the human provocations of transplanting and hybridization. Moreover, the nature capital of grapes and the material capital of wine also necessarily exist beyond the limits of probabilistic human science, and are therefore always potentially less or differently 'solid' than our current knowing. Accordingly, vines, grapes and wine are also significantly liquid or ever changing in the Ritzerian (2004) sense, and this solid-liquid dynamic also endures no matter what manner of human augmentation or amplification is brought to bear.

These naturally enduring, materially-bounded but ever-evolving, universal but always particular, banal but often extraordinary, characteristics, alert us to similar potentialities in the transmigratory and globalizing histories of wine. Wine has a significant history – at least 350 years (possibly 3500 years) – of aesthetic recognition and appreciative consumption, mastery of which has routinely denoted elite status. Furthermore, wine has long been produced and traded as a commodity for profitable market sale, to the point where 'home wines' or 'free wines' now exist in only a few domestic and socially intimate enclaves.

The enduring fidelities of commodified wine production, market exchange and socially distinct consumption, together with the last few decades of globalized wine worlds, fields and cultures, and the emergence of a global middle class that is wine-attuned, mean that analysis of wine's global specificities and glocal pluralities is not enough to substantively comprehend wine variance. Variance in wines produced by different people, places and times has long been 'business as usual', a naturally underscored and socially amplified component of evolving wine tastes, quality assertions and associated status distinctions. Beyond noting and analysing variance in commodified wines from a variety of interconnected natural, material, historical, sociocultural and global-glocal-local perspectives, it is also necessary to deploy critical, benchmark comparisons (implicit or explicit) with the moralities, practices and socialities of 'free wine' – or indeed any other similarly radical alternatives (fraudulent, stolen or even spontaneous wines). Otherwise, the risk of tacitly reproducing both the logics of capital and logics of glocal variance remains very real.

And while it is unlikely that any entirely free wines exist (i.e. without the use of any commodified materials such as land, bottles, presses), even partially free wines, made with free labour and/or freely given or gifted away to reproduce the intimate sociality of family, friends and neighbours, can provide a practical contrast with commercially produced and transacted wines in any global or historical context. Moreover, comparisons with free wines can serve to highlight where and how the commodification of wine plays out in different scales from the artisanal, *terroir*-orientated to large-scale, industrial enterprises. And if ever found, those moments when the commodification fundaments of wine are eloquently ignored, resisted or transcended should be celebrated alongside all other glocal pluralities, hybridities and deterritorializations that may also signal hope for a better, more civil, future.

Notes

1. Nature capital and material capital are additions to Bourdieu's (2010 [1984]) nexus of cultural, symbolic, social and economic capitals. Significantly, nature capital – genetic, biochemical, molecular, physiological systems to physical forms – exists with, and just as importantly without, human recognition, value or intervention. The material capital of any entity, however, ranges from the wholly natural (e.g. wild grapes) to being generated and enacted via a variety of transformative interventions or other capital inputs. Interventions range from the necessary (e.g. the technical, physical, etc., inputs required to produce grape wine) to the radical (e.g. the inputs required to transform grapes into unicorns).
2. Cellar doors are wine sale sites on a vineyard.
3. Ancient China is a notable exception, with wine being made from a variety of fruits (including grapes) and rice, with 'no distinction' (Johnson 2004 [1989]: 20) recorded.
4. *Mondovino* is a 2004 documentary that examines the influence of large transnational wine producers and acclaimed wine critics such as Robert Parker in standardizing wines globally.
5. http://www.tacama.com/en/history.html, accessed January 2016.
6. Prosumers are individuals (e.g. web creators) who produce (often commercially) what they also consume.
7. http://www.tacama.com/en/history.html, accessed January 2016.
8. http://www.tacama.com/en/land.html, accessed January 2016.

References

Anderson, K., and Neglen, S. (2011), *Global Wine Markets, 1961 to 2009: A Statistical Compendium*, Adelaide: University of Adelaide Press.

Badiou, A. (2007), *Being and Event*, London: Bloomsbury.

Bourdieu, P. (2010 [1984]), *Distinction: A Social Critique of the Judgement of Taste*, London: Routledge & Kegan Paul.

Bourdieu, P. (2010 [1990]), *The Logic of Practice*, Cambridge: Polity Press.

Charters, S. (2006), *Wine and Society: The Social and Cultural Context of a Drink*, Oxford: Elsevier.

Del Pozo, J. (2004), *Historia del vino Chileno*, Santiago: Editorial Universitaria.

Demossier, M. (2010), *Wine Drinking Culture in France: A National Myth or a Modern Passion?*, Cardiff: University of Wales Press.

Demossier, M. (2011), 'Beyond Terroir: Territorial Construction, Hegemonic Discourses and French Wine Culture', *Journal of the Royal Anthropological Institute*, 17(4):685–705.

Farrington, I., and Urry, J. (1985), 'Food and the Early History of Cultivation', *Journal of Ethnobiology*, 5(2):143–57.

Fielden, C. (1999), 'Literature of Wine', in Robinson, J. (ed.), *The Oxford Companion to Wine*, Oxford: Oxford University Press, 409–11.

Fuller, R. (1996), *Religion and Wine: A Cultural History of Wine Drinking in the United States*, Knoxville: University of Tennessee Press.

Harvey, D. (2014), *Seventeen Contradictions and the End of Capitalism*, Oxford: Oxford University Press.

Hannickel, E. (2013), *Empire of vines: Wine culture in America*, Philadelphia: University of Pennsylvania Press.

Heiman, R., Freeman, C., and Liechty, M. (eds) (2012), *The Global Middle-classes: Theorizing through Ethnography*, Santa Fe: SAR Press.

Holton, R.J. (2005), *Making Globalization*, Basingstoke: Palgrave Macmillan.

Howland, P.J. (2012), 'Euro-chic, Benign Cosmopolitanism and Wine Tourism in Martinborough, New Zealand', in Boscoboinik, A., and Horakova, H. (eds), *From Production to Consumption: Transformation of Rural Communities*, Berlin: LIT Verlag, 113–30.

Howland, P.J. (2013), 'Distinction by Proxy: The Democratization of Fine Wine', *Journal of Sociology*, 49(2–3):325–40.

Howland, P.J. (2014), 'Wines of Distinction: From Elite Refinement to Reflexive Democratization', in Howland, P. (ed.), *Social, Cultural and Economic Impacts of Wine in New Zealand*, Abingdon: Routledge, 175–90.

Howland, P.J. (2019), 'Plain-sight Utopias: Boutique Winemakers, Urbane Vineyards and *Terroir*-torial Moorings', in Dutton, J., and Howland, P.J. (eds), *Wine, Terroir and Utopia: Making New Worlds*, Abingdon: Routledge.

Inda, J.X. (2001), *The Anthropology of Globalization: A Reader*, Malden: Blackwell.

Inglis, D., and Gimlin, D. (eds) (2009), *The Globalization of Food*, London: Berg.

Jacobsen, J. (2003), 'The Tourist Bubble and the Europeanization of Holiday Travel', *Tourism and Cultural Change*, 1(1):71–97.

Johnson, H. (2004 [1989]), *Story of Wine*, London: Mitchell Beazley.

Jones, G.V. (2006), 'Climate and Terroir: Impacts of Climate Variability and Change on Wine', in Macqueen, R.W., and Meinert, L.D. (eds), *Fine Wine and Terroir – The Geoscience Perspective*. Geoscience Canada Reprint Series Number 9, St. John's, Newfoundland: Geological Association of Canada, 1–14.

Koo, H. (2016), 'The Global Middle-class: How Is It Made, What Does It Represent?', *Globalizations*, 1(1):1–14.

Leichty, M. (2012), 'Middle-Class Déjà Vu: Conditions of Possibility, from Victorian England to Contemporary Kathmandu', in Heiman, R., Freeman, C., and Liechty, M. (eds), *The Global Middle-classes: Theorizing Through Ethnography*, Santa Fe: SAR Press, 271–99.

Lopez, R.A., and Weinstein, B. (eds) (2012), *The Making of the Middle-class: Towards a Transnational History*, Durham: Duke University Press.

Ludington, C. (2013), *The Politics of Wine in Britain: A New Cultural History*, London: Palgrave MacMillan.

Miller, D. (1987), *Material Culture and Mass Consumption*, Oxford: Basil Blackwell.

Mitchell, R. (2004), *Scenery and Chardonnay: An Exploration of the New Zealand Winery Visitor Experience*, PhD Thesis, Dunedin: University of Otago.

Olmo, H. P. (2005 [1996]), 'The Origin and Domestication of the Vinifera Grape', in McGovern, P.E., Fleming, S.J., and Solomon, H.K. (eds), *The Origins and Ancient History of Wine*, Amsterdam: Taylor and Francis, 29–43.

Overton, J., and Murray, W.E. (2012), 'Class in a Glass: Capital, Neoliberalism and Social Space in the Global Wine Industry', *Antipode*, 45(3):702–18.

Overton, J., Murray, W.E., and Banks, G. (2012), 'The Race to the Bottom of the Glass? Wine, Geography, and Globalization', *Globalizations*, 9(2):273–87.

Peterson, R. (2005), 'Problems in Comparative Research: The Example of Omnivorousness', *Poetics*, 33(5–6):257–82.

Ray, R. (2007), *Globalization and Everyday Life*, London: Routledge.

Ritzer, G. (2004), *The Globalization of Nothing*, London: Thousand Oaks.

Saleh, E. (2013), 'Pursuits of Quality in the Vineyards: French Oenologists at Work in Lebanon', in Black, R.R., and Ulin, R.C. (eds), *Wine and Culture: Vineyard to Glass*, London: Bloomsbury, 245–60.

Shepherd, G. (2015), 'Neuroenology: How the Brain Creates the Taste of Wine', *Flavour*, 4(1): DOI10.1186/s13411-014-0030-9.

Shortell, T. (2016), *Everyday Globalization: A Spatial Semiotics of Immigrant Neighborhoods in Brooklyn and Paris*, New York: Routledge.

Sigala, M., and Bruwer, J. (2016), 'Does Location of Origin Differentiate Wine Tourists? Findings from McLaren Vale, Australia', in Bruwer, J., Lockshin, L., Corsi, A., Cohen, J., and Hirche, M. (eds), *9th Academy of Wine Business Conference Proceedings*, Adelaide: University of Adelaide, 621–34.

Simpson, J. (2011), *Creating Wine: The Emergence of a World Industry, 1840–1914*, Princeton: Princeton University Press.

Smith Maguire, J. (2018), 'The Taste for the Particular: A Logic of Discernment in an Age of Omnivorousness', *Journal of Consumer Culture*, 18(1):3–20.

Smith Maguire, J., and Lim, M. (2015), 'Lafite in China Media Representations of "Wine Culture" in New Markets', *Journal of Macromarketing*, 35(2):229–42.

Srivastava, S. (2012), 'National Identity, Bedrooms, and Kitchens: Gated Communities and New Narratives of Space in India', in Heiman, R., Freeman, C., and Liechty, M. (eds), *The Global Middle-classes: Theorizing Through Ethnography*, Santa Fe: SAR Press, 57–85.

Stewart, K. (2010), *Chancers and Visionaries: A History of Wine in New Zealand*, Auckland: Godwit.

Taylor, A. (2018), *How Then Could We Live? Towards the Pragmatic Creation of Sustainable Ecological Habitus in Cities*, PhD Thesis, Palmerston North: Massey University.

Tie, W. (2015), *In the Place of Utopia: Affect and Transformative Ideas*, Bern: Peter Lang.

Turner, B. (ed.) (2010), *The Routledge International Handbook of Globalization Studies*, Abingdon: Routledge.

Unwin, T. (1991), *Wine and the Vine: An Historical Geography of Viticulture and the Wine Trade*, London: Routledge.

Williamson, J. (1978), *Decoding Advertisements: Ideology and Meaning in Advertising*, London: Marion Boyars.

Woodward, I., and Skrbis, Z. (2013), *Cosmopolitanism: Uses of the Idea*, London: Sage.

10 Natural Wine and the Globalization of a Taste for Provenance

JENNIFER SMITH MAGUIRE

Introduction

This chapter examines the globalization of wine from the perspective of taste. To the initiated and uninitiated alike, it is clear that wine has everything to do with taste. The organoleptic and chemical properties of wines are the mainstays of wine evaluation and appreciation. A wine's acidity, tannins, flavours and aromas of fruit, smoke, spice and so on: these are the material properties (alongside the social-lubricating properties of alcohol) that underpin the experience (if not also pleasure) of the consumption of wine. However, the taste of and for wine is not only about how it registers on the palate; it is also bound up with social conventions of legitimacy and value. These two domains of taste are not mutually exclusive (nor exhaustive): what tastes good is influenced by what is considered to be 'good taste', and vice versa. Nevertheless, it is towards the latter set of concerns with legitimacy and social value that this chapter is oriented.

The boundaries demarcating the category of natural wine are relatively porous and contested. Indeed, some would argue that such a label is nonsense: all wines are 'natural' in that they come from an agricultural crop, and at the same time, no wine is 'natural', in that it requires human interventions with regard to pruning, picking and so forth. Such wines are characterized by an explicit focus on giving an authentic expression of their *terroir* (Inglis and Almila in this volume). This tends to mean minimal chemical and mechanical interventions in the vineyard and cellar – an approach to production that cuts across those who would self-identify as making organic, biodynamic, raw and natural wines. For the purposes of this chapter, I use an inclusive notion of natural wine, within which falls a range of producers who might not consider themselves to be part of the same 'camp'. Yet they share a concern with small-scale, *terroir*-focused, minimal intervention winemaking. Examining the commonalities within this genre of wine offers insights with regard to how the globalization of an emergent genre of 'natural' wine has hinged on wider patterns of taste and legitimacy.

In general terms, the production of natural wines is associated with low-yield vineyards in which the use of chemical fertilizers and pesticides, and much of the technology associated with modern-day agriculture, is avoided or outright rejected. This typically results in hand-picking grapes rather than using mechanical pickers, and may extend to using horses and ploughs rather than tractors. These practices may conform to official frameworks of sustainable agriculture for which there are various certifications, but not necessarily so (and where they do conform, they may not necessarily be practised under the banner of a certification, since official designations and labels are generally eschewed). Similarly in the cellar, the ethos of production means that chemical interventions are kept to a minimum, be that in terms of using naturally occurring rather than commercial yeast, and minimizing or eliminating the use of sulphur dioxide (a traditional stabilizer/preservative) and other additives. Proponents of natural wines claim that these production parameters result in wines that give the purest possible expression of their place of production, or *terroir*, thereby aligning them with the wine world's established terms of quality production, while also aligning with quality conventions within wine cultures – and consumer culture more broadly – with regard to the value and authenticity of wines *from somewhere*.

A focus on taste and value is perhaps an especially apt focus for the chapter, as the cultural legitimacy of natural wines is by no means secure. Natural wine production entails particular risks: crops are more vulnerable to failure, vintages can be highly variable, and the wines themselves can be less stable and can confound established product expectations. Thus, natural wines are unstable objects of value. For example, a wine writer for *The Globe and Mail* refers to her difficulty in coming to grips with natural wines (Gill 2012: n.p.): 'If not faulty (which some obviously were), these wines seemed almost self-consciously odd.' Elsewhere, a wine writer for *The Independent* notes in relation to two natural wine fairs:

> Natural wine polarises opinion not just because of a vagueness of definition but because the-less-done-to-wine-the-better approach can on occasion lead to vinegary wines. The hit rate at both fairs, though, was higher than many a mainstream wine tasting, even if the handcrafting of natural wines can sometimes make them pricey. (Rose 2012: n.p.)

Despite such obstacles, natural wine has undergone a process of global expansion, particularly since the early 2010s. This is a process that I argue is inextricably connected to ways in which natural wine is situated within wider legitimacy frameworks of good taste. In the terminology of this volume, I am concerned with the globalization of natural wine from the perspective of the wine field: how the production and consumption – or wine world and wine culture – of natural wine have hinged on particular regimes or conventions of taste, quality and value. I examine, first, the taste regimes within which natural wines are situated; second, the cultural field elements that have accreted legitimacy for natural wines; and third, the particular alignments between discourses of legitimacy for fine wines (as circulated in specialist wine media) and the attributes of natural wines, as identified by actors in the field of natural wine.

Therefore, the chapter proceeds with a consideration of the taste regimes within which natural wine is situated: the established notion of *terroir* and the contemporary trend of cultural omnivorousness. I look at the intersection between these framings of good taste in the form of the conventionalization of a 'taste for the particular' (Smith Maguire 2018b): a principle of categorization and legitimation that privileges the specificity of provenance (e.g. details of how, where, when,' and by whom a wine was produced). I suggest that the rise of omnivorousness has been significant in reframing notions of *terroir* within a more expansive notion of provenance, and that an omnivorous taste for provenance has provided a significant framework of legitimacy for the globalization of natural wine.

The chapter then turns to an overview of natural wine as an 'institutional field' (Zukin and Smith Maguire 2004). By calling attention to the significance of cadres of producers and intermediaries, spaces of production and consumption, and other aspects of the global formation and consolidation of natural wine, we can start to identify some of the factors associated with the legitimation of a not-yet-legitimate cultural good (Bourdieu 1990). The final section of the chapter looks in more detail at how the properties of natural wine serve as points of 'attachment' (Callon et al 2002) for the taste for provenance. Here I draw on my previous research on fine wine media, and wine producers and intermediaries, to highlight how the discourse of legitimacy circulated in specialist wine magazines intersects with the preferences and practices of professional natural wine market actors (e.g. winemakers, importers, retailers and writers). I explore the articulation of transparency, heritage, genuineness and external validation as legitimacy frames for fine wine generally and natural wine specifically.

Terroir and good taste

To understand the globalization of particular cultural phenomena, attention must be given to the wider discourses of legitimacy within which the goods and activities circulate. For wine, quality claims about prestige and value have long been couched in terms of *terroir*. From the mid-eighteenth century, wine regions – and especially those of France – have institutionalized various systems of classification for the production of quality wine, which hinged on the designation and ranking of specific vineyards and wine-producing regions (Charters 2006). Bound up with these classifications is the notion of *terroir*, which connotes quality by virtue of linking a wine to its particular vineyard or place. Formed through historic, economic and sociological forces, *terroir* and appellation systems more generally were market devices for securing competitive advantage and monopoly rents (Fourcade 2012; Guy 2001; Harvey 2002; Smith 2002 [1776]).

As a corollary to the construction of *terroir* as an Old World – especially French – wine product attribute, New World competitors were excluded from making related quality claims. Thus, *terroir* was regarded in the New World as anti-democratic

(Fourcade 2012; Guy 2001). This Old/New World opposition is neatly captured in a 2004 advertisement[1] for 'the great wines in Burgundy' that depicts 'John' wistfully sniffing his wine glass:

> John, the discerning New World grower, knows all about the bouquet of white Burgundy. He just can't get it in his glass. The bouquet of a truly memorable white Burgundy stems from the 'terroir'. That's how wine growers in Burgundy describe the alchemy of local soil, climate and wine-making traditions that draw the best out of the Chardonnay grape. As for getting it into the glass, that's what the discerning drinker might call savoir-faire or know-how.

The message is clear: Old World (French) wines 'have' *terroir*; others do not. However, rather than an objective reflection of an Old World monopoly on *terroir*, the advertisement can best be understood as a defensive response. Much has changed since the 1976 blind wine-tasting in Paris, when French judges were shocked to have scored Californian wines more highly than their French counterparts (Taber 2005). Place, regionality, tradition and small-scale production methods have become increasingly common as quality claims for New World wines (e.g. Pinney 2005; Resnick 2008), and the term *terroir* itself has been absorbed into marketing and broadened in scope to include notions of personality and identity (Charters 2006; Fourcade 2012). If France once was clearly at the core of the global fine wine world, that position has eroded over time. While the following section will spell out some of the structural field factors underlying the democratization of wine worlds, my focus here is on what happens to *terroir* in the face of wider changing patterns of taste. That is, the democratization of *terroir* – with regard to a weakened Old World monopoly on *terroir* as a basis for value claims – is bound up with the much larger change to tastes associated with the rise of cultural omnivorousness.

Over twenty years of scholarship has documented the breakdown of established boundaries between the culturally legitimate and illegitimate, marking an era of 'cultural omnivorousness' in which seemingly anything is worthy of discerning consumption (e.g. Peterson 2005; Peterson and Kern 1996). Much of this research has noted the decline of univorous snobs and instead the more common profile of high diversity of tastes (preferences that cross high/low boundaries) and high volume of tastes (preferences that span multiple genres). For example, Purhonen et al (2010), examining Finnish music and literary tastes, find that the univorous snob is practically non-existent: 40 per cent of Finns report likings that include highbrow, middlebrow and lowbrow musical tastes, and highly educated older women are the most common omnivores. Similarly, Katz-Gerro and Sullivan (2010) highlight the relationship between omnivorousness and cultural voraciousness (a blurring of high and low tastes, and the quantitative scale of heterogenous tastes), finding both to be stratified by social status. Looking at leisure consumption in the UK, they find that the highest levels of economic and cultural capital are associated with the highest levels of cultural voraciousness. Omnivorousness is also patterned by gender, such that the greatest gap occurs 'between men with the highest social status and women with the lowest' (Katz-Gerro and Sullivan 2010: 193). Although omnivorousness is found across the class spectrum, it is a taste repertoire that concentrates in elites.

To be omnivorous, however, is not to like everything indiscriminately. Rather, as Warde et al suggest, the 'omnivore might be a person who is prepared to consider the merits of any cultural artefact or genre, and who is capable of discrimination among them' (2008: 150). As such, scholarly attention is required to document both the decline of old elite/low boundaries and also the emergence of new logics of evaluation and legitimation (Lamont 2012). Recent research has identified a number of evaluative dynamics through which good taste and discernment are performed, including oppositions between old and new/trendy (Bellavance 2008; Taylor 2009), modest and opulent (Daloz 2010; Schimpfossl 2014), cosmopolitan and traditional (Cvetičanin and Popescu 2011) and authentic and mass (Beverland et al 2008; Johnston and Baumann 2007). Indeed, Johnston and Baumann go so far as to suggest that authenticity is a 'near-essential part of the omnivorous ... discourse' (2007: 179).

Whither *terroir* in such a climate in which preference for *both* elite and low, old and new/trendy is prized? As a clue, we might look to other cultural fields such as gastronomy, where changing taste regimes are reflected in the rise of the 'New Nordic Cuisine' (NNC), which adheres to the principles of 'purity, freshness, and simplicity; with local, seasonal ingredients from the Nordic terroir; and with a healthy, green, and environmentally friendly profile' (Byrkjeflot et al 2013: 44). Restaurants in the NNC vein draw credibility from, and – in the light of their success in the established currency of Michelin stars – affirm the prestige of, impeccable provenance and meticulous sourcing as links to heritage, established notions of quality, *and* popular fashion and quotidian authenticity.

As for countless other cultural fields, the wine market has been profoundly impacted by the rise of cultural omnivorousness. Former divides between elite and low (or Old and New World) have broken down; *terroir* is no longer a term reserved for Old World producers (John, the 'discerning New World grower,' has his revenge!). The terms of *terroir* have become more expansive and inclusive; from narrow criteria of local soil and climate, *terroir* expands to include notions of cultural and regional heritage, personality and authenticity (Charters 2006; Vaudour 2002). Thus, wine quality claims have undergone democratization: *terroir* has been joined by, or folded within, a more expansive notion of provenance that is linked to wider concerns with, and desires for, authenticity rooted in the particularities of production (Inglis 2015; Smith Maguire 2013), the impact of which is by no means restricted to the world of wine. Emergent, aestheticized, authenticity-focused niches of food and drink markets have emerged more widely, such as craft beer and small batch spirits, artisanal cheese and salt (Maciel and Wallendorf 2017; Ocejo 2017; Paxson 2010; Singer 2018). Thus, natural wine is situated within both established and emergent notions of *terroir* and provenance as bases for legitimacy.

The legitimation of a natural wine field

As noted in the introduction, natural wine has not been an altogether stable object of value. Various critics have decried natural wines as a fad and little more than marketing hype. Such voices come from within the 'mainstream' wine world. For example, the renowned wine critic Robert Parker called natural wine 'one of the major scams being foisted on wine consumers' (Asimov 2012: n.p.). Critical voices also come from within the 'alternative' wine world. For example, Nicolas Joly – a proponent of biodynamic winemaking – described the term 'natural wine' as 'nothing more than a drawer in which to put all the winemakers who didn't make enough effort to convert to organics and biodynamics' (Robinson 2012: n.p.). Nevertheless, natural wine has readily gained visibility, thanks in part to high-profile, media-savvy champions and widely publicized events, such as the global franchises of the natural (RAW) wine fair. To unpack the formation of a global natural wine market, I utilize Bourdieu's notion of a *cultural field* – a network of sites, texts, producers, and consumers that generates practices, meanings and values of particular cultural objects and activities (Bourdieu 1984, 1993; Ferguson 1998; Zukin and Smith Maguire 2004). In the case of natural wine, four field dimensions bear specific mention.

First, the emergence of a cultural field is made possible through new social and cultural conditions, which stimulate and sustain the production of new cultural goods, and also popular interest and participation in new activities (Ferguson 1998: 601). External stimuli are necessary for fields to break with the earlier traditions and institutions that are their foundation. A field is made possible by new political pressures, economic models, technological possibilities and social movements, and the same cultural and social conditions that stimulate the emergence of a field also continue to produce interest in it (Jenkins 1992: 85). Several social and cultural conditions have served as relevant catalysts for the emergence of natural wine. Several of these conditions are captured in Howland's (2013) excellent account of the democratization of fine wine since the 1970s. He notes in particular the rise of varietal labelling, which reduces the need for expert knowledge of vineyards and regions; more accessible information about wine (via the web, wine clubs, classes and service personnel), which opens up access to previously elite knowledge; a proliferation of quality assurances, such as wine awards, points rankings and wine columnists, making expert guidance widely available; the emergence of more affordable entry points to fine wine, including tiered product offerings from vineyards and restaurant wine lists; greater proximity to the formerly elite spaces of wine, via winery tourism; and greater openness and ordinariness of the elite makers of wine, via media profiles and public events.

If such factors underpin the democratization of wine cultures and the *consumption* of fine wine, other factors have contributed to the democratization of wine worlds and the *production* of fine wine. As discussed in the preceding section, the democratization of the membership of the fine wine category is inseparable from the rise of omnivorousness, which has opened up access to producers from non-established regions to make quality claims based on notions of *terroir*, while simultaneously affirming the capacity of non-mainstream cultural goods to operate as markers of distinction and good taste. In addition, the increasing awareness of the environmental unsustainability of mainstream agri-business has reinforced the validation of natural wine (see Inglis in this volume). Indeed, concerns with ecological sustainability were central to the much earlier emergence of many of the production techniques now associated with natural wines, such as Rudolf Steiner's impact on the development of biodynamics in the 1920s (Paull 2011).

Second, the emergence and globalization of natural wine requires a critical mass of passionate, legitimate market actors: a cadre of consumers, producers and cultural intermediaries who regard the field's rules and rewards as both legitimate and desirable. Participation in cultural fields is not universal. The taste for certain fields (such as art, gastronomy, sport) is patterned by individuals' habitus, their embodied, class-bound dispositions (Bourdieu 1984), such that fields entail a stratification of actors by virtue of their relative command of field-specific forms of capital and prestige. An emergent cultural field thus must offer means by which participation can serve as tools in wider games of distinction. The cultural legitimacy of the consumers and producers serves as guarantor for the field, creating a 'transmission belt' effect, pulling new middlebrow market actors into the field (Bourdieu 1984: 1990).

In the case of consumers, the consumption of natural wine 'fits' the hallmarks of the omnivorous taste profile found disproportionately among affluent and educated consumers. For example, an interest in natural wines can demonstrate a disregard for 'elitist' notions of fine wine, thereby serving as a means for exercising aesthetic distance (Bourdieu 1984). Natural wines, while often more expensive than their mainstream competitors, are typically more affordable than established, elite wine producers such as those in Burgundy, who have long pursued small-scale, minimal interventionist winemaking. As such, natural wines also offer the chance to make a 'virtue of necessity' (Bourdieu 1984) for the intelligentsia and other middle-class consumers, whose stocks of cultural capital tend to outpace those of economic capital.

In addition to a cohort of affluent, educated consumers who seize on the emergent field as a means of demonstrating aesthetic distance and distinction, natural wine also requires a cadre of professional market actors who draw on their expertise to frame natural wine and its associated practices, places and properties as worthy points of attachment for others. This will include high-profile spokespeople, as well as legions of 'invisible' intermediaries who work to filter and qualify the goods that make it to market (Callon et al 2002; Smith Maguire 2013): winemakers, importers, distributors and retailers, restaurateurs and sommeliers, educators and writers. One very visible example of an intermediary shaping the natural wine market is the *New York Times* writer Alice Feiring. Feiring has written favourably about natural wines for over fifteen years (e.g. Feiring 2001), making a pedagogical intervention in the market with regard to what consumers should expect from such wines. In addition, she served as an early bridge between markets, bringing the emergence of Parisian natural wine bars to the attention of her American readers (e.g. Feiring 2005), thereby setting natural wine within a repertoire of cosmopolitan cultural capital. Another highly visible 'celebrity' of the natural wine field is Isabelle Legeron, or 'That Crazy French Woman' as she is known via her online blog and website, media appearances (e.g. the BBC's Food Programme), and events (including the Raw Wine Fair she founded in 2012). Legeron's website (http://www.thatcrazyfrenchwoman.com/) constructs legitimacy for natural wine via personal charisma and genuineness, as well as established credentials (e.g. her 'country-bumpkin' roots, status as the first French woman to be awarded a Master of Wine qualification, receipt of multiple awards and recognition from within the wine world).

Third, the relative autonomy of a field, both from its antecedents and in its external relations to contemporaneous fields, is signalled by the production of 'institutionally constituted points of entry' (Jenkins 1992: 85). These points of entry establish the boundaries around, and approved ways into, the arena of action. In particular, fields tend to develop distinct social spaces, dedicated to production and consumption of new products and practices (Ferguson 1998: 601), such as the restaurant, art gallery or private health club. By taking the field's activities out of the private sphere of the home and bringing participants together in a public domain, these sites allow the mutual display and affirmation of membership, status and resources. The boundaries of a site provide a literal division between participants and non-participants, while the competition between sites results in a hierarchy of elite and non-elite producers and consumers (Ferguson 1998: 605–6).

Distinct social spaces in which consumers interact with producers and intermediaries have played a key role in the emergence and globalization of natural wine. High-profile wine bars and restaurants have affirmed natural wine as part of a constellation of urban, cosmopolitan consumption practices – as when Feiring (in the 2005 article noted above) cites La Muse Vin and Autour d'un Verre in Paris, or when globally prestigious restaurants such as the Michelin-starred Noma, the epicentre of 'New Nordic Cuisine' (Byrkjeflot et al 2013), feature wine lists dominated by natural wines. Similarly influential are wine events or fairs, such as the first 'Natural Wine Fair' in London in 2011 which begat in 2012 both the 'Real Wine Fair' (organized by Doug Wregg of Les Caves de Pyrène, an importer/distributor specializing in organic and biodynamic wines) and Legeron's Raw Wine Fair. The Raw event has since expanded to Berlin, Vienna and New York. Indeed, the 2016 New York Raw wine fair attracted 2,300 visitors (Asimov 2016: n.p.). Various wine bars, stores, restaurants and events confer legitimacy (via their own status, be it conferred by awards, reviews, clientele or location) on the natural wines they feature, and provide the nodes in a global network of distribution from producer to intermediary to consumer, creating a loose network with winemakers and intermediaries globally circulating, formally and informally, through tastings, workshops, lectures and award presentations.

Fourth, fields require a 'second order' product of field-specific media (Ferguson 1998: 600). Such media contribute to standardization and institutionalization of a field's stakes, knowledge and hierarchy of positions, providing relatively stable, durable channels through which field actors exchange views, debate practices, and confirm common assumptions. This dimension is bound up with the others. Blogs, wine fairs, wine lists and wine columns are all examples of mediating devices that circulate the discourse of natural wine: a discourse that affirms the value of authenticity, discerning omnivorousness and a taste for provenance.

In sum, adopting a field perspective on natural wine calls attention to the interconnected dimensions that have underpinned the emergence of the natural wine field and the increasing durability of its cultural legitimacy and links to conventions of good taste: a cohort of educated, affluent consumers and cadres of professional market actors, visible spaces that bring together production and consumption, and field-specific mediated discourse, set against wider structural, symbolic and cultural changes in the organization and valuation of wine and consumption more generally.

Natural wine and the taste for provenance

In this final section, I look in more detail at how natural wine is embedded in and aligned with an omnivorous taste regime that prizes provenance and authenticity. This entails looking back and forth between the wider discourse of legitimacy that circulates in relation to fine wine (based on an analysis of two fine wine magazines), and the particular attributes of natural wine that are singled out by its focal field actors (based on interviews with natural winemakers and intermediaries). What emerges is a picture of how natural wine – despite often being framed as a more authentic alternative to or rejection of 'mainstream' wine (see Inglis in this volume) – complies with the expected attributes of fine wine, suggesting how its globalization has been facilitated with the established conventions and expectations of wine worlds, cultures and fields. Before turning to those findings, let me first briefly outline the research underpinning this section.

On the one hand, I draw from an analysis of how the legitimacy of fine wines is constructed for cultural omnivores (Smith Maguire 2018b). The research involved an analysis of the editorial and advertising content of *Wine Spectator* and *Decanter*, two of the most influential fine wine magazines. The magazines' readerships[2] are exemplary of the profile of upper middle-class cultural omnivores: professional/managerial individuals with an average annual income of approximately US$150,000, whose consumption patterns confirm their high levels of economic and cultural capital. For example, 86 per cent of *Decanter* readers have been on a wine-related holiday, and 59 per cent have been on a wine course; 70 per cent of *Wine Spectator* readers have travelled outside of the United States in the past three years, and at least 60 per cent claim attending live theatre, museums and attending wine and food events/festivals as passions and hobbies. These magazines – and other connoisseurship media more broadly – form part of the 'economy of qualities' (Callon et al 2002), through which particular legitimacy frames are circulated and specific product properties are singularized and made available as points of attachment. The alignment of repertoires of cultural legitimacy, and the material and symbolic properties of consumption fields (their objects and associated practices), is part of the complex qualification of goods and the tessellation of production and consumption on which globalization (in part) rests.

Cultural omnivorousness was operationalized in the analysis via the comparison of representations of Old and New World wines, coded in terms of four legitimacy frames based on prior research on authenticity, wine and other cultural goods: transparency (biographic and geographic specificity of production), heritage, genuineness, and external validation (such as appellation designations and wine awards). The findings confirmed a cultural omnivorization of the fine wine field. On the one hand, there was evidence of democratization. For example, there was no Old World monopoly on the category of legitimate fine wines. On the other hand, there was evidence of the reproduction of hierarchies of legitimacy. While representations of Old World producers could 'double dip' into established/elite and omnivorous repertoires of cultural legitimacy, representations of New World provenance as legitimate continued to be underpinned by the external referent of Old World *terroir*.

On the other hand, I draw from interpretive research involving forty interviews with natural winemakers and intermediaries (Smith Maguire 2018a). Data collection extended over several years and rounds of fieldwork in New York (2010 and 2012), Western Australia (2012), France's Champagne region (2012) and South Africa's Cape Winelands (2015). Natural wine explicitly informed the selection of respondents, all of whom are involved with natural wine (e.g. making and selling raw, biodynamic, organic, or natural wine, or on- and off-trade retailers and distributors specializing in such wines). However, natural wine per se (definitions and virtues thereof) was not a direct focus of the interview questions. Rather, interview questions focused broadly on an individual's market context (e.g. generic responsibilities linked to their present occupation, length of time and different work experiences within the wine market); the characteristics of their work (e.g. usual work practices, major obstacles to accomplishing desired ends, perceptions of their typical consumer); and their engagement with wine in their personal lives (e.g. their 'consumer' attitudes and practices). Discussions of natural wine, *terroir*, quality, taste and so forth emerged organically in the course of the interview through probing questions that followed up on respondents' comments. In terms of respondents' primary role within the market, twenty were winemakers (active in either the cultivation of grapevines, making of wine, or both), thirteen were distributors/retailers (including those selling wine to restaurants, and to consumers in restaurants or wine stores/bottle shops), six were sommeliers (qualified experts in wine, often responsible for the wine lists in restaurants), and there was one wine writer (presenting information about wine to consumers). All respondent names used below are pseudonyms.

With that methodological context as the backdrop, let us now look in more detail at the intersection of the contemporary regime of cultural omnivorousness and the attributes of natural wine, as articulated in the discourse of the fine wine field, and understood from the point of view of the natural wine field's cadre of cultural producers and intermediaries.

Transparency

The most common legitimation frame in the media analysis was that of transparency, found in 82 per cent of the advertising and 74 per cent of the columns. Through representations of the geographic specificity (via details of the context of production) and biographic specificity (via details of the specific producer) of a wine's provenance, wine magazines perform a crucial function in the construction of legitimacy. Common examples included mention of the specific geographic location of the winery and pictures of, or quotes from, winemakers. On the one hand, the origins for particular wines come to seem known or knowable (Trubeck 2005), and thus trustworthy and credible (Sassatelli and Scott 2001). On the other hand, wine in general is reproduced as the object of intellectual and aesthetic discernment – an object for which origins matter. Moreover, transparency as a legitimizing frame offers a potentially high volume of diverse choices, thus affirming wine as a legitimate field of omnivorous taste. All wines have some form of geographic or biographic specificity, and thus all wines can, by virtue of transparency, be potentially legitimate.

In my interviews with natural winemakers and intermediaries, transparency was an omnipresent quality mentioned in articulations of what distinguished natural wine from other wines, what was highlighted to others in processes of qualification (e.g. what information a wine writer or sommelier might choose to convey), and what were the aspects of natural wines that they found personally engaging. For example, Griffin is a retailer in New York specializing in natural and other small-scale production wines. He highlights both biographic and geographic transparency in his characterization of the wines he works with (as opposed to mainstream, or 'magazine', wines):

> I've taken to calling them magazine wines. They're everywhere and I'm not interested. I'm interested in showcasing *terroir*. … I'm of the view that you can't talk about *terroir* or microclimates if you're not also talking about people who are doing everything they can for the health of their land. But I'm not looking for certification. You should be able to prove it without having to be governmentally regulated or certified. So you have to find the proof yourself. As someone who buys and sells wine, you *should* be able to know. You should do that *anyway* if you're going to properly represent these families and this wine. You should really know what you're selling.

Transparency both serves as a point of attachment for Griffin in his search for wines to represent through his store, and also frames his role in the process of qualification: he is charged with preserving and transmitting that transparency to the end consumer.

Heritage

In the media analysis, the legitimation frame of heritage was found in 35 per cent of the advertising and 39 per cent of the wine columns. By providing visual and textual information on heritage, the wine magazines add value to particular wines through links to tradition and an anti-modern nostalgia (e.g. Peñaloza 2000; Zukin 2009). The most common provenance element to be framed in this way was the producer, via references to the history behind the winery, winemaker, wine brand or region. However, there were some significant differences: heritage frames were far more likely for Old World wines in terms of regional heritage (in the wine columns) and heritage of the style of winemaking (in the advertisements). This difference may reflect that Old World regions have, on the whole, longer-term histories of winemaking. However, heritage is not exclusive to the Old World. There was no significant difference in frequency in advertising representations of heritage of the winery or brand (the most common form of heritage) between Old and New World wines. The heritage of the winemaker (e.g. being a second or third-generation winemaker) was included in the feature articles more frequently for New World wines (a point of difference confirmed above with regard to biographic transparency).

Heritage was also a common point of attachment for the respondent natural winemakers and intermediaries. Consider Antoine, a natural Champagne vigneron, and the current generation of a long-standing Champenois family historically focused on growing grapes for the large Champagne houses. His account of practice (including transforming the family concern of less than 10 hectares into a small house producing 85,000 bottles annually, half of which are exported) references not only his own heritage (thus intersecting with biographical transparency for the Champagnes he makes) but traditional knowledge and practice as well. At first, he characterizes his father's generation:

> The big houses, Moët and Chandon, Clicquot, like that, they use this system [of chemical-intensive viticulture]. My father, his friends, this type of wine growers, this generation, they look at that. They think if these big brands do that, it's ok, it's perfect. Because big brands use that, put that [fertilizer, herbicide] in the soil, for the growers they think it's ok. It's normal. For this generation, a beautiful vineyard is a vineyard without any grass. And [*knocks on table*] like that, like macadam. It's too difficult for this type of people to work without herbicide. You need a new tractor. You need a new system of agriculture. You need the *savoir faire*. ... And the growers of big brands, they lose that, they lose that *savoir faire*.

In contrast, Antoine works with sustainable, organic methods in the vineyard – but this requires a different mode of production:

> We have 9 hectares and one half; and we have nine workers. One person, one hectare. ... It's difficult for the workers to work in a different way, without herbicide. ... The [local grower committee, they] don't like that. They say it's not possible. 'Don't you understand. It's completely *fou*, crazy. I can't do that.'

Heritage for Antoine is not a static referent from which legitimacy is drawn, but an active process of moving against the dominant tide of chemical-intensive agriculture. Like many of the respondents, he is not merely drawn to and affirmed by the heritage dimensions of his natural winemaking, but is also actively involved in the resurrection and development of endangered practices and values, leap-frogging over his father's post-war generation to reclaim the knowledge of a mode of agriculture associated with his grandparents.

Genuineness

The third frame from the media analysis, genuineness, was found in just over a quarter of both the advertising and columns. Previous research links authenticity to economic disinterestedness, the hand-crafted, a lack of artifice or homogeneity, and an opposition to the mass market (e.g. Beverland et al 2008; Johnston and Baumann 2007). In the magazines, genuineness was most commonly used as a frame for the producer: 29 per cent of wine columns mentioned the producer's character or philosophy. Also common was the genuineness of product attributes: reference to a wine's genuine expression of where it is from appeared in 26 per cent of wine columns, and 17 per cent of the advertising sample. However, advertising for New World wines was significantly more likely to use genuineness as a frame in this way. In the feature articles, discussions of wine as genuine (commonly in relation to being innovative) occurred only in relation to New World wines.

For the natural winemakers and intermediaries, genuineness was omnipresent as a self-claimed attribute: a guarantor of their own legitimacy. For example, Christie is a New York-based importer of natural wines. She describes how she became focused on natural wines:

> Well I always go back to the beginnings of our company when we were just discovering all of these wines and at the time we didn't know how they were made or that there were natural wines, it's just [we] would go to Paris to visit this bistro or this specific store ... and be completely intrigued and bowled over and just in love with what the wines had to say. And the more questions we asked about how they were made the more we realised that they were all made with the same philosophy, the ones we actually liked to drink happened to be natural wines. It wasn't 'Oh, here's our ethics and ... we want to go and start an organic wine company.'

Similarly, Maurice elaborates on his motivation to have converted his family's medium-scale Champagne house to natural methods in the vineyard and cellar:

> I would like to answer the question of why. Our only target, our only goal, is to make the best wines possible. Everything which would go in the direction of sustainable agriculture, or something like that, would just be a consequence of that choice. ... Our idea is to make good wines, the best wine possible, and if it helps to be sustainable, then fine. If it doesn't, then too bad. But obviously it does.

For Christie and Maurice, natural wines materially embody genuineness (e.g. both refer to such wines giving the purest expression of place), but also afford opportunities for their own personal self-authentification as social actors. More broadly, articulations of genuineness, transparency and heritage are significant for a process of consecration of the product and producer/intermediary, through which economic/instrumental motivations and commercial dimensions of the product are disavowed in order to construct symbolic capital and trust in the value of the wine (Bourdieu 1993: 81–2).

External validation

The final legitimation frame in the media analysis was external validation. Devices such as lists, wine awards and reviews (Allen and Germov 2010; Karpik 2010) remain central for rendering provenance credible and valuable for both Old and New World wines. Nevertheless, there were internal differences. Wine reviews were cited in significantly more advertising for New World wines; this difference was also found in the feature articles. Furthermore, external validation of the context of production (reference to registered designations of origin, such as *Appellation d'Origine Contrôlée*, or AOC status) was found in 52 per cent of the advertising, but was present in significantly more Old World wine advertisements (68 per cent, compared with 26 per cent of New World ads).

From the perspective of the natural wine respondents, however, external validation was a markedly different point of attachment than in the media analysis. Rather than citing awards or certification schemes, respondents were far more likely to reject such forms of legitimacy. For example, Griffin, introduced above, eschews certifications in favour of his capacity to guarantee the transparency and value of the wines he sells. Similarly, Benjamin (a New York-based retailer of natural wines) privileges provenance (genuineness, heritage, transparency) over certifications:

> By and large, we like to go with wines that are certified, but we're not caught up in glorifying 'organic' or 'biodynamic.' Here, it's really about method: smaller production, lower yields, hand-picked grapes, naturally occurring yeasts. These tend to be, by default, people who are also organic or biodynamic.

Similarly, Antoine notes that he chooses not to pursue organic certification:

> Because my importer, my customers don't need … the back label having that. They have a lot of confidence in my family, in the quality of the house. They know we make the maximum flavour, good quality Champagne. And I don't like the customers, like they look at the label and say 'Oh it's bio, I buy that because it's organic.' I don't like this type of customers. I prefer you like my wine, you taste, you're ok with the quality.

In each case, forms of embedded, personal validation are privileged over disembedded trust regimes (Sassatelli and Scott 2001). The exercise of a taste for provenance filters what goods make it to market, positioning particular market actors to monopolize gatekeeper and arbiter roles.

In both the magazines and the accounts of natural wine producers and intermediaries, the taste for provenance underpins the construction of new boundaries between the legitimate and illegitimate (from Old vs. New World wines, to geographically and biographically specific vs. mass, 'magazine' wines). In the case of transparency, heritage and genuineness, the material and symbolic properties of the provenance of natural wine (who made it, how, when, under what conditions) align with the expected markers of legitimacy for fine wine. Natural wine has no monopoly on these attributes, but its context of production (small-scale, hand-crafted, site-specific) arguably makes such points of attachment more available for articulation, both by producers and intermediaries, and for consumers. At the same time, the provenance of natural wine also provides the material foundations for alternative, embedded validation schemes that run parallel to, if not take the place of, more institutionalized frameworks for regulation and legitimacy, such as organic or biodynamic certifications.

Conclusion: From *terroir* to provenance

The chapter has explored how the globalization of natural wine has hinged on the alignment of its material and symbolic properties and field elements with the legitimacy of taste regimes – both the established prestige of *terroir* for fine wine, and the emergent omnivorous taste for provenance and authenticity. A taste for provenance – on the part of multiple wine world and field actors – serves as a tool of qualification through which specific attributes of natural wines are singularized and converted into forms of value, prestige and legitimacy. The legitimation of natural wine is bound up with the wider-reaching rise of cultural omnivorousness. The globalization of natural wine has rested in part on a democratization of access to the category of 'fine wine' such that Old World producers no longer have exclusive claims to quality or *terroir*. For both Old and New World wines, transparency, heritage and genuineness are deemed credible and valid criteria for evaluation and credibility. These product attributes have clear material anchors in the case of natural wines, given that they are small-scale, hand-crafted, oriented towards expressing *terroir*, and bound up with extinct and/or endangered modes of agricultural and viticultural production. However, I have also tried to provide an anti-exceptionalist account of the globalization of natural wines. Natural wines largely align with the expected field structure and taste criteria of fine wine, and the market development for them largely mirrors changes happening in relation to speciality food and drinks more broadly (e.g. Maciel and Wallendorf 2017; Ocejo 2017; Paxson 2010; Singer 2018). This underlines the importance of looking at how the globalization of production and consumption of wine is bound up with and mediated by more encompassing legitimacy frameworks and taste regimes.

By drawing on various data sources, I have attempted to demonstrate how the material and symbolic properties of natural wine offer points of attachment for the legitimacy frames associated with 'good taste' in the fine wine field more broadly. It is through the particularities of provenance (product, producer, context of production) that *terroir* is effectively democratized, becoming a seemingly universally available quality claim for all wines, regardless of region of origin. At the same time, the minutiae of provenance – a sort of *terroir max* – retain a capacity to serve as a device for discernment, implicated in the categorization and legitimation of some wines as fine wines, and supporting natural wine's migration from not-yet-legitimate to legitimate cultural good (Bourdieu 1990).

In closing, I would like to suggest that attention to provenance as a market device is useful for resisting the temptation to reduce people's valorization of *terroir* as being 'just' about a quest for status and distinction. Rather, the taste for provenance acts as a logic of action (Bourdieu 1977), enabling producers and intermediaries to make decisions, devise practices and discern quality. Their actions are taste-led in a way that cannot be reduced to the pursuit of social esteem. The taste for provenance is a device that enables and constrains the construction of a natural wine market in ways that do and do not overlap with the wine market more generally. That is, we can see how the same principle of division operates to construct parallel symbolic boundaries in other cultural fields, which allows natural wine to exist not only within the terms of comparison and competition set by the wine market, but also within the terms of competition for, for example, craft beer and spirits or artisanal cheese and salt.

Moreover, a focus on provenance resists the reduction of *terroir* to being essentially located in the soil, or *savoir faire*, or conversely, 'just' about a marketing pitch. Rather, notions of *terroir* are enfolded within the more expansive, yet highly specific notion of provenance, which is circulated as a global aesthetic regime by cadres of cultural producers, intermediaries, and elite cosmopolitan consumers, and represented and reproduced by the media of connoisseurship and specialist spaces of production/consumption. In this way, a field perspective enables an appreciation of how the globalization of natural wine is intimately bound up in processes of intense localization through the hyper-specification of provenance.

Notes

1. Bourgogne print advertisement. 2004. *The Times* (London) 23 October: no page.
2. Information on magazine readership composition was obtained from the magazines' media kits (available online: http://content.yudu.com/A1qxnf/DecanterMediaInfo/resources/index.htm?referrerUrl=http%3A%2F%2Fwww.decanter.com%2F; http://www.mshanken.com/winespectator/ws/WSM_Reader11.pdf), which cite various market research sources for the information: NOP 2009 for *Decanter* readership demographics and IPC Media Insight Decanter survey, January 2010 for *Decanter* reader hobbies; and MRI Fall 2010 Survey for *Wine Spectator* readership demographics and Mendelsohn Affluent Study 2010 for *Wine Spectator* reader hobbies.

References

Allen, M.P., and Germov, J. (2010), 'Judging Taste and Creating Value: The Cultural Consecration of Australian Wines', *Journal of Sociology*, 47(1):35–51.

Asimov, E. (2012), 'Wines Worth a Taste, But Not the Vitriol', *The New York Times*, 24 January, http://www.nytimes.com/2012/01/25/dining/natural-wines-worth-a-taste-but-not-the-vitriol.html?_r=0 (accessed 20 March 2017).

Asimov, E. (2016), 'Wine That's Not Only Natural, It's Alive', *The New York Times*, 23 November, https://www.nytimes.com/2016/11/23/dining/natural-raw-wine-fair.html?_r=0 (accessed 20 March 2017).

Bellavance, G. (2008), 'Where's High? Who's Low? What's New? Classification and Stratification Inside Cultural "Repertoires"', *Poetics*, 36(2–3):189–216.

Beverland, M.B., Lindgreen, A., and Vink, M.W. (2008), 'Projecting Authenticity through Advertising: Consumer Judgments of Advertisers' Claims', *Journal of Advertising*, 37(1):5–15.

Bourdieu, P. (1977), *Outline of a Theory of Practice*, Cambridge: Cambridge University Press.

Bourdieu, P. (1984), *Distinction: A Social Critique of the Judgment of Taste*, Cambridge, MA: Harvard University Press.

Bourdieu, P. (1990), *Photography: A Middle-brow Art*, Cambridge: Polity Press.

Bourdieu, P. (1993), *The Field of Cultural Production: Essays on Art and Literature*, New York: Columbia University Press.

Byrkjeflot, H., Pedersen, J.S., and Svejenova, S. (2013), 'From Label to Practice: The Process of Creating New Nordic Cuisine', *Journal of Culinary Science & Technology*, 11(1):36–55.

Callon, M., Méadel, C., and Rabeharisoa, V. (2002), 'The Economy of Qualities', *Economy and Society*, 31(2):194–217.

Charters, S. (2006), *Wine & Society: The Social and Cultural Context of a Drink*, Oxford: Elsevier.

Cvetičanin, P., and Popescu, M. (2011), 'The Art of Making Classes in Serbia: Another Particular Case of the Possible', *Poetics*, 39(6):444–68.

Daloz, J.P. (2010), *The Sociology of Elite Distinction: From Theoretical to Comparative Perspectives*, Basingstoke: Palgrave.

Feiring, A. (2001), 'For Better or Worse, Winemakers Go High Tech', *The New York Times*, 26 August. Section 3, Column 1; Money and Business/Financial Desk: 4.

Feiring, A. (2005), 'Bevy of Wine Bars Go Au Naturel', *The New York Times*, 25 September. Section 5, Column 1; Travel Desk: 4.

Ferguson, P.P. (1998), 'A Cultural Field in the Making: Gastronomy in 19th-century France', *The American Journal of Sociology*, 104(3):597–641.

Fourcade, M. (2012), 'The Vile and the Noble: On the Relation between Natural and Social Classifications in the French Wine World', *The Sociological Quarterly*, 53(4):524–45.

Gill, A. (2012), '"Natural" Wine: Fabulous or Faddish Scam?', *Globe and Mail*, 7 August, http://www.theglobeandmail.com/life/food-and-wine/food-trends/natural-wine-fabulous-or-faddish-scam/article4467582/ (accessed 15 March 2017).

Guy, K.M. (2001), 'Wine, Champagne and the Making of French Identity in the Belle Epoque', in Scholliers, P. (ed.), *Food, Drink and Identity: Cooking, Eating and Drinking in Europe Since the Middle Ages*, Oxford: Berg, 163–77.

Harvey, D. (2002), 'The Art of Rent: Globalization, Monopoly and the Commodification of Culture', *Socialist Register*, 38:93–110.

Howland, P.J. (2013), 'Distinction by Proxy: The Democratization of Fine Wine', *Journal of Sociology*, 49(2–3):325–40.

Inglis, D. (2015), 'On Oenological Authenticity: Making Wine Real and Making Real Wine', *M/C Journal*, 18(1), http://journal.media-culture.org.au/index.php/mcjournal/article/view/948

Jenkins, R. (1992), *Pierre Bourdieu*, London: Routledge.

Johnston, J., and Baumann, S. (2007), 'Democracy Versus Distinction: A Study of Omnivorousness in Gourmet Food Writing', *American Journal of Sociology*, 113(1):165–204.

Karpik, L. (2010), *Valuing the Unique: The Economics of Singularities*, Princeton: Princeton University Press.

Katz-Gerro, T., and Sullivan, O. (2010), 'Voracious Cultural Consumption', *Time & Society*, 19(2):193–219.

Lamont, M. (2012), 'Toward a Comparative Sociology of Valuation and Evaluation', *Annual Review of Sociology*, 38:201–21.

Maciel, A.F., and Wallendorf, M. (2017), 'Taste Engineering: An Extended Consumer Model of Cultural Competence Constitution', *Journal of Consumer Research*, 43(5):726–46.

Ocejo, R. (2017), *Masters of Craft: Old Jobs in the New Urban Economy*, Princeton: Princeton University Press.

Paull, J. (2011), 'The Secrets of Koberwitz: The Diffusion of Rudolf Steiner's Agriculture Course and the Founding of Biodynamic Agriculture', *Journal of Social Research & Policy*, 2(1):19–29.

Paxson, H. (2010), 'Locating Value in Artisan Cheese: Reverse Engineering *Terroir* for New-World Landscapes', *American Anthropologist*, 112(3):444–57.

Peñaloza, L. (2000), 'The Commodification of the American West: Marketers' Production of Cultural Meanings at the Trade Show', *Journal of Marketing*, 64:82–109.

Peterson, R.A. (2005), 'Problems in Comparative Research: The Example of Omnivorousness', *Poetics*, 33:257–82.

Peterson, R.A., and Kern, R. (1996), 'Changing Highbrow Taste: From Snob to Omnivore', *American Sociological Review*, 61:900–07.

Pinney, T. (2005), *A History of Wine in America: From Prohibition to the Present*, Berkeley: University of California Press.

Purhonen, S., Gronow, J., and Rähkönen, K. (2010), 'Nordic Democracy of Taste? Cultural Omnivorousness in Musical and Literary Taste Preferences in Finland', *Poetics*, 38(3):266–98.

Resnick, E. (2008), *Wine Brands: Success Strategies for New Markets, New Consumers and New Trends*, Basingstoke: Palgrave Macmillan.

Robinson, J. (2012), 'Nature's Way', *Financial Times*, 2 June, https://www.ft.com/content/778be4a4-aab3-11e1-9331-00144feabdc0 (accessed 15 March 2017).

Rose, A. (2012), 'Natural Wine Polarises Opinion', *The Independent*, 16 June, http://www.independent.co.uk/life-style/food-and-drink/features/anthony-rose-natural-wine-polarises-opinion-7848536.html (accessed 15 March 2017).

Sassatelli, R., and Scott, A. (2001), 'Novel Food, New Markets and Trust Regimes: Responses to the Erosion of Consumers' Confidence in Austria, Italy and the UK', *European Societies*, 3(2):213–44.

Schimpfossl, E. (2014), 'Russia's Social Upper Class: From Ostentation to Culturedness', *The British Journal of Sociology*, 65(1):63–81.

Singer, A. (2018), 'Strategies of Distinction: Aesthetic Materiality and Restrained Discourse', *Poetics*, 67:26–38.

Smith, A. (2002 [1776]), 'Of the Rent of Land', in Mazlish, B. (ed.), *The Wealth of Nations: Representative Selections*, Mineola, NY: Dove Publications, 103–04.

Smith Maguire, J. (2013), 'Provenance as a Filtering and Framing Device in the Qualification of Wine', *Consumption, Markets and Culture*, 16(4):368–91.

Smith Maguire, J. (2018a), 'Taste as Market Practice: The Example of "Natural" Wine', in Venkatesh, A., Cross, S., Ruvalcaba, C., and Belk, R. (eds), *Consumer Culture Theory Research in Consumer Behavior*, Bingley, West Yorkshire: Emerald Publishing, 71–92.

Smith Maguire, J. (2018b), 'The Taste for the Particular: A Logic of Discernment in an Age of Omnivorousness', *Journal of Consumer Culture*, 18(1):3–20.

Taber, G.M. (2005), *Judgement of Paris: California vs. France and the Historic Tasting That Revolutionized Wine*, New York: Scribner.

Taylor, T.D. (2009), 'Advertising and the Conquest of Culture', *Social Semiotics*, 19(4):405–25.

Trubeck, A.B. (2005), 'Place Matters', in Korsmeyer, C. (ed.), *The Taste Culture Reader*, Oxford: Berg, 260–71.

Vaudour, E. (2002), 'The Quality of Grapes and Wine in Relation to Geography: Notions of Terroir at Various Scales', *Journal of Wine Research*, 13(2):117–41.

Warde, A., Wright, D., and Gayo-Cal, M. (2008), 'The Omnivorous Orientation in the UK', *Poetics*, 36(2–3):148–65.

Zukin, S. (2009), *Naked City: The Death and Life of Authentic Urban Places*, New York: Oxford University Press.

Zukin, S., and Smith Maguire, J. (2004), 'Consumers and Consumption', *Annual Review of Sociology*, 30:173–97.

11 Wine, Women and Globalization: The Case of Female Sommeliers

ANNA-MARI ALMILA

Introduction

The research presented in this chapter started in the early 2010s on a winter afternoon in Helsinki, Finland. I was sitting in a large hotel's wine bar and glancing through a Swedish wine magazine: just glancing, as I was not in the mood to read. What I noticed, however, struck me quite forcefully. In the whole magazine, there was just one woman featured in just one of the pictures. She was walking behind two men in a vineyard. If this absence of female presence was the case in a *Swedish* magazine, I found myself thinking, what would be the situation elsewhere?

I have since found that this magazine may have been an exception and that even in places where one would least expect women to feature strongly in traditionally male-dominated wine-related professions, one may find surprising numbers of women operating in wine worlds, cultures and fields today. However, the first push for me to conduct research on (globalizing) wine and women had been given. I wanted to understand both my own experiences as a female wine lover (who often both eats and has a drink alone when travelling), and also the relations that pertain today between women and wine more generally. One thing I came to notice was that a lot of female wine experiences are shaped by forms of *mobility*: geographical, social and cultural. In fact, women's relationships with wine are often enabled in the first place through trans-border movements of wine, people, ideas and knowledges. Things that would have been impossible in relatively closed and apparently unchanging socio-cultural settings are increasingly possible for cosmopolitan women as they travel, move abroad and claim new spaces and experiences in globalized wine environments.

Globalization processes often operate in ways that are highly gendered (Acker 2004; Chow 2003). Many of the consequences of these processes are unpredictable and unintended. One interesting consequence of the increasing interconnectedness of wine worlds, cultures and fields across the planet has been the rise of women inside the wine industry (Matasar 2006). When winemaking operated as a solely or primarily agricultural, traditional and earth-bound practice, it remained highly bound by localized patriarchal structures (Lem 2013). Such structures might, for example, define women's roles as involving supplying specific types of alcohol for the men who consume them

(Dietler 2006), or they might define certain parts and areas of wine production, such as labour in wine cellars, as out of bounds for women (Matasar 2006). And while many such long-standing structures (as well as new forms of gender discrimination) abound, yet various changes in the processes of wine production, distribution, mediation and consumption have created new opportunities for women to operate in wine worlds and cultures. Formal education has been one such factor. University degrees in oenology and wine management have been helpful for substantial numbers of women in establishing themselves as winemakers, often focused on producing high-quality wines (Brenner 2007; Matasar 2006). On the other hand, globalization processes have also enabled multinational corporations to gain power in wine production and supply, and these big businesses are usually not very keen on having women in higher management and leadership positions. Indeed, even when women working in such businesses often think there is no significant gender discrimination present, nonetheless 'masculine' organizational cultures and hierarchical gender differences remain obdurate facts (Bryant and Garnham 2014). Wine is gendered in a myriad of ways, and this is reflected in levels of professional and other forms of involvement in wine worlds: for example, wine professionals are more likely to be male than female. Gendered power operates in wine cultures in terms of shaping behaviours (women and men often buy wine differently, as discussed below) and also shapes the discourses to be found in wine fields (connotations in regard to the tastes and smells of wine commonly evoked by femininity often differ from those that masculinity invokes (Inglis 2019)).

In the first two sections of this chapter, I draw together different factors to do with wine and gender, which today are thoroughly bound up with globalization processes. I examine how wine has been gendered throughout the centuries and remains so today, although in changing ways. I focus here primarily on how women have drunk wine, and how women have been supposed to taste wine. Female winemakers have been the focus of academic writing before now (e.g. Matasar 2006), but accounts of women drinking wine are much more scattered. I here seek to gather these writings together. Thereafter, I discuss how wine has also been marketed differently to women, particularly in cases where (middle-class) women have been the sole target group of a particular wine. I then turn to discuss how gender operates in wine mediation, in the particular case of sommeliers, which as a professional category is highly globalized and exists across diverse locations and national contexts.

In my discussion I draw upon a variety of data gained through a number of methodological orientations. My work is partly ethnographic and auto-ethnographic. I have spent time over the last decade observing professional settings such as restaurants, wine-tastings and wine fairs. I have interviewed eight professional women (introduced later in this chapter) who work as sommeliers and wine experts in Helsinki, Tampere (Finland), Rome and Copenhagen. I have also spoken informally with many wine professionals, both women and men, across Europe. In addition to field data, I draw upon books and journalistic accounts written by and about women in the wine industry. These sources throw light on the fact that many of the struggles, and sometimes successes, of female wine professionals are similar across different geographical locations, as well as showing that the ways these women make sense of their experiences are often shared across national boundaries.

Women drinking wine

The history of women and wine could be narrated as a series of more or less strict prohibitions, restrictions and moral concerns, both formal and informal. While there are no comprehensive histories in this regard, and proof of how exactly wine has been gendered throughout the centuries is often little more than anecdotal, some general points can be drawn from the available literature.

These especially involve moral concerns to do with different kinds of laxity women have been considered to be prone to when consuming alcoholic beverages. For example, in Ancient Egypt, women's drinking of wine was often associated with intoxication, excess and sexual license (Phillips 2000). In ancient Greece, female alcohol consumption was considered a threat to the household by men – mostly because alcohol consumption was seen to lead to financial ruin and neglect of domestic duties: 'O great blessing for the wine-merchants, and a curse in turn for us! And what a curse again for the household utensils and the weaving!', says a male character in a play by Aristophanes (in Davidson 1998: 191).

In ancient Rome, documents from earlier periods of the city's history indicate that women were not allowed to consume wine, and although some of those restrictions loosened with time, still wine consumption was a socially risky business for women. Those women dwelling in, or associated with, venues of wine consumption were likely to be prostitutes or were otherwise considered sexually available to patrons (Purcell 1994). The Roman poet Juvenal said as much: 'When she is drunk, what matters to the Goddess of Love? She cannot tell her groin from her head' (in Matasar 2006: 6). Some have also claimed that the most valued wines were considered too strong for women, even when diluted with water, and instead women turned to alternative 'wines' made specifically for them, concorted from asparagus or various herbs (Soyer 2004 [1853]: 333).

Wine's survival in Europe during the medieval period is attributed largely to the Catholic Church, whose gender views came to be established such that women were often excluded from wine worlds and cultures. Such gender exclusion is not necessarily Biblically-derived, as Jewish law does not exclude women from drinking wine in celebrations (Matasar 2006).

Moralistic gender distinctions survived in Europe in different forms for a long time (and still do to a certain extent). For example, while in the late eighteenth and early nineteenth centuries in Britain, Port wine was much favoured by both middle and upper classes, it was drunk only in small amounts by women in those classes. Instead, women were expected to leave men to drink Port (and to reach considerable levels of drunkenness), while having tea and pursuing more prudent conversational topics among themselves. While women both bought and drank wine, they were likely to do so at home, as drinking outside the domestic domain was associated with prostitution. Meanwhile, men consumed both wine and women simultaneously, for an alcoholic drink bought for the prostitute was considered part of her payment (Ludington 2013). Such spatial division had not always been in place: in fifteenth century Britain, upper-class women could go to taverns to drink wine along with their menfolk (Colquhoun 2007: 77). As the nineteenth century went on, the British taste for drink, and how wine was gendered, started shifting. Upper- and middle-class women were increasingly drinking sherry, including outside the domestic sphere, for example at the theatre. Yet some wines remained gender restricted: Port was considered a man's drink, while women regularly had (small amounts of) sherry and champagne (Ludington 2013).

One element which is significant here is that fermented grape juice is both a *wine* – with sometimes mythical and mystical associations – and an alcoholic drink like other forms of alcohol. In many cases, wine's position as available only to some types of people rather than others has been connected to its position as a *luxury* drink. According to Veblen (1994 [1899]: 51),

> In communities where the popular habits of thought have been profoundly shaped by the patriarchal tradition we may accordingly look for survivals of the tabu on luxuries at least to the extent of a conventional deprecation of their use by the unfree and dependent class. ... [W]omen are to the greatest extent subject to a qualified tabu on narcotics and alcoholic beverages ... [where] the general rule is felt to be right and binding that women should consume only for the benefit of their masters.

In other words, women should not enjoy the luxury of drinking (especially a relatively luxury product like wine) for their own benefit. Moreover, women have also often been considered to become sexually loose if they are allowed to drink alcohol in excess. What could be more disturbing to a patriarchal social order than women indulging not just in alcohol but in high-quality wine? And conversely, what could be a clearer indication of changing moral and gender attitudes than the increasing social acceptability of a woman drinking wine *alone*, in a public place, and for her own pleasure?

Alcohol has often been associated with men and masculinity, and women's relationships to alcohol have either been ignored (as if they did not exist), or condemned, or even accepted as less problematic than male alcohol consumption (McDonald 1994a). It is also the case that many restrictions on alcohol drinking that have existed historically have concerned upper- and middle-class women who needed to guard their reputations. Conversely, lower-class women's alcohol consumption has caused various sorts of moral panics, which seem often to have been voiced by elites rather than socially enforced by people of the lower classes themselves (Thom 1994). Just as attitudes towards alcohol and drunkenness in general have varied across different times and places (McDonald 1994a), so too have attitudes towards female consumption of alcohol, and specific alcoholic drinks, varied. For example, in Soviet Georgia, (foreign) prostitutes were the only women supposed to drink alcohol in excess, and drunkenness was supposed to happen legitimately only among male groups. Women were also expected not to touch spirits, even when consuming alcohol during celebrations (Dragadze 1994). In another example, this time from western France in the

1990s, young women could enjoy 'cosmopolitan' light beers and cocktails in bars, local red wines being drunk mostly by elderly men, while a generation or two earlier, only sweet liquors and fine wines would have been (very occasionally) available for women in celebrations (McDonald 1994b).

So, in most cultural contexts, women are supposed to be able to take smaller amounts of alcohol than men, in terms of both the strength and amount of the drink (Dietler 2006). This is a dogma that continues to be embodied in governmental recommendations as to levels of permitted alcohol consumption, which typically recommend different limits for men and women. (In 2017, the UK became a notable exception to this rule, recommending the same limits for everyone.) But for a female wine lover who prefers to consider a restaurant's whole wine list – not only wine-by-the-glass and half bottles – as an opportunity for engaging in pleasurable consumption, it is sometimes difficult to get what one orders. Elizabeth David, legendary English food writer, lamented in 1962 in an essay called 'Ladies' Halves' that she struggled to get a full bottle of wine even to share with a female friend, let alone when she ordered it for herself. She recalled a male staff member in a railway restaurant carriage exclaiming: 'A bottle madam? A whole bottle? Do you know how large a whole bottle is?' (David 2009 [1962]: 46). When in 2016 I was asked by a confused-looking waiter in a London restaurant that in my order I surely had meant a half bottle – the wine that I wanted was not available in half bottles – I excitedly messaged a colleague, 'I was offered a ladies' half!!!'.

Women tasting and choosing wine

The belief that women have different tastes, and prefer different drinks, from those favoured by men has a long history. In the 1870s, during a visit to North America, the French botanist Jules-Émile Planchon[1] described a local wine in his tasting notes: *'Diluted syrup in which the ladies delight.* No vinosity; no strength; no bouquet. Very inferior' (cited in Campbell 2004: 135, emphasis mine). The assumption that women 'naturally' prefer sweet flavours has survived into later times. Sweeter white wines have been described as 'womanly' (as opposed to 'manly', robust red wines) until quite recently (e.g. Cowan 1991: 184), and also some sommeliers I spoke with indicated that particularly older generations of women tend to prefer their wine sweet.

Although the habit of describing wines as 'feminine' and 'masculine' has been found unhelpful and uninformative by wine drinkers (Inglis 2019), and is practically abandoned altogether today in globalized wine fields and cultures (Gallo 2007), some gender distinctions are still taken for granted by many wine professionals and amateurs. Some of these are claimed to be based on biology, such as the sense of smell, which has great significance for how wine is experienced (Matasar 2006). While women in general have been found in tests to be better at distinguishing and sensing smells than men are, the training of smelling is actually a more significant factor than gender. Those trained in distinguishing certain scents can smell more accurately than untrained individuals, irrespective of their gender (Fox n.d.). And while it is true that, for example, hormones influence sensory experiences, sensory dispositions are also largely shaped by individual experiences:

> The perception of smell consists not only of the sensation of the odours themselves but of the experiences and emotions associated with these sensations. Smells can evoke strong emotional reactions. In surveys on reactions to odours, responses show that many of our olfactory likes and dislikes are based purely on emotional associations. (Fox n.d.: 4)

As seen above, the supposed preference for sweetness on the part of women has a long history. Thus in sixteenth-century Britain, wine was 'sweetened with sugar for the ladies' (Colquhoun 2007: 100), and a few hundred years later, women were still considered to prefer a glass of something 'strong and sweet' (Ludington 2013: 235). But more global changes have happened in terms of sweetness in wine, which has come to be considered old-fashioned, unsophisticated, parochial and anti-cosmopolitan in many locations across the world (see e.g. Taplin and Kjellgren, both in this volume). At the same time, wine drinking in general has come to be coded as more 'female' (with perhaps the exception of appreciation of heavy reds and serious wine connoisseurship more generally) (Matasar 2006). In some locations, such as the United States, wine has become the preferred alcoholic drink more for women than for men (Barber et al 2006).

Women have also been found to buy wine in different ways from men, with a different level of engagement (Barber et al 2010), and with more reliance on mediators such as wine shop staff, sommeliers and visible information, such as about wine awards (Atkin et al 2007). An Australian study indicated that women with low levels of wine expertise drank significantly more sparkling and white wine than men or high-expertise women (Johnson and Bastiani 2007). According to one UK-based study, women buy more wine than men, but their buying is more casual and 'safe', and is likely to happen in supermarkets rather than in specialist shops. Women often perceive their wine knowledge as low level, consider buying for special occasions as risky, and thus are likely to pass the responsibility onto male members of their family (Ritchie 2009). In a study from the early 1990s, now perhaps somewhat dated, it was found that men are special occasion buyers and decision makers (often aided by staff, who, for example in restaurants, customarily used to hand the wine list to a male member of the party). The ritual of wine serving and tasting has been associated with men rather than women, while men were not particularly good at coping with wine-savvy women (Nicolson 1990).

Such patterns of wine serving and drinking are, in my experience, changing, particularly among younger service staff. Wine serving usually follows one of two rules today: either tasting is done by the person who ordered the wine, or the staff member asks who will taste the wine. But before such changes in service culture, I needed many times to fend off a waiter from my father (a teetotaller), when they expected him to taste the wine I had ordered. And while practically all my female friends and colleagues happily pass the responsibility of choosing wine to me (a forty-something white woman), such is not the case with all male acquaintances, especially those senior to myself.

Marketing wine to women

Wine marketing today follows increasingly globalized scripts (Inglis in this volume). Gendered marketing devices are worth paying some attention to in this light. Given the differences in patterns of female and male wine buying and drinking, it is perhaps not altogether surprising that some producers of wine have decided to target female consumers with special products aimed especially at them. There seem to be two assumptions in play here (partly supported by consumer research, as indicated above). First, women find wine-buying challenging and want it to be easier and 'safe'. Second, women would on the whole prefer low alcohol and calorie levels. Here the target group seems to be middle-class women who are assumed to be highly diet-conscious. For example, the Californian company Beringer Blass launched *White Lies Chardonnay* in 2005, with the idea that women would want specific things from wine. As explained by their representative Tracey Mason, 'as wines are becoming so alcoholic, it is difficult to drink a glass of wine during the week, especially with women's busy lives and having kids'. 'Women would really like to have a glass of wine but might forego it because of the demands on their lifestyles.'[2] Mason further claimed that wine is 'unapproachable' for women and that this new wine spoke to women using 'our language'.[3] This apparently involved the idea of wine being a sort of guilty secret, the drinking of which required the telling of little white lies towards one's family and peer group (and perhaps oneself). The wine being launched was made out of under-ripe grapes, which results in naturally low alcohol and sugar.[4]

Other producers have targeted more directly the hidden calories often today associated with wine. For example, Bethenny Frankel from the Skinnygirl company in the United States is primarily concerned with this: 'I'm not a wine connoisseur, but I do love a refreshing, great-tasting glass of wine and that's what I've created. There is a selection of red, white and rosé varietals [actually they are generic blends, not grape or region varietals] ... and each serving is only 100 calories – 15 per cent lower than most other brands.'[5] Skinny Prosecco, more recently launched by the Englishwoman Amanda Thomson, targets sugar levels from another, slightly different angle. She taps into current globalized health trends, attracting celebrity interest, useful media coverage and consequent buoyant sales in the UK, where her offerings sell in higher-end supermarkets.[6] However, not all media coverage has been friendly. She noted: 'We laughed when we were called the "basic bitch drink of the summer" in the media but demand has been off the scale. It said something quite significant about the gap we'd discovered in the wine market.'[7] Therefore it seems that while low-calorie, low-alcohol and low-sugar 'healthy' wines may be associated with women and femininity, the recent trend of marketing them seems to be less focused on gender per se and more on gendered lifestyle. (I am not sure what to make of the fact that the first occasion I met this drink was in a London airport champagne bar, where the advertisement showed a piccolo bottle with a stripey straw. I have never seen this drink offered there since then, so it probably was not a success in that location.) But what is interesting is that the old assumption of women's preferences for sweeter wines seems to have become dated today, at least for the aspirational middle classes in the wake of transnational health trends. At the same time, global trends in wine flavour preferences have moved from sweet to dry more generally, while women are buying more wine than ever before.

The origins and globalization of the sommelier

Having looked at broader patterns concerning gender and wine consumption, I will now home in on a particular case of how women operate in globalized wine worlds, cultures and fields, namely working as sommeliers, a traditionally male-dominated profession. A sommelier, the *Oxford Online Dictionary* informs us, is a 'wine waiter'. The word originated in French in the early nineteenth century and meant literally 'butler'.[8] 'Butler', on the other hand, is a Middle English word deriving from the Old French term 'bouteillier' – 'cup-bearer', deriving from 'bouteille', meaning 'bottle'. 'Butler' meant 'the chief manservant of a house'.[9] While professional sommelier associations still tend to stress high levels of knowledge about wine as a key defining factor of the profession, particularly in Anglo-Saxon contexts the term 'sommelier' is nowadays often considered to be a sales and service person, doing a job that can also be called 'wine steward' (see e.g. Manske and Cordua 2005).

The history of the sommelier is traceable to France, and it is there that the first professional association (the *Union des Sommeliers*) was established in 1907. Many other wine professional bodies, both national, regional and international, have been established since then, such as the *Wine & Spirit Education Trust* (WSET). This London-based educational body, which offers a range of wine-related certificates, was first created for the purposes of the British wine trade, but its certificates have since become a globalized form of recognition of wine expertise. While the numerous qualifications offered by the WSET are sought by many other wine professional groups, a WSET award or diploma is certainly a form of high cultural capital for a professional sommelier, and such awards and diplomas can today be secured in a number of locations beyond London, and in a number of languages beyond English. This is in itself a sign of the globalization of wine-related professions, in line with broader processes to do with the transnationalization of wine education today (Inglis in this volume). These kinds of qualifications (and also those offered by the *Court of Master Sommeliers*) are also important steps en route to the highly regarded award of the Master of Wine, granted since 1955 by the *Institute of Masters of Wine*.[10]

Examining webpages belonging to professional sommelier associations, based throughout Europe, North America, Australasia and other locations, it is hard not to come to the conclusion that being a sommelier is largely a 'male and pale' type of occupation, at least when it comes to representation at the higher end of the field. So, for example, the *Court of Master Sommeliers* currently has an all-male, all-white executive board with one (white) female administrator.[11] The *Association de la Sommellerie Internationale* is slightly less exclusively male in composition, but their sommelier competitions have until recently been dominated by men, which in turn has created a competition panel, formed by previous winners, that is all-male. Women seem to be allowed to serve in managerial roles.[12]

Another area of male over-representation is the realm of the 'celebrity sommelier', a concept that was promoted, and to a certain extent created, by the US documentary film *Somm* (2012). The film follows the attempts of four male sommeliers (three white, one black) in the United States to pass the demanding Master Sommelier (MS) exam, which is awarded by the UK-based but internationally present *Court of Master Sommeliers*. While the film seeks to document the protagonists' journey towards passing the exam (or failing it), in practice it also engages in certain forms of myth-creation, such as declaring some individuals as outstanding tasters with apparently almost superhuman abilities. The film received a standing ovation from an audience of wine professionals when it was first shown at the Napa Valley Film Festival.[13] While supposed to be an investigative documentary, the film actually moulds and confirms myths rather than taking them apart, and so is essentially a film that constructs a new breed of wine-related celebrities. The film was popular enough to spawn a sequel about winemakers (*Into the Bottle*, 2015). A second sequel was announced in March 2018 with three celebrity wine professionals featuring in it: Steven Spurrier (former wine merchant, the organizer of the (in)famous *Judgment of Paris* wine-tasting in 1976 – see Inglis in this volume), Jancis Robinson (MW, wine critic, journalist, author, and one of the highest profile women in the global wine field) and Fred Dame (MS, with numerous other recognitions, who was already featured in the first film).

In the original *Somm*, gender roles are sometimes displayed in a markedly unquestioning manner. For example, one of the candidates very seriously tells the camera that he wants to pass the exam for his wife's sake, and well may he say so: the woman in question had told us earlier in the film that she would constantly come home to find full spittoons (a bucket where you spit the tasted wine, to avoid intoxication while tasting), which her husband and his friends – all restaurant professionals – had left behind, and which she would end up cleaning by herself. This, apparently, was not considered as problematic by anyone, including the film-makers, who seem to expect a similar non-response to this patriarchal situation on the audience's behalf.

However much the representation of sommeliers involves the foregrounding of the 'male and pale', actual working life can be different, including professionals from different backgrounds, genders and ethnicities. This situation is likely to continue to shape both restaurant service culture and the increasingly globalized wine world in the future. One important element here is how restaurant service is viewed more generally, both by professionals within it and by the publics being served by it.

For example, over a decade ago, Natalie MacLean (2007: 243), a Canadian wine writer, described an encounter with a particular sommelier, 'a dour gentleman', in an unnamed European country. 'As he waited for me to try the wine, he tapped his index finger on the bottle – waiter code for "Hurry the hell up, I've got larger groups to serve, for better tips"'. MacLean found the (high prestige, and therefore pricey) wine corked, but was so intimidated by the sommelier that she at first failed to tell him so. When she finally had the courage to suggest that the sommelier taste the wine for himself, he denied there was anything wrong with it. Eventually the situation was resolved by a female restaurant manager, and dinner, with an unspoiled bottle of wine, was served in a private room. While this narrative is of course anecdotal, it does illuminate changes that have happened in the restaurant world in recent times. The sommelier profession today is about much more than just possessing high levels of wine knowledge, with customers expecting a different kind of service than they likely did in previous decades.

Some people in fact argue that broader changes in customer expectations are a major reason why women may nowadays perform well as sommeliers, as they may not intimidate their customers as much as old-style male sommeliers did (or do still), and can also be less hazardous in terms of handling sometimes fragile customer egos (see e.g. Matasar 2006: 154). A sommelier is now expected both to persuade the customer to buy wine, and to make them feel comfortable (Manske and Cordua 2005). There has been a corresponding shift in the sommelier's defined role: from merely having wine knowledge, towards a broader service ethos, where selling wine involves many other elements too, such as creating user-friendly wine lists that give easily accessible information (e.g. grouping wines according to character or listing what is available by well-known grapes), and offering wine in different quantities (by the glass, or carafe, or half bottle) (Dewald 2008). In line with this, the WSET has until recently offered an Award in Wine Service qualification in addition to more traditional knowledge-based wine and spirit qualifications.

Yet the strong knowledge element of the job remains in place, meaning that at the pinnacle of the profession, it has been found by researchers that 'sommeliers' brains show specialization in the expected regions of the olfactory and memory networks, and also in regions important in integration of internal sensory stimuli and external cues' (Banks et al 2016: unpaginated). It is certainly true that to be a sommelier today is much more demanding in terms of knowledge than it has been previously. One can no longer only master the classic wine regions of the world. One has to be able to know in detail about emerging regions in established countries, as well as new regions in countries just recently emerged onto the global wine radar. Keeping a track on ever-changing developments across the world can be very challenging. In essence, a sommelier today has to have a constantly updating map of wine globalization in their heads, and must use that knowledge to guide clients within an ever more demanding globalized service culture. There is a level of gendering involved here: the idea of 'mastering' anything is in itself a gendered concept, evoking a 'masculine' idea(l) of detailed and extensive knowledge. One of my informants called this a 'geek' element in the sommelier job, another concept associated with a type of masculinity and masculine 'mastery'.

Sommeliers influence patterns of wine consumption in various ways. They enhance wine sales both in terms of persuading more people to order wine and also through encouraging them to try higher quality and more highly priced wines (Dewald 2008; Manske and Cordua 2005). They may also influence clients to try more 'adventurous' wines from hitherto more obscure regions, thus contributing to the globalization of palates. And it is certainly the case that in choosing which wines to sell in the restaurant, they have direct influence on what it is possible for customers to order in the first place.

In this regard, many sommeliers are influenced by transnational wine trends. An illuminative example of this is that well over a third of London restaurant wine lists currently feature organic, biodynamic and/or natural wine,[14] whereas a decade ago one would have found hardly any wines of these categories (see Inglis in this volume). Whether this relatively rapid change is due to similar processes which Blumer (1969) called 'collective selection' in clothing fashion buying remains to be empirically proven. The following quote from one of my Finnish sommelier informants seems to indicate that it may be so. She was speaking of natural, organic and biodynamic wines, considered very fashionable in Finland today. She declared that she was not *seeking* to make a wine list explicitly based on these types of wine, stating that 'what wines I've tasted, and what feel good, by chance they have happened to be of these styles'. Smith Maguire (this volume) shows how a wide variety of media and influencers are involved in making something like 'natural wine' ever more widely known in and across multiple locations. It is certainly the case that trends spread through globalized wine cultures very quickly today, and this cannot be fully explained by the attempts of wine corporations to push their products as fashionable (see Unwin 1991: 352).

When one looks at the roles played by sommeliers, one can see that other things are going on too. Tastes that are shared by multiple actors – here, by a large number of sommeliers who all start to put 'natural' wines onto their lists at about the same time – can emerge through various mechanisms, beyond being influenced by critics and other influential people. Collectively held tastes emerge in shared lifeworlds – here, the shared symbolic universe of sommeliers – that can be more specific or more global in nature. Actors in that lifeworld often are not 'following fashion' in any explicit or conscious sense. Instead, a new style of wine will only pique their interest if it somehow taps into and resonates with the tastes that are already collectively distributed across the sommelier lifeworld. Once a style has been widely taken up in, and disseminated through, that lifeworld, then the shared taste culture alters in subtle ways, which in turn will shape how other styles in future will be received, made sense of, and either embraced, or decried, or ignored altogether. Part of the professional code of the sommelier involves great reluctance to say something like 'I chose this wine for my wine-list just because I am following a trend'. Instead, more subtle and hidden judgement processes are at work in ways analogous to the mechanisms that Blumer (1969) described for clothing fashion buyers. These processes are intertwined with globalization processes in delicate ways, an issue that needs further empirical investigation. Such reflections may help us to understand the deeper significance of natural winemaker Philippe Pacalet's declaration: 'We used to struggle. People weren't ready. But chefs change, sommeliers change, whole generations change. Now they are ready.'[15] Their 'readiness', which is transnational in nature and spread across multiple locations, emerges through complex collective processes irreducible to fashionability and promotion alone.

Sommeliers across transnational Europe

After the profession was established in France, sommeliers came to be professionally established in Italy in the *Associazione Italiana Sommelier*, founded in 1965. The association still offers sommelier training, focusing particularly on Italian wines and regions (and including knowledge of the provenance of olive oils, understood as being very akin to wines). Sommeliers have also come to be professionally established in other European countries, particularly being found in high-end restaurants across increasingly cosmopolitan European cities. The process of establishing the profession is underpinned by various background factors, including the role of the EU in facilitating labour mobility, the internationalization of education systems, and the appearance of new forms of social mobility, all of which are changing the restaurant industry.

For this part of the chapter, I interviewed eight women who have worked as sommeliers in four different cities:[16] Helle Hasting (Copenhagen), Laura Koskenkari (Helsinki), Katrina Laitinen (Helsinki), Hande Leimer (Rome), Heidi Mäkinen (Tampere), Mia Stjerna (Helsinki), Christina Suominen (Tampere) and Angelika Trägårdth (Rome). Most of the women worked as sommeliers in restaurant service. In addition, Christina Suominen is a founding co-owner of the restaurant she works in, and Hande Leimer runs a company that organizes wine-tastings with educational elements for tourists visiting Rome. In terms of their background, they can be divided into three groups: (a) those who grew up in a restaurant family: Katrina Laitinen, Laura Koskenkari and Christina Suominen (who is the mother of Katrina Laitinen); (b) those with little or no family background in wine: Hande Leimer, Heidi Mäkinen, Mia Stjerna and Angelika Trägårdth; and (c) those who grew up in a family where the parents were very interested in food and wine as amateurs: Helle Hasting.

These different backgrounds obviously coloured each woman's experiences with restaurant work and their path to becoming a wine professional. For example, a family background in the restaurant world provides an individual with certain levels of social and cultural capital (Bourdieu 1984) that are likely to help in her career path. Katrina Laitinen, who tried to rebel against the inherited pull towards wine by focusing on other drinks (such as coffee) instead, initially trained as a waitress in her mother's restaurant. Her mother, Christina Suominen, claims she herself had 'no alternative' to a restaurant career, having practically grown up in a restaurant setting. Laura Koskenkari, whose father is a chef, recalls the normality of having wine with dinner – not a sentiment widely shared in Finland at the time. But the parents' wine interests outside their professional engagements could have had effects on an individual's cultural capital too. Helle Hasting, who comes from an upper middle-class background, remembers travelling through the Champagne region at the age of eight and through the Mosel valley at the age of thirteen, and being allowed to taste wine from a very early age (not that she liked it much at that time).

A very different early experience with wine was described by Mia Stjerna:

> I stole a bottle of wine from my mom, [but] we couldn't open it ... [I] pushed the cork in with something like a screwdriver and we probably drank it from the bottle or perhaps some plastic cup ... and I looked at it like 'this is super good' ... a sort of 'I see' moment. Later [the wine] turned out to have been kept for my 20th [birthday], it was a bit finer wine. I may have been 16 or so [at the time].

All the women with less inherited cultural capital actually started their career somewhere other than restaurants: Mia Stjerna and Angelika Trägårdth worked in the wine retail trade, Hande Leimer was originally in business and marketing (a skill that serves her well in her new wine career), and Heidi Mäkinen has no basic restaurant training but instead studied theatre and drama research at university before embarking on her sommelier career.

Around the world, formal education has been an important factor for women becoming wine professionals, and wine education has been increasingly globalized and transnationalized too (Matasar 2006). For example, in Finland sommelier training is a fairly recent development, only beginning in 1999, and can be taken in three major vocational schools/polytechnics, one in Turku and two in Helsinki. All these training programmes have international connections, and the two Helsinki programmes follow WSET award requirements, which allows for significant geographical mobility for those who hold such qualifications. The WSET award held particular appeal for those who work in a foreign country, such as Helle Hasting (a Norwegian working in Denmark), and Hande Leimer (a Turkish/German working in Italy), who both hold such mobility-enhancing qualifications. But the transnational recognizability of a certificate is significant also for people working in their home country, for it holds the possibility of working outside the country, as became clear when I spoke with some of my Finnish informants.

Other factors allowing for geographical mobility include EU citizenship (held by all my informants), which allows for both travelling and working in other EU countries, and language skills. For example, Angelika Trägårdth (Swedish working in Italy) won her job in Rome partly through her language skills. Many Italians are not particularly skilled in English, which is nowadays necessary in the restaurant business where an increasing number of customers are tourists. Similarly, Helle Hasting had an easier time getting a job in Copenhagen than many others might, as one of the requirements was knowledge of a Scandinavian language (Swedish, Norwegian, Danish). The Finnish women working in Finland had also often worked abroad previously: Katrina Laitinen in Norway, Heidi Mäkinen in the UK, and Mia Stjerna in France and the UK. All of them acknowledged that due to an increasingly international clientele, both in Helsinki and Tampere, it is not enough to speak only Finnish in Finland's globalizing restaurant world today. In fact, restaurants in Helsinki have recently, and for the first time, started hiring people who do not speak Finnish, which indicates a high level of internationalization, and perhaps also a need for a skilled workforce that the Finnish labour market is not fully capable of meeting.[17]

These women interestingly reflect more general recent changes in professional restaurant work. If working in vineyards and wine production has come to be acceptable for middle-class people, since the previous association between these and socially 'backward' agriculture and rural areas has dissolved (Robinson 1997: 1), so too has the restaurant become a place where people from different class backgrounds can work together: those with a long-standing family background in restaurants, such as Christina Suominen and her daughter Katrina Laitinen, and those from academic upper middle-class families, such as Helle Hasting. Indeed, I have often noticed when speaking with restaurant staff in the UK that many hold university degrees in completely unrelated fields, such as literature. With few graduate-level jobs available in more established middle-class professions, restaurant work has become more socially acceptable, as ever more middle-class graduates migrate towards it, in so doing collectively redefining such labour as both more bourgeois and more hip than it ever was in the past. In this sense, Heidi Mäkinen with her university degree and passion for wine and restaurant work is part of a much wider transnational trend, rendering sommelier work acceptable for even the upper middle classes.

Yet, despite global and transnational trends, different geographical and national locations still operate differently. To work as a sommelier in a traditionally wine-growing country, such as Italy, differs from working in locations with little or no viticulture and viniculture, such as Finland and Denmark. It is also different to work in an internationally fashionable culinary city, such as Copenhagen, and increasingly Helsinki, or in a less well-known location, such as Tampere: tourists often travel to the former two primarily because of the food scene. Along with the emergence of Helsinki as a food city, consumers willing to pay more for wine and to taste new wines have appeared and, according to Laura Koskenkari, now can form a significant part of the clientele in a restaurant that has a strong wine focus and reputation. And while in Rome Hande Leimer and Angelika Trägårdth both build their wine selections by almost exclusively drawing upon (all) Italian regions, in Copenhagen relatively few Danish wines end up on restaurant wine lists. And although I have found certain Finnish green currant sparkling wines (made in *Méthode Classique* style) delightful, I have yet to find them sold by any restaurant in Finland.

But there are also many similarities in operation across all these cities. The same trends operate in different locations. For example, 'natural' wines have become popular quite simultaneously in different locations across Europe. The clientele differs not so much between locations as between types of restaurants. As sommeliers tend to work in higher-end restaurants, they face relatively similar sorts of clientele everywhere: cosmopolitan, relatively affluent, and increasingly young and adventurous. All my informants recognized increasing wine knowledge and wine curiosity among their customers, and declared that the younger generation of diners is often more willing to experiment and trust the sommelier than are the older generations who have more stabilized wine preferences. This was equally true in all locations, including in Italy, where some younger consumers are, according to Hande Leimer, starting to realize that 'there is wine outside of Italy'. The younger generation of diners is also likely to be less rigid in their gender assumptions, both as comes to their own wine-drinking and -enjoyment, and to the gender of the person who serves the wine.

Gender and the globalized sommelier

A few years after the film *Somm* came out, a wave of celebratory stories about women working as sommeliers emerged in the United States.[18] Some of these presented female sommeliers as a new phenomenon, although many women had done pioneering work in the field for years already.[19] Some women took issue with being framed as 'female sommeliers', as they considered themselves as professionals who just happen to be women.[20] Coping with gender is indeed an element that women working with wine usually have to encounter, as they tend to become highly visible in professional environments due to their gender. When already well established in her profession, British wine critic Jancis Robinson (1997: 66) asked her male colleague (and friend) what his peers, 'traditional wine merchants', thought about her when she first built her career in London. To her surprise, she learned that she had been viewed by her male colleagues as underlining her gender unnecessarily ('you had a bit of a chip on your shoulder about being a woman'). Many other wine professionals, who happen to be women, have found themselves reflecting upon their careers in terms of their gender – something that, for obvious reasons, male professionals rarely do (see Brenner 2007; Matasar 2006). The women I interviewed are no exception.

Gender, according to my analysis, matters at least in four ways: with colleagues, with customers, in terms of workplace dress and behaviour, and in terms of the gender of customers. Although some of the informants considered women to taste wine differently from men, they largely considered gender irrelevant for the purposes of professionalism. However, they acknowledged that in more or less subtle ways, gender still matters in their working life. For example, many of them had needed to develop an 'attitude' in order to survive in male-dominated environments. Such an attitude involved elements such as humour and self-irony, ignoring forms of discrimination and winning a positive reputation through hard work. The latter was, it seemed, easier in Finland and Denmark than in Italy. Hande Leimer admitted that her start in the Roman wine world was not smooth and that she still struggles with some male colleagues. Undoubtedly, it is challenging to be a non-Italian claiming to know about Italian wine, 'and then you're a woman!'. She consequently has sometimes been dismissed by some male winemakers:

> I was at a trade tasting ... at the table of a winery the wine maker [was there] himself. [There were a] couple of wines, and I'm tasting. One of the wines ... was corked, [it's a] mistake, failure. And I said so, and he was like 'No no, this is a grape of the region ... you don't know this grape, this grape smells like that' ...

Ok good. I went away, and I talked about this with a friend of mine who was there, and he went and tasted the wine, and told the wine maker the wine [is] cork[ed]. And he goes like 'Really? Are you serious?', and immediately tasted himself. With me he didn't bother ... He tasted it and was 'You're right, it's corked'.

This narrative forms an interesting parallel with Natalie MacLean's experience described above – a tendency by some male professionals to dismiss a woman's wine views, especially when they claim to find a flaw in a wine. Yet despite such experiences, Hande Leimer has managed to win the respect of several Italian male colleagues, but her business model targeting tourists also ensures that she does not really need such respect as much as if she tried to work in local restaurants.

Things were not always easy for a pioneering woman in Finland either. Christina Suominen was often the only professional woman in wine events, particularly when she started participating in competitions. But she also was a source of inspiration. In a Nordic sommelier competition in the mid-1990s, where she was the first woman participating, she found how important role models are for the younger generation: 'I was surrounded by a group of girls who quizzed me: how dare you, how did you get started with this?'

With customers, gender operates differently. On the one hand, customers have gendered expectations, while on the other, sommeliers seek to manage customers through managing their own behaviour and particularly through their dress. To communicate one's status as a sommelier through explicit visual markers, most commonly a sommelier's pin,[21] is often not very effective due to issues to do with the small size of the pin. So, when Helle Hasting gets asked by customers that she call the sommelier, she does not think it has much to do with her gender: 'I don't really think they see I wear the pin ... I just find it a little funny, I'm not offended or anything.' Mia Stjerna sometimes reads surprise in customers' eyes and counters it directly: 'I go there, a young girl, relaxed ... they might stare or even ask – especially foreign men – "are you the sommelier?," and I've always joked that "I know you were expecting an older gentleman with a belly"'. Laura Koskenkari recognizes the look of surprise too, but she muses: 'It might be that it's just inside my head, maybe they didn't look at me differently, it might be my own uncertainty [of what they think].' While there may be no direct discrimination, there may still be little hints that women read and may be left reflecting upon, something their male colleagues are highly unlikely to experience.

Some of the women acknowledged that men may have certain advantages with customers. Katrina Laitinen feels that 'men are able to be a bit more charismatic with customers' and that 'men are able to more easily achieve authority'. Especially at the beginning of her career, Heidi Mäkinen felt that she 'wasn't appreciated' because she was a young woman. But nowadays she feels she has achieved a professional habitus that works well with customers. When she reflected upon this, she also thought that men probably had an easier time and also had tools to deal with customers that would not work for women, such as making naughty or slightly dirty jokes to create a bond with customers.

Dress also operates differently for women than for men. While one would think that wearing a uniform-like suit – which could work towards downplaying visual indicators of femininity – would be easy, there are challenges with this kind of dress style too. Heidi Mäkinen explained some of these: 'If I were a man, I'd shave my head bald, I wouldn't need to think how to dress [my hair] for service.' Women, according to her, need to think of their appearance and dress more than men: 'Men look so much better when they put on a suit.' This, she felt, was partly due to poor availability of garments: finding a fitting shirt suitable for work is more difficult for a woman than for a man. Also, finding shoes is easier for men, as women's low-heeled shoes tend to have a more limited selection. Shoes are understandably important for restaurant workers, and most of my informants wore no heels. The exception, Laura Koskenkari, prefers a small heel, for it helps her to feel that her 'back is a bit straighter'. On the other hand, she does not want to wear a skirt. The one time she did she felt 'this just doesn't work, it's really difficult to unpack a load [of bottles and bottle cases] or lift heavy cases with a skirt'. Helle Hasting also noted that male and female garments often have different functional qualities. For example, female garments usually do not have pockets – a crucial detail for anyone working the front of house in a restaurant (where do you put the corkscrew?).

Interestingly, jackets were not considered as causing problems by all the Finnish informants but were considered somewhat intimidating by informants based in Italy – hinting at national differences in otherwise transnational sartorial expectations and practices. Hande Leimer elaborated upon the balancing act she has engaged in this regard: she called it 'playing around', where the right balance must be found between looking not too serious, too sloppy or too sexy. She felt she would look a bit too scary with a blazer, but if she did not have formal enough attire, she would not achieve the authority she needs in her work. She did not wish to be like 'the sommelier in black and white in a restaurant, where [the customers] are so intimidated, and do not dare [to] ask any questions'.

Angelika Trägårdth had similar considerations:

When I started in this restaurant, I introduced myself with my jacket and my suit, that I used to have when I worked for the [Italian Sommelier] Association … and it's a very classic thing, it's … jacket, white shirt and black pants … and they liked it … [but] sometimes people can be a bit, they think it's a bit too elegant for a restaurant, [customers don't] come inside if they see you wear it … [so] I don't wear the jacket anymore.

The expectation of a certain level of formality, and wearing black-and-white suit attires in restaurant work, is a transnational and globalized element of high-end restaurant work (although the norms are increasingly relaxing in this regard). These reflections indicate that women may be particularly likely to be seen as overdressed if they wear suits or jackets, but this varies from one country to another, and even from one city to another, within one country. Indeed, Christina Suominen in Tampere said she wanted her dress to make her look 'approachable', adding that people in the Tampere restaurant world dress in more relaxed ways than their counterparts in Helsinki. By contrast, in Helsinki Mia Stjerna found that a jacket gives a sense of 'credibility' for both male and female members of staff, while Katrina Laitinen appreciated the 'anonymity' of a work uniform, which she finds helps her put on her professional persona to customers. Laura Koskenkari felt the same about workwear, and said she might wear a jacket even in a private wine-tasting, as it communicates a business-like attitude and respect towards the customers.

These are important considerations, for dress has major influences on the interactions between the restaurant worker and the customer (Kaiser 1985). Communicating one's gender can also have further risks and benefits for one's work. Female and male customers may react differently to the same person doing the same things. As indicated above, some male customers are still surprised to be served by a female sommelier. And conversely, some women may actually prefer to operate with a female sommelier. Hande Leimer experiences this often in her work in Rome, as most of her guests are female and bookings are made mostly by women, even when a male–female couple is visiting her tasting together. According to her, women feel 'better coming to a wine tasting held by a woman, I've heard this more than once that they feel more comfortable about it, and ask me questions, and they don't feel stupid doing that'.

Conclusion

This chapter has reflected upon some aspects of the long and often vexed history of women and wine. For centuries, women in different locations either had only limited access to wine, because of male fears to do with drunkenness and possible licentiousness, or instead were compelled to operate within social contexts characterized by strong assumptions about appropriate wine consumption. Forceful social norms guided how much and which types of wine women could legitimately drink, such wines often tending towards small portions of sweeter and more liqueur-like styles. But a range of socio-cultural changes in the later twentieth and early twenty-first centuries – a period of complex globalization in all manner of ways – have meant that at least some women, mostly from middle-class social positions, have been able to embrace wine connoisseurship as a profession and to pursue viable wine-related careers.

The globalization of wine fields, cultures and worlds has not totally transformed age-old gendered assumptions about women and wine. It is still widely believed in some quarters that women have markedly different *tastes in wine* from men and that they also *taste wine* differently from men. Yet various new trends run counter to those old forms of bias. It is increasingly recognized that female consumers are far from a homogeneous group, and that ever more women make wine, often very successfully (Matasar 2006). These trends are bound up with broader wine globalization processes in complex manners which require further investigation. Nonetheless, what this chapter has been able to show is that, in the case of women working in the particular type of cultural mediation called the sommelier profession, globalization and changing gendered norms and practices go together in certain specifiable ways. Certain broad processes of globalization have facilitated the entry of women into a hitherto very male-oriented and -dominated professional world, where masculinist forms of mastery and possession of technical knowledges have historically been at a premium. These globalization processes include access to wine education and professional training programmes, which are themselves transnational in scope and reach; increased capacities for social and geographical mobility, the latter being particularly pronounced in the right of EU citizens to work anywhere within the European Union; changes in restaurant service cultures, involving shifts towards increasing informality; and the entrance into the dining world of new types of middle-class consumers with new expectations of the type of service and treatment desired in restaurant settings.

As expectations among mutating consumer groups have changed as to what wines should be drunk and in which manners, this has opened up spaces for new kinds of sommelier practice, including those which are recognizably less masculinist than was the case before. Such changes can be found across multiple locations, especially in the very largest cities, but also in more medium-sized and smaller urban environments. The opportunities for, and challenges faced by, women working in sommelier jobs have many similarities across locations and national borders: the situation in Tampere in Finland is in many ways not that different from the situation in London, for example. This is not to deny that national, regional or city-specific differences persist in this regard. Diverse wine cultures still exist in different places, and thus the environment in which a female wine professional is compelled to operate within will be in certain ways different depending on whether she is in Rome or Helsinki. Nonetheless, the globalization of wine can be discerned precisely in those cases where there are strong similarities between diverse locations in terms of what such women do and think, and how they navigate the problems attendant upon working within a professional context that is still dominated by men.

A further interesting element here concerns globalized wine fashions. Through the increasingly interconnected, transnational nature of both restaurant and wine worlds, cultures and fields, wine trends today can spread astonishingly quickly. But it is yet not fully clear how such spreading actually happens, although sommeliers certainly play a part in this, as do other wine mediators such as magazine critics and retailers. For future scholarship concerned with wine, it would be advisable to consider both the gendered *and* fashion-driven nature of wine in more depth than has been the case so far.

Notes

1. Planchon played an important role in the nineteenth-century European battle against the phylloxera insect (Campbell 2004).
2. https://business.highbeam.com/138368/article-1G1-134677701/woman-world-beverage-companies-creating-products-specifically, accessed 13 February 2018.

3. https://business.highbeam.com/137330/article-1G1-131319409/beringer-fabricates-new-ladies-wine, accessed 13 February 2018.
4. https://business.highbeam.com/3003/article-1P2-11941097/wishywashy-toast-little-white-lie, accessed 13 February 2018.
5. https://www.wine-searcher.com/m/2012/04/-don-t--let-them-eat-cake, accessed 13 February 2018.
6. https://www.telegraph.co.uk/news/2016/10/03/diet-prosecco-to-go-mainstream-next-year-as-middle-class-drinker/, accessed 13 February 2018.
7. http://www.telegraph.co.uk/food-and-drink/news/is-skinny-prosecco-really-better-for-you/, accessed 13 February 2018.
8. https://en.oxforddictionaries.com/definition/sommelier, accessed 15 May 2018.
9. https://en.oxforddictionaries.com/definition/butler, accessed 15 May 2018.
10. The first examinations took place in 1953 and the institute was formed two years later. The first non-UK MW was Michael Hill Smith from Australia in 1988; the first female MW was Sarah Morphew Stephen in 1970. The exam was opened for people outside the wine trade in 1984, when Jancis Robinson became the first non-trade MW. The institute currently has activities in twenty-eight countries. http://www.mastersofwine.org/en/aboutus/history-of-the-institute.cfm, accessed 22 May 2018.
11. http://www.courtofmastersommeliers.org/the-court/the-board/, accessed 21 March 2018.
12. https://www.sommellerie-internationale.com/en/board_members/; https://www.sommellerie-internationale.com/en/asi_winners/, accessed 21 March 2018.
13. http://www.decanter.com/wine-news/opinion/guest-blog/film-review-somm-24043/, accessed 6 April 2018.
14. https://www.theguardian.com/news/2018/may/15/has-wine-gone-bad-organic-biodynamic-natural-wine, accessed 20 May 2018.
15. In https://www.theguardian.com/news/2018/may/15/has-wine-gone-bad-organic-biodynamic-natural-wine, accessed 20 May 2018.
16. The interviews were conducted between November 2014 and March 2018 in Finnish and English. All translations are mine. All the women consented to their real names being used in research reports, such as this chapter.
17. In London, where the restaurant sector has greatly expanded recently, there is a shortage of skilled workers, and the situation is expected to get more challenging with Brexit. Helsinki, however, is in a very different situation in terms of the need for foreign staff. https://www.theguardian.com/business/2018/mar/18/great-british-chef-shortage-eating-out-under-threat-brexit, accessed 21 March 2018.
18. https://www.wsj.com/articles/the-rise-of-female-sommeliers-1439214769; https://www.bloomberg.com/news/articles/2015-07-02/sex-and-the-sommelier-make-way-for-women, accessed 21 March 2018.
19. https://www.guildsomm.com/public_content/features/articles/b/weblog/posts/nyc-pioneering-sommeliers, accessed 21 March 2018.
20. https://vinepair.com/articles/hate-female-somms/, accessed 21 March 2018.

21. A sommelier's pin is a pin worn as part of one's attire when in service. There are different kinds of pins, including those given by the *Court of Master Sommeliers*, which indicate the level of expertise of the individual sommelier. Restaurants may also choose to have all their sommeliers wear the same kind of a pin, which typically would feature a bunch of grapes to indicate wine expertise.

References

Acker, J. (2004), 'Gender, Capitalism and Globalization', *Critical Sociology*, 30(1):17–41.

Atkin, T., Nowak, L., and Garcia, R. (2007), 'Women Wine Consumers: Information Search and Retailing Implications', *International Journal of Wine Business Research*, 19(4):327–39.

Banks, S.K., Sreenivasan, K.R., Weintraub, D.M., Baldock, D., Noback, M., Pierce, M.E., Frasnelli, J., James, J., Beall, E., Zhuang, X., Cordes, D., and Leger, G.C. (2016), 'Structural and Functional MRI Differences in Master Sommeliers: A Pilot Study on Expertise in the Brain', *Frontiers in Human Neuroscience*, https://doi.org/10.3389/fnhum.2016.00414.

Barber, N., Almanza, B.A., and Donovan, J.R. (2006), 'Motivational Factors of Gender, Income and Age on Selecting a Bottle of Wine', *International Journal of Wine Marketing*, 18(3):218–32.

Barber, N., Taylor, D.C., and Strick, S. (2010), 'Selective Marketing to Environmentally Concerned Wine Consumers: A Case for Location, Gender and Age', *Journal of Consumer Marketing*, 27(1):64–75.

Blumer, H. (1969), 'Fashion: From Class Differentiation to Collective Selection', *The Sociological Quarterly*, 10(3):275.

Bourdieu, P. (1984), *Distinction*, London: Routledge.

Brenner, D. (2007), *Women of the Vine: Inside the World of Women Who Make, Taste, and Enjoy Wine*, Hoboken, NJ: Wiley.

Bryant, L., and Garnham, B. (2014), 'The Embodiment of Women in Wine: Gender Inequality and Gendered Inscriptions of the Working Body in a Corporate Wine Organization', *Gender, Work and Organization*, 21(5):411–26.

Campbell, C. (2004), *Phylloxera: How Wine Was Saved for the World*, London: Harper.

Chow, E.N. (2003), 'Gender Matters: Studying Globalization and Social Change in the 21st Century', *International Sociology*, 18(3):443–60.

Colquhoun, K. (2007), *Taste: The Story of Britain through Its Cooking*, London: Bloomsbury.

Cowan, J.K. (1991), 'Going Out for Coffee? Contesting the Grounds of Gendered Pleasure in Everyday Sociability', in Loizos, P., and Papataxiarchis, E. (eds), *Contested Identities: Gender and Kinship in Modern Greece*, Princeton: Princeton University Press, 180–202.

David, E. (2009 [1962]), 'Ladies, Halves', in David, E., *An Omelette and a Glass of Wine*, London: Grub Street, 41–45.

Davidson, J. (1998), *Courtesans and Fishcakes: The Consuming Passions of Classical Athens*, London: Fontana.

Dewald, B.W.A.B. (2008), 'The Role of the Sommeliers and Their Influence on US Restaurant Wine Sales', *International Journal of Wine Business Research*, 20(2):111–23.

Dietler, M. (2006), 'Alcohol: Anthropological/Archaeological Perspectives', *Annual Review of Anthropology*, 35:229–49.

Dragadze, T. (1994), 'Gender, Ethnicity and Alcohol in the Former Soviet Union', in McDonald, M. (ed.), *Gender, Drink and Drugs*, Oxford: Berg, 145–52.

Fox, K. (n.d.), *The Smell Report: An Overview of Facts and Findings*, Social Issues Research Centre.

Gallo, G. (2007), 'Foreword', in Brenner, D. (ed.), *Women of the Vine*, Hoboken, NJ: Wiley.

Inglis, D. (2019) 'The Mutating and Contested Languages of Wine: Heard on the Grapevine', in Brunn, S. and Kehrein, R. (eds) Handbook of the Changing World Language Map, Basel: Springer, https://link.springer.com/content/pdf/10.1007/978-3-319-73400-2_205-1.pdf.

Johnson, T.E., and Bastian, S.E.P. (2007), 'A Preliminary Study of the Relationship between Australian Wine consumers' Wine Expertise and Their Wine Purchasing and Consumption Behaviour', *Australian Journal of Grape and Wine Research*, 13:186–97.

Kaiser, S. (1985), *Social Psychology of Clothing*. New York: MacMillan.

Lem, W. (2013), 'Regimes of Regulation, Gender, and Divisions of Labor in Languedoc Viticulture', in Black, R.E., and Ulin, R.C. (eds), *Wine and Culture: Vineyard to Glass*, London: Bloomsbury, 221–40.

Ludington, C. (2013), *The Politics of Wine in Britain: A New Cultural History*, Basingstoke: Palgrave MacMillan.

MacLean, N. (2007), *Red, White, and Drunk All Over: A Wine-soaked Journey from Grape to Glass*, London: Bloomsbury.

Manske, M., and Cordua, G. (2005), 'Understanding the Sommelier Effect', *International Journal of Contemporary Hospitality Management*, 17(6–7):569–76.

Matasar, A.B. (2006), *Women of Wine: The Rise of Women in the Global Wine Industry*, Berkeley: University of California Press.

McDonald, M. (1994a), 'Introduction – A Social-anthropological View on Gender, Drink and Drugs', in McDonald, M. (ed.), *Gender, Drink and Drugs*, Oxford: Berg, 1–32.

McDonald, M. (1994b), 'Drinking and Social Identity in the West of France', in McDonald, M. (ed.), *Gender, Drink and Drugs*, Oxford: Berg, 99–124.

Nicolson, P. (1990), 'Gender, Power and Wine Selection: A Pilot Study', *Journal of Wine Research*, 1(3):235–42.

Phillips, R. (2000), *A Short History of Wine*, London: Penguin.

Purcell, N. (1994), 'Women and Wine in Ancient Rome', in McDonald, M. (ed.), *Gender, Drink and Drugs*, Oxford: Berg, 191–208.

Ritchie, C. (2009), 'The Culture of Wine Buying in the UK Off-trade', *International Journal of Wine Business Research*, 21(3):194–211.

Robinson, J. (1997), *Confessions of a Wine Lover*, London: Penguin.

Soyer, A. (2004 [1853]), *Food, Cookery, and Dining in Ancient Times: Alexis Soyer's Pantropheon*, Mineola: Dover Publications.

Thom, B. (1994), 'Women and Alcohol: The Emergence of a Risk Group', in McDonald, M. (ed.), *Gender, Drink and Drugs*, Oxford: Berg, 33–54.

Unwin, T. (1991), *Wine and the Vine: An Historical Geography of Viticulture and the Wine Trade*, London: Routledge.

Veblen, T. (1994 [1899]), *A Theory of the Leisure Class*, New York: Dover Publications.

Index

Actor Network Theory 5, 9
advertising 75, 92, 179, 181–4
   contemporary forms of 161
   global 158
   for New World wines 184
agriculture 1, 7–8, 37–8, 68–9, 84, 90–1, 171–2, 181–2
   'backward' 204
   Chinese 115
   economies 14, 29
   European 89, 159
   'farm to table' movement in 75
alcohol 26, 125, 141, 193, 194
   consumption of 13, 79, 134, 142, 193–5
   drinking, restrictions on 194
   and drunkenness 194
   forms of 194
   opposition to 68
   overconsumption of 142
   women's relationship to 194
alcoholism 68
Algeria 12, 28–9, 54, 122
Alsace 15, 39
American Viticultural Areas (AVAs) 76
Anderson, K. 99 n.9, 128
anthropology 15, 47, 49
   American 50
   Chinese 121
   European 49–50
Appadurai, A. 145
Appellations d'Origine Contrôlées (AOCs) 54, 127, 184
   panels 40–1
   regulations 26
   rules 37
Argentina 12, 27–9, 141, 144, 149
Asda 6, 34
Asian financial crisis 127
assemblages 26, 48, 156, 160
   bio-neural-cultural 155

austerity policy 115, 128
Australian wine
   exports of 12
   prominence of 32
   supply of 27
Austria 39, 141
authenticity 4, 16, 26, 57–60, 73, 76, 125, 134, 172, 175, 179–80, 183, 185
AVAs. *See* American Viticultural Areas (AVAs)

Balkan Non-Associated Countries (BNAC) 83, 87
bankruptcy 90
barrels 9, 22–4, 26, 33, 155, 157
B2B interaction. *See* business-to-business (B2B) interaction
B2C interaction. *See* business-to-consumers (B2C) interaction
beer consumption 78, 93
   European 140
Beijing Winery 122, 125
biodynamic winemaking 40, 176
Blumer, H. 201
Bordeaux 8, 13–14, 16–17, 24–5, 30–2, 75, 125, 134
   place market 108
   producers 24
   transformation 112
Bordeaux wine 103–4, 157
   capitalistic transformations of 110–11
   classifications of 104–6, 157–8
   hierarchy of 106
   in institutional arena 103
   institutions and professional structures of 111
   in market arena 107–10
   in media arena 106–7
   merchants of 103, 153
   production and taste 103
   in productive arena 103, 110–13

reputation dynamics 108
reputation system 103
types of evaluations 103
value and reputation dynamics for 108
Bosnia 87
bottles 1–3, 8, 22, 24, 36, 56, 60, 92,
    138–9, 141–2, 145, 157, 160, 163,
    165, 168, 195, 197–8, 200, 203, 207
  brands on 34
  of 'drinkable' wine 69
  labels on 8
  origin of 110
  sizes 24
  technology 24
Bourdieu, P. 140, 143–4, 167 n.1, 176–7
boutique winemakers 79, 88, 162
Bové, J. 37
brands/branding 78, 127–8, 136, 144
  tasting 144–6
  of wine 136, 144–6
British wine trade 198
Burawoy, M. 98 n.8
Burgundy 9–10, 14–15, 24–5, 48, 134, 177
  comforting image of 52
  investments of 55
  viticulture 49
Burgundy wines 51, 53–7
  geographic origins for 61 n.7
  political economy of 56
business-to-business (B2B) interaction 136
business-to-consumers (B2C) interaction 136

California 25, 30–1, 72, 77, 94, 100, 134,
    157, 159, 174, 197
  grapes/juice from 69
  wine from 35, 174
  in world winemaking 35
capitalism 50–1, 58
  global 37, 165
  industrial 153
  post-industrial 51
  Western 165
Champagne 25, 31, 182–4, 197–8, 202–3
  climatic conditions for 39
  luxury-branded 31
Chiffoleau, Y. 51
Chile 1–2, 12, 29–30, 77, 144, 159
  vineyards in 159
China 13, 15–16, 27, 34, 42, 134, 138, 159
  beer industry 125
  beverages 121

culinary patterns of 116
foreign companies 127
market 117, 127
medicine 139–40
modern history 116
reconstruction and re-establishment of
    117
socialism 119
strength and flourishing trade 123
tradition 122
'universal recognition' of 121
vineyards of 122
wine production 129 n.1
Yunnan Highland Wine 125
Chinese wine 115–17
  history 120
  industry 117
  and legitimacy 117–20
  trajectories of 120–8
clusters/clustering 66–7, 72–4, 77, 134
  industrial 134
collective organizational learning 72–3, 77
collective selection 201
commodification 41, 50, 153, 165, 167
  transnational 54
communion wine, production of 25
Communism 30
Confucian ideology 117–18
Constantia wine 25
consumers 1, 3–6, 12, 17, 39–40, 163, 177–8
  in Europe 13
  in Germany and United States 14
  in Hong Kong 141, 143
  international 135
  niche markets of 15
  scepticism 74
  subjectivity of 165
consumption of wine 3, 29–30, 48–9, 54,
    57–8, 65, 67–8, 92, 103, 134–6,
    139–44, 146–7, 153, 160, 163, 171,
    185, 189
  in Europe 13, 30
  fields, material and symbolic properties
      of 179–80
  in non-wine-producing countries 13
conventionalization, form of 173
cork technology 24, 157, 200, 205–6
cosmopolitans 16, 71, 83, 139, 153, 165,
    175, 177–8, 186, 191, 195–6, 202,
    204
'cost-intensive' techniques 151

214 Index

cultural capital 17, 135, 140, 142–4, 146, 174, 178–9, 198, 202–3
cultural legitimacy 172, 179–80
cultural omnivorousness/voraciousness 173–5, 179–80, 185

Danish wine 204
David, E. 195
Defoe, D. 24
deindustrialization processes 13
de-localization
  commodity 2
  dietary 1
  of winemaking practices 33
democratization
  taste and 134
  of terroir 174–6
  of wine drinking 3
Demossier, M. 10, 14–15, 135
de Rothschild, Baron P. 104
deterritorialization 7, 155–6
Diageo 6
digital technology 53
Dion, R. 24, 50
Douglas, M. 142
dress 139, 164, 206–8
  and behavior 205
drinkers/drinking 1, 14, 26–7
  constructive 142
  culture of 68, 133
  luxury of 194
  restrictions on 194

EBRD. *See* European Bank for Reconstruction and Development (EBRD)
economic
  capital 111, 177
  disinterestedness 183
  pragmatism 118
  of qualities 179
education 13, 16, 52, 54, 68, 74, 136–7, 142–3, 146–7, 159–60, 192, 198, 202–3, 209
  European-modelled 116
  formal 192, 203
  and knowledge 174
  levels of 136, 142–4
  systems 202
  tertiary 160
Egypt 22, 154, 156–7, 193

English wine industry 31, 35, 39, 48, 134
'en primeur' campaigns 106–8
entrepreneurs of reputation 111
environmental degradation 38–9
EU. *See* European Union (EU)
Eurasia 21–2
European Bank for Reconstruction and Development (EBRD) 93–4, 98 n.2
Europeanization 84, 86
European Union (EU) 16, 31, 36, 84, 88–97, 202, 209
  Common Agricultural Policy (CAP) 84, 88–9
  citizenship 203
  funding 31
  Instrument for Pre-accession Assistance (IPA) 84, 89
  IPA for Rural Development (IPARD) programme 90
  wine regions 96
Europe/European 23–4, 28
  anthropology 49–50
  colonialism 26
  consumers in 13
  consumption in 30
  elites, flows and networks of 50
  producers in 92
  production trends in 29
  quality wines 153
  vineyards 24
  winemaking in 27, 29
  wine regions 49–50

family violence 68
FDI. *See* foreign direct investment (FDI)
Feiring, A. 177–8
female. *See* women
Ferguson, P. P. 8
fermentation 9, 33, 40, 161
  Chinese 121
  of embodied sugars 154
feudal land tenure 25
filtering 9, 40
Finland 13, 191–2, 201–6, 209
flavours, wine 3, 21, 28, 33–4, 36, 67, 71, 154, 157–8, 171, 184, 195, 198
food globalization 115–16
foreign direct investment (FDI) 30–1, 88, 136
foreign foods, omnivoristic consumption of 165
forward integration 29

Index 215

Fourcade, M. 51–2
France 9–12, 134, 173, 202
　brandy exporters of 26
　colonial wine production of 28
　quality wines 153
　vineyards 53, 127
　wine industry 134
　wines in 11–12, 28, 35, 141
Franklin, B. 156
free markets 86, 90, 95
Friedman, J. 50

Gallo, G. 31–2, 36, 195
gender/gendering 141, 192–5, 197–8, 200, 205. See also female; women
genuineness 17, 173, 178, 183–4
Georgia 1, 22, 41–2, 138, 152, 194
Germany 12, 15, 23–4, 27, 39, 67, 89–90, 129–30, 135, 141, 144
　consumers in 14
　wines 27
glassware 3
global economy 30
global financial crisis 133
global hierarchy of values 15, 49, 51–2, 58–9
global interconnectedness 48
globalization 22–3, 37, 41, 49–52, 115, 134, 145–6, 153, 166, 171–3, 185–6, 192, 195
　anthropological studies of 152
　Bordeaux wines (see Bordeaux wine)
　industry 65
　legitimation of field 176–9
　market dynamics 14
　marketplace 88
　natural wine market 176
　of palates 201
　quality wines 161–6
　reputation 23–4
　scales and levels of 7
　service culture 200
　of signature 112
　Soviet wine production 31
　of taste 112, 173–5, 179–85
　trade, perspectives 136
grain-based drinks 126–7
grape-growing 68, 74
　idiosyncrasies of 78
　scientific approach to 77

grapes 5, 8, 28, 38, 41, 115, 151
　climate for cultivation of 22
　criteria of 104
　cultivation of 39
　evidence of making 22
　Eurasian 120, 122
　farming 31–2
　forms and types 9
　fragmented production 87
　growers/growing 22, 38, 86–7, 91–2
　Horse Nipple 123
　hybrid 74
　natural capital of 151, 166
　price for 89
　production and growers 90
　species 21
　varieties 33
Great Leap campaign 126
Greece 23, 84, 90, 93, 95, 99, 99 n.14, 152, 193

Harvey, D. 57
heritage 47–8, 50, 53, 57–60, 66, 74, 94, 173, 175, 182–3
　legitimation frame of 181–3
hipster-style drinkers 3
Hong Kong 133–4
　availability of wine in 143
　consumers in 141–3
　drinking culture and alcohol industry 133
　and emerging wine businesses 136–9
　exporting goods from 138
　Food and Wine Festival 144–5
　global wine trade perspective 136–7
　International Wine & Spirits Fair 136
　local branding and tasting of wine 144–5
　marketing image of wine in 139
　popularization of wine consumption 139–42
　supermarket chain in 138
　Tourism Board 136
　Trade and Development Council (HKTDC) 136
　Wine and Dine Festival 136
　wine trade in 136–9
Hungary 26, 32
hygiene 90

Iberia 21–3, 80, 153
imbrication 7, 48–9, 58–9, 154

INAO. *See* Institut National des Appellations d'Origine (INAO)
indigenization 7, 119, 135m 147, 145
industrial wineries 28
innovations 21, 29, 33, 65–6, 79, 110, 115, 152, 155, 157, 162
Institut National des Appellations d'Origine (INAO) 26
intermediaries 16–17, 107–8, 160, 173, 177–86
International Financial Centre 139
international market 16, 53
   demands 83
   dynamics in 108
international merchants 107, 113 n.1
international trade 12, 29, 85, 115
IPA for Rural Development (IPARD) programme 90, 92, 94, 97
Italy 11–14, 22–4, 34, 37, 202
   wines 66, 105, 202

Jefferson, T. 105
Jinping, Xi 115
   anti-corruption campaign 128

Karpik, L. 56–7
knowledge 17, 31–3, 47, 51, 53–7, 66, 77–8, 80–1, 111, 136, 142–4, 155, 158–60, 196, 200, 202–6, 209
   brokering 72–4
   cultural 94
   and education 142–6
   elite 176
   embeddedness, interdependency of 73
   of geographical origin 93
   levels of 200
   local 136
   scientific 9
   traditional 182
   of vineyards and regions 176
   winemaking 23
kombinati 85, 88
Kosovo 87
Kurniawan, R. 56

Laferté, G. 50, 52–3
Laporte, C. 51

Macedonia
   agricultural products and exports 83, 90–1
   branding and international market 92–6

EU agricultural policies on redevelopment 88–92
financial deepening 83–5
Tikveš wine region 84–8
wine industry 85
Macedonian wine/wineries 88–9, 91, 93, 95, 99 n.14
   branding 92–6
   exports and sales 89
   family-labour holdings of 91
   international market 92–6
MacLean, N. 199–200, 206
Madeira vineyards 25–6
market/marketing 3–5, 8–10, 14, 16, 29, 31–4, 36–40, 51–7, 66–9, 71, 74, 76–80, 83–4, 86–98, 103, 105–9, 111, 113, 115–19, 126–30, 135–41, 144–7, 151–3, 155, 158–9, 165–6, 173–80, 183–6, 192, 196–8, 203–4
   commodification of wine 165
   commodity wine production 152
   economy 116–17, 119
   growth of 52
   strategies 5
   trend of 197–8
mass-market factory production 37
mass-market wines 10, 25, 33–4, 39
McDonaldization' trends 34
media visibility 110
medical wine 130 n.7
Mediterranean diet 70
Médoc wine 157
merchants 5–6, 23, 26, 34–5, 49, 52, 58, 103–10, 116–17, 127, 137, 153, 157, 193, 205
   of Bordeaux wine 103, 153
   international 107, 113 n.1
   traditional wine 205
Mexico 25
micro-wineries 166
mobility 17–18, 54, 123, 202–3, 209
   forms of 191
modernization 116, 118, 120
Mondavi, R. 30, 35, 37
Mondovino (film) 106
monopoly rent 51, 173
mountain grapes 130 n.5
muscadines 73
   growers 74
   popularity of 71

producers 71
   resurgence of 69–70
myth-creation, forms of 199

Napa Valley Film Festival 199
national banquet beer 125
natural wine 17, 35, 40–1, 171–3, 177, 179–81, 183, 185, 201
   consumption of 177
   cultural legitimacy of 172
   emergence of 176–7, 179
   global formation and consolidation of 173
   globalization of (see globalization)
   legitimacy for 172, 178, 185
   material and symbolic properties of 185
   producers and intermediaries 184–5
   production of 171–2
natural winemakers/winemaking 180–3
neo-liberal economy 14, 41
'New Nordic Cuisine' (NNC) 175, 178
New World 15, 35–7, 180
   business and academic actors from 36
   exports 12
   styles 23
   wines 13, 174, 184
New York 26–7, 58, 67, 69–70, 88, 95, 133, 178, 180–1
   Raw wine fair 178
New Zealand 153, 158, 165
   vineyards of 161–4
   wine tourism 152
North Carolina 15
   attaining maturity 78–9
   clustering and knowledge brokering 72–4
   history of wine in 67–9
   institutional support and leader firms 76–8
   Winegrowers Association 77
   wine's resurgence 69–72
Nossiter, J. 106

oenophiles 70–1
Old World 15, 31, 35–7
   producers 12–13
   styles 23
   wines 182
omnivorousness 173–6, 179–80, 185

palates, globalization of 201
Parker, Robert 4, 106–7, 112, 154–5, 176

Pérignon, Dom 133, 155
Peru 22, 25, 27, 164–5
   wine exports 162
   winemakers in 153
   wine tourism 152
pests 9, 27–8, 134
phylloxera 27–8, 53, 124, 134, 209 n.1
placelessness 57
place making 48–9, 54, 59
Planchon, J.-É. 195
political economies of wine 161–2
politics of scaling 48–9
popularization of wine 136, 139–42, 146
Portugal 12–13, 24, 26, 47, 141
Port wines 26, 193
post-industrial capitalism 51
post-Marxist analyses 153
premium wine 13, 25
   Bordeaux 106
   community 112
   consumption of 13
   industry 110
   wine markets and trade into 25
pricing strategy 109–10, 112
principal selection criteria 109–10
privatization 16, 31, 86–8, 90, 93, 96–7
production of wine. See wine production
progressive crystallization 105
promotion of wine 3, 10, 34, 60, 71, 74, 92, 94, 96, 136, 139, 146, 156, 160, 162, 202
Prosecco 197
proto-globalization 11, 21–5. See also wine globalization
provenance 4, 9, 26, 36, 54, 158, 173, 175, 185
   taste for 171, 173, 179–86
   terroir to 185–6
public drunkenness 68
public visibility 110

quality of wine 14, 66, 79–80, 84, 88, 90, 158, 160, 163–5, 175
   ascription of 157
   aspects of 162
   contemporary notions of 157
   globalized culture of 165
   globalized practices of 165
   hegemonic efficacy of 153
   narratives 160
   possession of 155–6, 158–9

quantities of wine 109, 137
qvevri wine 41

Real Wine Fair 178
rebranding 84, 92–3
red wine 70, 88, 108, 140, 142, 146, 195
    health effects of 124
    Macedonian 93
reflexivity 50
'regional' food culture 10
regional identity 79
religious conservatism 65
resurgence of wine 69–72
retail outlets 3, 31
Robinson, Jancis 199, 205

sacramental wine 159, 161
Sainsbury's 34
science 10, 28, 33, 38, 40, 154, 160, 166
Serbia 87, 89
shipping 29
singularity 56–9, 109, 113, 156–7
Sino-Western dichotomy 115–16, 128
'slow-food' tourism 91
social capital 32
    interdependency of 73
    levels of 202
socialism 85–7, 95–6, 98, 98 n.8, 119, 122
social mobility, forms of 202
social relations 6–7, 22, 59, 73, 91
social reproduction 52, 57
Somm (film) 199
sommelier 3, 17, 58, 95, 111, 177, 180–1,
    192, 195–6, 200–9
    celebrity 199
    history of 198
    origins and globalization of 198–202
    patterns of wine consumption 200–1
    representation of 199
    in restaurant service 202
    training 203
South American wines 153, 161
Spain 11–14, 24, 112, 134, 141, 153
Spurrier, Steven 35, 199
standardization 24, 152, 178
Steiner, R. 40, 177
Strategy 2025 policy 32
sulphites 9, 40
supermarkets 34
surplus wine 89, 151

sweeter wines 195, 198
Sylvestris 21
symbolic capital 111, 184

table wines 13–14, 25, 27, 29–31, 128
Tacama 162, 164
    high-quality wines with 161
    vineyards of 161, 163, 165
taste of wine 3–4, 23, 27–8, 31, 33–5, 136,
    144–6, 151, 171, 173, 177
    aesthetics of 156
    domains of 171
    globalization of 112
    homogenization of 40–1
    legitimacy frameworks of 172
    perceived variations in 155
    preferences of 65
    for provenance and authenticity 185–6
    terroir and 173–5
tasting
    courses 144
    serving and 195
    technique 144
techno-scientific winemaking 40
Teil, G. 11
terroir 4, 9–11, 36, 39, 47–9, 52–3, 105,
    158, 173
    authentic expression of 171
    authenticity and singularity 57–9
    birthplace of 52–3
    in Burgundy 49
    characteristic of 134
    construction of 173
    democratization of 174
    globalization of 48
    ideology 57
    international cult of 9–10
    marketing 10, 36, 40
    notions of 173, 176–7
    people's valorization of 186
    to provenance 185–6
    reduction of 186
    specific properties of 112–13
    and taste 173–5
    transnational spread of 73
Tesco 6, 34
Tikveš 90–7, 99 n.9
    contradictions and confusion in 89
    with domestic policies 89
    families in 90

post-socialist social and economic change in 84–8
Winery 93, 95
Tong Hua Winery 125–6
trade 3, 11–12, 22–3, 25–6, 29, 123, 133, 136–9, 153
 companies 25–6
 cross-border 29
 in Hong Kong 136
 hub 133–4
 international 12, 29, 85, 115
 wine retail 203
traditional wine merchants 205
transmission belt' effect 177
transnational alcohol corporations 159
transnational wine trends 201
transparency 88, 92, 173, 181–2, 184–5
transportation of wine 5, 24
trial-and-error system of production 72
Tuscany 14, 26

Ulin, R. C. 24, 50
United Nations Food and Agriculture Organisation (FAO) 93
United States 14, 27, 29, 31, 35–6, 67–70, 88, 92, 95, 110, 137, 141, 144, 179, 196–7, 199, 205
US strip labels 110

vanguard wines 156–61
Vardar River valley 84, 93–4
'Vardar Valley' wines 94
variance in wines 166–7
varietal labelling 176
Veblen, T. 143–4, 194
Veseth, M. 88
vinegar 154, 166, 172
vineyards 3, 6, 9, 17, 22, 24–5, 31–4, 39–40, 204
 in Chile 159
 of China 122
 Europe/European 24
 France 53, 127
 knowledge of 176
 Madeira 25–6
 monitoring and control of 28
 of New Zealand 164
 organic methods in 182
 topography of 28
 water shortages in 39
 workers of 163

vintibusinesses 31
Virginia Dare 67–8
Vitis rotundifolia 67
Vitis vinifera 21–2, 65, 67, 69–74, 120, 130, 154–5, 158
 grapes 70, 74, 161
 growers of 71–2
voluntary quality alliance programme 74–5

Westernization 117–19
white wine 1, 15, 127, 140, 142–3, 146, 161, 195–6
wine 121–4, 154
 fundamental aspects of 156
 globalizations of 151–3
 market trade of 153
 nature and material capitals 154–6
 production 151, 156
wine auction 55
wine consumption 78, 163, 193
 gender and 198
 in Hong Kong 136, 139–42
 patterns of 200–1
 venues of 193
wine culture 78, 103, 105, 107, 110, 158, 191–2
 defined 49
 democratization of 176
 integration of 76
 international 108
wine fairs 135, 192
wine field 11, 23–4, 103, 105, 107
 integration of 76
 international 108
wine frauds 54
wine globalization 4–8, 21–2, 32
 complexity of 15
 definitions of 9, 15
 dynamics and phenomena of 2
 features of 6
 history of 4–5
 long-term development of 21
 Marxist political-economic and neo-Marxist accounts of 7
 'natural' concerns 38–41
 neo-liberalization 30–5
 old world/new world 35–7
 pioneers of 27
 process of 6
 'proto-globalization' 22–5
wine-growing areas 28

wine industry
   in Europe 134
   institutional support for 77
   obstacles in 90
   privatization of 88
   redevelopment of 88–92
   representation of 96
winemakers/winemaking 3, 11, 22, 31, 38, 68, 71, 74, 110, 158, 176, 178, 181–2, 191–2
   climate change on 3
   creativity 163
   dissemination of 77–8
   European 29
   exports 32
   facilities, integration of 2
   female 192
   'golden rules' of 154
   histories of 182
   innovations of 29
   intervention 171
   knowledge of 23
   male 205
   maturation and storage 33
   methods 26, 38
   in Peru 153
   process of 5, 30
   scientific and technical basis of 10
   spread of 26
   styles of 21–2
   techniques 23, 27, 158
   technologies 27
   traditions 158
wine management 192
wine production 2–3, 8, 11–12, 25, 87–8, 94, 126, 141, 154, 156, 166, 173, 176, 204
   climate change role in 38–9
   collective nature of 66
   domestic 30
   elite 16, 156–61, 177–8
   globalization of 185
   investment for 25
   market-commodity 152
   particularities of 175
   patterns of 11
   political economy of 48
   process of 51, 192
   source of 28
   trends in Europe/European 29
   university qualifications in 31
   volume of 11–12
wine retail trade 203
wineries 28, 33, 75, 91–2
   growth in 71
   locations for 79
   mortality rate of 79
   owners 75
   triad of 126
   types of 79
Wine & Spirit Education Trust (WSET) 198, 200
   award 203
wine tourism 15–17, 66, 74–5, 94–7, 134, 136–7, 152
women 191, 193–5, 202, 206. *See also* gender/gendering
   alcohol consumption 193
   alcohol supplying 191–2
   'anonymity' of work uniform 208
   cultural capital 203
   discrimination 206
   dress style for 207
   education for 203
   marketing wine to 197–8
   shoes for 207
   sommeliers 202–8
   tasting and choosing wine 195–7
   winemakers 192

Xiaoping, Deng 119

yeasts 9, 40
   artificial 33, 36
   on grape skins 154
Yugoslavia 83, 85, 89, 94, 98

Zedong, Mao 118, 120